ENVIRONMENTAL SCIENCE ACTIVITIES KIT

MICHAEL L. ROA

**THE CENTER FOR APPLIED
RESEARCH IN EDUCATION**
West Nyack, New York 10995

Library of Congress Cataloging-in-Publication Data

Roa, Michael L., 1946–
    Environmental science activities kit : ready-to-use lessons, labs,
and worksheets for grades 7–12 / Michael L. Roa ; illustrated by
Ginny Allen.
        p.   cm.
    Includes bibliographical references.
    ISBN 0-87628-304-0
    1. Environmental education—Activity programs.   2. Environmental
sciences—Problems, exercises, etc.   I. Allen, Ginny.   II. Title.
GE77.R63   1993   93-12227
363.7—dc20   CIP

Printed in the United States of America

10   9   8   7   6   5   4

ISBN 0-87628-304-0

ATTENTION: CORPORATIONS AND SCHOOLS

Prentice Hall books are available at quantity discounts with bulk purchase for educational,
business, or sales promotional use. For information, please write to: Prentice Hall Career &
Personal Development Special Sales, 113 Sylvan Avenue, Englewood Cliffs, NJ 07632. Please
supply: title of book, ISBN number, quantity, how the book will be used, date needed.

**THE CENTER FOR APPLIED RESEARCH
IN EDUCATION**
West Nyack, NY 10994
A Simon & Schuster Company

On the World Wide Web at http://www.phdirect.com

Prentice-Hall International (UK) Limited, *London*
Prentice-Hall of Australia Pty. Limited, *Sydney*
Prentice-Hall Canada Inc., *Toronto*
Prentice-Hall Hispanoamericana, S.A., *Mexico*
Prentice-Hall of India Private Limited, *New Delhi*
Prentice-Hall of Japan, Inc., *Tokyo*
Simon & Schuster Asia Pte. Ltd., *Singapore*
Editora Prentice-Hall do Brasil, Ltda., *Rio de Janeiro*

Acknowledgments

This book is the product of the efforts and influences of many people. The sincere interest and concern about our environment shown by the students with whom I have been priviledged to work has been an inspiration and a challenge. To all young people everywhere: Thank you for caring!

The ideas for activities in this book came from many sources, many of which are listed as references in the activity descriptions. One especially useful source of information is G. Tyler Miller's environmental studies text *Living in the Environment*. A most useful source of activities is *Conserve and Renew,* written by Leeann Tourtillot.

Many thanks to the following who reviewed some of the activities included in this book: Dr. John DeMartini, professor of Biological Sciences, Humboldt State University, Arcata, CA; Cathy Dickerson, science teacher, Blue Lake School, Blue Lake, CA; Dr. James Marshall, professor of Science Education, California State University, Fresno, CA; and last, but not least, my longtime friend and mentor, Frank Schiavo, instructor in Environmental Studies, San Jose State University, San Jose, CA.

Others who made helpful suggestions include Dr. Rocky Rohwedder, Dr. Erv Peterson, Dr. Steven Orlick, Dr. Stephen Norwick, all of Sonoma State University in Rohnert Park, CA, and Dr. Esther Railton, of California State University in Hayward, CA.

The artist, Ginny Allen, in addition to showing great flexibility, skill, and imagination in her artwork, made many helpful suggestions.

Sandra Hutchison, my editor at Prentice Hall, has also made many helpful suggestions and provided support and guidance through the production process.

My wife, J. T. O'Neill, has shown great patience and support during the many hours spent on this book. She has also made many helpful suggestions.

Finally, I want to acknowledge you, the user of this book, for caring about our world and for seeking to find ways to pass on your knowledge and concern for it. I hope that this book helps.

About the Author

MICHAEL ROA has been a teacher since 1969. He has taught grades 4 to 12, as well as workshops for preservice and inservice teachers. He received his B.A., M.A., and Secondary Teaching Credential from San Jose State University in San Jose, California. He earned his Elementary Teaching Credential at Sonoma State University in Rohnert Park, California.

Mr. Roa, a frequent presenter at local, state, and national science teachers' conventions, is also the co-author (with Donnell Tinkelenberg) of *Biology Teacher's Instant Vocabulary Kit* (The Center, 1991).

I don't know who first said "We do not inherit the Earth from our parents . . . We borrow it from our children," but I would like to thank him or her.

This book is dedicated to my children, Alexander O'Neill Roa and Megan O'Neill Roa. Thanks for the loan. I hope I can repay it with interest.

Love,
Papa

About Environmental Education and This Resource Book

Now, as never before, there is a need for Environmental Education. Our concern for the environment was awakened in the 1960s. That concern blossomed into a hue and cry for action in the 1970s. The 1980s saw the actual work of protecting the environment proceeding without much fanfare. As our understanding of and concern for the environment matures, our students need to continue to grow in their understanding of our environment, its problems, and how they can be instrumental in protecting it.

The term "Environmental Education" means many things to many people. Most commonly, it means what I call "Outdoor Education." There are at least three forms of Outdoor Environmental Education: nature study, residential outdoor education camp programs, and living history programs.

Outdoor Education is a very important part of Environmental Education. Without actually experiencing their natural world outside of the classroom, the students will neither truly appreciate nor understand the world in which they live.

Environmental Education can also mean what I would call "Conservation Education." To me, Conservation Education deals with environmental problems and working toward solutions, or at least understandings of potential solutions.

As used in this resource, Environmental Education is education that is intended to enable students to understand and appreciate their environment (both natural and man-made), to increase their knowledge of environmental problems, and to teach ways to approach reducing or solving those problems. The *Environmental Science Activities Kit* is about Conservation Education.

Environmental Education not only enables the student to learn about solutions, but involves him or her in actually working toward solutions. Environmental Education allows the student to be informed, concerned, and involved. The involvement, though, is intended as a learning experience in itself. A caveat: There is a possibility that students can become pawns in the teacher's campaign in a particular environmental cause. While it is good that students learn how to become involved, and it is important that they be able to actually become involved, the teacher must use discretion in his or her steering of the students. The teacher must not use the students to advance his or her own environmental goals, however well intentioned they may be.

There are currently a great many Environmental Education resources available for Outdoor Education. Examples include Project Wild and Project Learning Tree materials. While many of the activities designed for Outdoor Ed programs can be adapted for use in the classroom, many are not very well suited for classroom use. There are other activities that are more appropriate for use in the classroom. This resource is a collection of some of the best activities I have found to use in the classroom or on school grounds.

My purpose with the *Environmental Science Activities Kit* is to provide activities that can be done in a classroom, or at least at a typical school site. Just as many of the Outdoor Education activities can be modified for use at a school site, most of these activities could easily be utilized by the Outdoor Educator. There are certainly many other excellent activities available.

When considering environmental issues and when teaching about them, it is important to keep the following axioms in mind. They provide the basis for many of the activities included in the *Kit:*

- There is no free lunch.
- All things are interconnected.
- More is not always better.
- Nature was at bat first, and bats last!
- There is no "away."
- It is better to be safe than sorry.
- Nobody is perfect, but we can all be better.
- Be not merely good. . . . Be good for something!
- Think globally, act locally.

When students learn about environmental problems, or any social problems, they often become quite concerned and want to work toward solutions. If we provide them merely with information about the problems, we run the risk of our students' becoming angry, frustrated, pessimistic, and feeling powerless and, therefore, hopeless. We must also teach the skills and attitudes necessary for positive involvement. Like other skills, this requires hands-on and minds-on experiences built upon a firm foundation of knowledge.

Thus, I see Environmental Education as a circular or triangular enterprise. Our students need to be informed. When informed, they will probably become concerned. When concerned, they will want to become involved. But the more concerned and involved they become, the more informed they will become; as they become more informed, they will become still more concerned and involved. The concern and involvement must be based on knowledge and understanding, but that knowledge does no good unless it results in concern and action.

Teaching about environmental issues raises the question of the teaching of values. I believe that we do not merely teach *about* values; we teach particular values every day. When we encourage our students to be punctual, honest, creative, kind, hard-working, and neat, we are teaching particular values. When we promote behaviors such as safe driving or we discourage behaviors such as smoking, we are also teaching particular values. As environmental educators, we should be encouraging our students to develop values and behaviors that will help protect and improve our world. We must also remember to teach by example. Our students learn the behaviors, attitudes, and values that we model.

Michael L. Roa

Using the Environmental Science Activities Kit

The activities in this resource require only common materials and equipment that is readily available to secondary school teachers. All are appropriate for use in secondary level (grades 7–12) science classes. They are generally suitable for Earth, Life, or Physical Science classes, and are usable by students of varying abilities. Many can be done in Social Studies, Home Economics, Health, or other classes. The activities could certainly be built upon for more in-depth scientific inquiry. Suggestions are given for expanding upon the activities and for showing how they are related to each other.

Some activities are best done by individual students. Others are best done by groups of students. In general, the groups for such activities are referred to as "teams" rather than "groups." Referring to them as teams reinforces the idea that each member needs to contribute to and participate in the activity, rather than to be merely part of a group watching someone else do it.

Each unit deals with a different Environmental Education topic, but, of course, all units are related. This separation into discrete units is intended only to facilitate use of selected activities. It is important, though, that you, the teacher, enable the student to see the interrelatedness of the activities. You can select the materials for a given topic or can select from a variety. Each can be utilized alone or in conjunction with others. As you plan your course, it would be useful for you to read the Activity Summary at the start of each activity. Since each activity can be used independently of the others, you may find it useful to do the activities in a different sequence. If students seem ready to undertake independent or group projects at any time, I would suggest that you get them started at that time. Activity 32 suggests many student projects and provides a format for students to use in doing projects. Consider having the students do small, simple projects early in the year and more complex projects later in the year.

All pages are suitable for reproduction. Many of the activities are suitable for cooperative learning groups, involve critical thinking, and "higher order" learning. Many also deal with the "affective" domain, rather than just with knowledge acquisition. The Extension activities, Discussion questions, and the Questions sheets provided with each activity are especially useful in teaching in the affective domain.

Some of the activities are open-ended, requiring the student to investigate a question to which he or she does not know the answer. Current science teaching emphasis is on the investigative nature of science. These open-ended activities should help the student develop investigative abilities and attitudes conducive to scientific inquiry.

While it is important to emphasize open-ended activities, it is also valuable for students to experience activities that help them to clearly understand concepts that they may have heard or read. The addage "I hear, I forget; . . . I see, I remember; . . . I do, I understand!" still holds true. Some of the activities in this book are designed to reinforce what the students have probably read or heard in their class or elsewhere.

Some of the activities are "original," having been developed by the author without knowledge of their being used elsewhere. Others are modifications of activities commonly done in science classes. My intention is to provide at least one activity for each of the major areas of environmental concern and to provide other ideas for further investigation.

For each topic, the following are included:

√ A brief summary of the activity
√ Suggestions for introducing the activity, including
   - suggestions for grouping of students
   - an estimate of the time required
   - anticipated outcomes
√ Materials list
√ Vocabulary (most of the vocabulary terms are highlighted in the student Background Information pages and in the activity Instructions)
√ Teacher preparation
√ Safety considerations
√ Step-by-step procedures for teaching the activity
√ Questions for discussion, which may be used in class discussions or as writing assignments
√ Answers for the questions that are included with the student pages
√ Extensions, which are projects or other activities that build upon the activity in the chapter
√ Suggestions for modifications of the activities
√ References
√ A one- (or two-) page Background Information sheet. This provides information for either the teacher *or student* to use as he or she approaches study. It is intended to be a brief summary of the important basic and general information on the subject, not a detailed technical report.
√ Depending upon the activity, there may be data recording tables, student activity guides, worksheets, transparency masters, or other reproducible materials for student or teacher use.
√ For each activity there are questions for the students to answer.

A couple of suggestions regarding duplicating of the materials in this resource: To save on duplicating, the Background Information sheets and Instructions to most of the activities might be shared among members of a group or team of students. If you collect them, you can use them again next year. The Questions sheets and Data Tables might be made into transparencies, and the students could answer the questions on their own lined paper. They could also be used as discussion questions. The questions could also be answered by groups of students as a collaborative writing assignment or in small group discussions.

Guest speakers can be a wonderful addition to your class. The following suggestions may be useful if you decide to invite guest speakers to your classroom:

• Check your district's policy regarding guest speakers, especially if the subject is a "controversial" one. You might discuss the controversy with the class prior to the speaker's presentation.

• Make your arrangements well in advance.

• Send a letter confirming the details such as time, date, place, topic, how long, how many classes, students' ages, what background they already have, how the presentation fits into your teaching, a map to your school and room, asking if there are any special needs such as slide projectors, giving your school and home phone numbers in case the speaker needs to get in touch, and telling where and when the speaker will be met at the school.

- Confirm the appointment two days before the event.
- Have an alternative lesson plan in case the speaker is delayed or doesn't show up.
- Have a student meet the speaker at the class to escort him or her to the class and carry materials. You may want to borrow a handcart from the custodian.
- Have a student escort the speaker back to his or her transportation.
- Write a thank-you letter promptly and have one or more students write letters for the class.

Some of the activities in the Kit include names, addresses, and telephone numbers of various organizations, companies, and agencies. These were obtained from a variety of sources, as indicated in the reference section of the lessons. Since addresses and telephone numbers often change, the accuracy of these cannot be guaranteed. It is a good idea, therefore, to check them before having students write to them, especially if there is not enough time to seek another source if these do not work out. When writing to a source for information, be sure to allow plenty of time for a response.

A Few Words About Safety

For each activity, appropriate safety precautions are given. However, the individual teacher must carefully consider safety when doing activities with students. No amount of forewarning will ensure complete safety. Both students and teachers must always use good judgment and common sense when doing hands-on activities.

Every science classroom should have at least an eye wash, fire blanket, fire extinguisher, and first aid kit available at all times. Students must wear proper clothing such as shoes that cover the entire foot, clothing that will not get caught in equipment or a flame, appropriate eye protection, and a hair band to keep long hair from catching fire. Whenever using chemicals, cleanliness must be emphasized to prevent possibly dangerous contamination, as well as to ensure accurate results.

WARNINGS, INSTRUCTIONS, AND RULES ARE ONLY AS GOOD AS THE TEACHER'S ENFORCEMENT OF THEM. SAFETY MUST BE THE FIRST CONCERN IN ALL LABORATORY SITUATIONS.

DISCLAIMER: These safety suggestions are offered only as general guidelines. They are not intended to be complete or inclusive. The teacher is solely responsible for safety precautions in the classroom. Neither the author nor the publisher assume any responsibility for actions or consequences resulting from doing activities suggested in this book.

Your local school district, state department of education, or other governmental agencies may have safety manuals or guidelines. Some science supply companies provide such manuals.

Contents

About Environmental Education and This Resource Book • xvii

Using the *Environmental Science Activities Kit* • vix

A Few Words About Safety • xii

UNIT I: LAND USE ISSUES I

ACTIVITY I. SURFACE MINING • 3

Activity Summary • Introduction • Grouping • Time • Anticipated Outcomes
• Materials • Vocabulary • Teacher Preparation • Safety Considerations
• Procedure • Discussion • Answers to 1.3, Surface Mining Questions
• Extensions • Modifications • References

Reproducibles

1.1 *Surface Mining: Background Information*

1.2 *Surface Mining: Instructions*

1.2 *Surface Mining: Data*

1.3 *Surface Mining: Questions*

ACTIVITY 2. WHY RECYCLE? • 14

Activity Summary • Introduction • Grouping • Time • Anticipated Outcomes
• Materials • Vocabulary • Teacher Preparation • Safety Considerations
• Procedure • Discussion • Answers to 2.3, Why Recycle? Questions • Extensions
• Modifications • References

Reproducibles

2.1 *Why Recycle? Background Information*

2.2 *Why Recycle? Instructions*

2.2 *Why Recycle? Data*

2.3 *Why Recycle? Questions*

ACTIVITY 3. SOIL COMPACTION • 24

Activity Summary • Introduction • Grouping • Time • Anticipated Outcomes
• Materials • Vocabulary • Teacher Preparation • Safety Considerations
• Procedure • Discussion • Answers to 3.3, Soil Compaction Questions
• Extensions • Modifications • References

Reproducibles

A Generalized Soil Profile (transparency master)

3.1 Soil Compaction: Background Information

3.2 Soil Compaction: Instructions and Data

3.3 Soil Compaction: Questions

ACTIVITY 4. WHAT PRICE OPEN SPACE? • 33

Activity Summary • Introduction • Grouping • Time • Anticipated Outcomes • Materials • Vocabulary • Teacher Preparation • Safety Considerations • Procedure • Discussion • Answers to 4.3, What Price Open Space? Questions • Extensions • Modifications • Reference

Reproducibles

4.1 What Price Open Space? Background Information

4.2 What Price Open Space? Instructions

4.3 What Price Open Space? Questions

Character Cards Sheets

ACTIVITY 5. MULTIPLE USE OR MULTIPLE ABUSE? • 42

Activity Summary • Introduction • Grouping • Time • Anticipated Outcomes • Materials • Vocabulary • Teacher Preparation • Safety Considerations • Procedure • Discussion • Answers to 5.3, Multiple Use or Multiple Abuse? Questions • Extensions • Modifications • References

Reproducibles

5.1 Multiple Use or Multiple Abuse? Background Information

5.2 Multiple Use or Multiple Abuse? Research Assignment

5.3 Multiple Use or Multiple Abuse? Questions

UNIT 2: WILDLIFE ISSUES 51

ACTIVITY 6. HABITATS—THE CHOICE IS YOURS • 53

Activity Summary • Introduction • Grouping • Time • Anticipated Outcomes • Materials • Vocabulary • Teacher Preparation • Safety Consideration • Procedure • Discussion • Answers to 6.3, Habitats: The Choice Is Yours Questions • Extensions • Modifications • References

Reproducibles

6.1 Habitats—The Choice Is Yours: Background Information

6.2 Habitats—The Choice Is Yours: Activity Instructions

6.2 Habitats—The Choice Is Yours: Planning Map

6.3 Habitats—The Choice Is Yours: Questions

ACTIVITY 7. MICROHABITATS • 63

Activity Summary • Introduction • Grouping • Time • Anticipated Outcomes • Materials • Vocabulary • Teacher Preparation • Safety Considerations • Procedure • Discussion • Answers to 7.3, Microhabitats Questions • Extensions • Modifications • Reference

Reproducibles

7.1 Microhabitats: Background Information

7.2 Microhabitats: Data

7.3 Microhabitats: Questions

ACTIVITY 8. ENDANGERED SPECIES I—WHAT'S HAPPENING? • 70

Activity Summary • Introduction • Grouping • Time • Anticipated Outcomes • Materials • Vocabulary • Teacher Preparation • Safety Considerations • Procedure • Discussion • Answers to 8.3, Endangered Species I—What's Happening? Questions • Extensions • Modifications • References

Reproducibles

8.1 Data Graphing Activity

8.2 Endangered Species—What's Happening? Information

8.3 Endangered Species—What's Happening? Questions

ACTIVITY 9. ENDANGERED SPECIES II—WHO CARES? • 78

Activity Summary • Introduction • Grouping • Time • Anticipated Outcomes • Materials • Vocabulary • Teacher Preparation • Safety Considerations • Procedure • Discussion • Answers to 9.3, Endangered Species II—Who Cares? Questions • Extensions • Modifications • References

Reproducibles

9.1 Endangered Species II—Who Cares?: Background Information

9.2 Endangered Species II—Who Cares?: Assignments

9.3 Endangered Species II—Who Cares?: Questions

UNIT 3. WATER ISSUES 87

ACTIVITY 10. OIL SPILL! • 89

Activity Summary • Introduction • Grouping • Time • Anticipated Outcomes • Materials • Vocabulary • Teacher Preparation • Safety Considerations • Procedure • Discussion • Answers to 10.3, Oil Spill! Questions • Extensions • Modifications • References

Reproducibles

10.1 Oil Spill! Background Information

10.2 Oil Spill! Data Table

10.3 Oil Spill! Questions

ACTIVITY 11. WATER TREATMENT • 99

Activity Summary • Introduction • Grouping • Time • Anticipated Outcomes • Materials • Vocabulary • Teacher Preparation • Safety Consideration • Procedure • Discussion • Answers to 11.3, Water Treatment Questions • Extensions • Modifications • References

Reproducibles

11.1 Water Treatment: Background Information

11.2 Water Treatment: Instructions

11.3 Water Treatment: Questions

ACTIVITY 12. "WATER" WE GOING TO DO? • 107

Activity Summary • Introduction • Grouping • Time • Anticipated Outcomes • Materials • Vocabulary • Teacher Preparation • Safety Considerations • Procedure • Discussion • Answers to 12.4, "Water" We Going to Do? Questions • Extensions • Modifications • References

Reproducibles

12.1 "Water" We Going to Do?: Background Information

12.2 "Water" We Going to Do?: Personal Water Use

12.3 "Water" We Going to Do?: Home Conservation Survey

12.4 "Water" We Going to Do?: Questions

UNIT 4. ATMOSPHERIC ISSUES 119

ACTIVITY 13. DETECTING AIR POLLUTION • 121

Activity Summary • Introduction • Grouping • Time • Anticipated Outcomes • Materials • Vocabulary • Teacher Preparation • Safety Considerations • Procedure • Discussion • Answers to 13.3, Detecting Air Pollution Questions • Extensions • Modifications • References

Reproducibles

13.1 Detecting Air Pollution: Background Information

13.2 Detecting Air Pollution: Instructions

13.2 Detecting Air Pollution: Data

13.3 Detecting Air Pollution: Questions

ACTIVITY 14.   ACIDIC PRECIPITATION • 130

Activity Summary • Introduction • Grouping • Time • Anticipated Outcomes
• Materials • Vocabulary • Teacher Preparation • Safety Considerations
• Discussion • Answers to 14.3, Acidic Precipitation Questions • Extensions
• Modifications • Reference

Reproducibles

14.1 Acidic Precipitation: Background Information

14.2 Acidic Precipitation: Instructions and Data Table

14.3 Acidic Precipitation: Questions

ACTIVITY 15.   GLOBAL WARMING • 139

Activity Summary • Introduction • Grouping • Time • Anticipated Outcomes
• Materials • Vocabulary • Teacher Preparation • Safety Considerations
• Procedures • Discussion • Answers to 15.3, Global Warming Questions
• Extensions • Modification • References

Reproducibles

15.1 Global Warming: Background Information

15.2 Global Warming: Instructions

15.2 Global Warming: Data

15.3 Global Warming: Questions

UNIT 5. ENERGY ISSUES 144

ACTIVITY 16.   FOOD CHAINS • 151

Activity Summary • Introduction • Grouping • Time • Anticipated Outcomes
• Materials • Vocabulary • Teacher Preparation • Safety Consideration
• Procedure • Discussion • Answers to 16.2, Food Chains Questions
• Extensions • Modifications • Reference

Reproducibles

16.1 Food Chains: Background Information

16.2 Food Chains: Questions

ACTIVITY 17.   HIDDEN ENERGY USES • 163

Activity Summary • Introduction • Grouping • Time • Anticipated Outcomes
• Materials • Vocabulary • Teacher Preparation • Safety Considerations
• Procedure • Discussion • Answers to 17.3, Hidden Energy Uses • Extensions
• Modifications • References

Reproducibles

17.1 Hidden Energy Uses: Background Information

17.2 Hidden Energy Uses: Instructions

17.3 Hidden Energy Uses: Questions

ACTIVITY 18. "WATTS" THE COST? • 170

Activity Summary • Introduction • Grouping • Time • Anticipated Outcomes
• Materials • Vocabulary • Teacher Preparation • Safety Consideration
• Procedure • Discussion • Answers to 18.3, "Watts" the Cost? Questions
• Extensions • Modifications • References

Reproducibles

18.1 "Watts" the Cost?: Background Information

18.2 "Watts" the Cost?: Instructions

18.2 "Watts" the Cost?: Data

18.3 "Watts" the Cost?: Questions

18.4 "Watts" the Cost?: Parent Letter

ACTIVITY 19. CONSERVE A WATT • 181

Activity Summary • Introduction • Grouping • Time • Anticipated Outcomes
• Materials • Vocabulary • Teacher Preparation • Safety Considerations
• Procedure • Discussion • Answers to 19.3, Conserve a Watt Questions
• Extensions • Modification • References

Reproducibles

19.1 Conserve a Watt: Background Information

19.2 Conserve a Watt: Instructions

19.2 Conserve a Watt: Data

19.3 Conserve a Watt: Questions

19.4 Some Ways to Conserve Energy

ACTIVITY 20. KEEP THE HEAT! • 193

Activity Summary • Introduction • Grouping • Time • Anticipated Outcomes
• Materials • Vocabulary • Teacher Preparation • Safety Considerations
• Procedure • Discussion • Answers to 20.3, Keep the Heat! Questions
• Extensions • Modifications • References

Reproducibles

20.1 Keep the Heat!: Background Information

20.2 Keep the Heat!: Instructions

20.2 Keep the Heat!: Data

20.3 Keep the Heat!: Questions

ACTIVITY 21. CATCH THE SUN! • 202

Activity Summary • Introduction • Grouping • Time • Anticipated Outcomes
• Materials • Vocabulary • Teacher Preparation • Safety Considerations
• Procedure • Discussion • Answers to 21.3, Catch the Sun! Questions
• Extensions • Modification • References

Reproducibles

21.1 Catch the Sun!: Background Information

21.2 Catch the Sun!: Instructions

21.2 Catch the Sun!: Data

21.3 Catch the Sun!: Questions

ACTIVITY 22. FOSSIL FUEL EXTRACTION • 210

Activity Summary • Introduction • Grouping • Time • Anticipated Outcomes
• Materials • Vocabulary • Teacher Preparation • Safety Consideration
• Procedure • Discussion • Answers to 22.3, Fossil Fuel Extraction Questions
• Extensions • Modifications • References

Reproducibles

22.1 Fossil Fuel Extraction: Background Information

22.2 Fossil Fuel Extraction: Instructions and Data

22.3 Fossil Fuel Extraction: Questions

ACTIVITY 23. THE NUCLEAR POWER PUZZLE • 218

Activity Summary • Introduction • Grouping • Time • Anticipated Outcomes
• Materials • Vocabulary • Teacher Preparation • Safety Considerations
• Procedure • Discussion • Answers to 23.3, The Nuclear Power Puzzle Questions
• Extensions • Modifications • References

Reproducibles

23.1 The Nuclear Power Puzzle: Background Information

23.2 The Nuclear Power Puzzle: Instructions

23.3 The Nuclear Power Puzzle: Questions

ACTIVITY 24. BIOGAS • 231

Activity Summary • Introduction • Grouping • Time • Anticipated Outcomes
• Materials • Vocabulary • Teacher Preparation • Safety Considerations
• Procedure • Discussion • Answers to 24.3, Biogas Questions • Extensions
• Modifications • References

Reproducibles

24.1 Biogas: Background Information

24.2 Biogas: Instructions

24.3 Biogas: Questions

ACTIVITY 25.   ENERGY ALTERNATIVES • 238

Activity Summary • Introduction • Grouping • Time • Anticipated Outcomes • Materials • Vocabulary • Teacher Preparation • Safety Considerations • Procedure • Discussion • Answers to 25.3, Energy Alternatives Questions • Extension • Modifications • References

Reproducibles

25.1 *Energy Alternatives: Background Information*

25.2 *Energy Alternatives: Instructions*

25.3 *Energy Alternatives: Questions*

UNIT 6. HUMAN ISSUES 247

ACTIVITY 26.   POPULATION—MORE IS LESS • 249

Activity Summary • Introduction • Grouping • Time • Anticipated Outcomes • Materials • Vocabulary • Teacher Preparation • Safety Consideration • Procedure • Discussion • Answers to 26.3, Population: More Is Less Questions • Extensions • Modifications • References

Reproducibles

26.1 *Population—More Is Less: Background Information*

26.2 *Population—More Is Less: Instructions*

26.3 *Population—More Is Less: Questions*

ACTIVITY 27.   FOOD? WHAT FOOD? • 263

Activity Summary • Introduction • Grouping • Time • Anticipated Outcomes • Materials • Vocabulary • Teacher Preparation • Safety Considerations • Procedure • Discussion • Answers to 27.3, Food? What Food? Questions • Extensions • Modifications • References

Reproducibles

27.1 *Food? What Food?: Background Information*

27.2 *Food? What Food?: Questions*

ACTIVITY 28.   WE "AUTO" DRIVE LESS • 270

Activity Summary • Introduction • Grouping • Time • Anticipated Outcomes • Materials • Vocabulary • Teacher Preparation • Safety Consideration • Procedure • Discussion • Answers to 28.3, We "Auto" Drive Less Questions • Extensions • Modification • References

Reproducibles

28.1 We "Auto" Drive Less: Background Information

28.2 We "Auto" Drive Less: Instructions

28.3 We "Auto" Drive Less: Questions

ACTIVITY 29.   TOXICS IN THE HOME • 281

Activity Summary • Introduction • Grouping • Time • Anticipated Outcomes • Materials • Vocabulary • Teacher Preparation • Safety Considerations • Procedure • Discussion • Answers to 29.3, Toxics in the Home Questions • Extensions • Modification • References

Reproducibles

29.1 Toxics in the Home: Background Information

29.2 Toxics in the Home: Instructions and Data Table

29.3 Toxics in the Home: Questions

ACTIVITY 30.   WANTS AND NEEDS • 290

Activity Summary • Introduction • Grouping • Time • Anticipated Outcomes • Materials • Vocabulary • Teacher Preparation • Safety Consideration • Procedure • Discussion • Answers to 30.3, Wants and Needs Questions • Extensions • Modification • References

Reproducibles

30.1 Wants and Needs: Background Information

30.2 Wants and Needs: Instructions

30.2 Wants and Needs: Data

30.3 Wants and Needs: Questions

ACTIVITY 31.   WHAT'S HAPPENING? • 300

Activity Summary • Introduction • Grouping • Time • Anticipated Outcomes • Materials • Vocabulary • Teacher Preparation • Safety Considerations • Procedure • Discussion • Answers to 31.3, What's Happening? Questions • Extensions • Modifications • Reference

Reproducibles

31.1 What's Happening?: Background Information

31.2 What's Happening?: Instructions

31.2 What's Happening?: Article cover Sheets

31.3 What's Happening?: Questions

ACTIVITY 32.   DO IT! • **308**

Activity Summary • Introduction • Grouping • Time • Anticipated Outcomes
• Materials • Vocabulary • Teacher Preparation • Safety Consideration
• Procedure • Discussion • Answers to 32.3, Do It! Questions • Extensions
• Modifications • References

Reproducibles

32.1 *Do It!: Background Information*

32.2 *Do It!: Instructions*

32.2 *Do It!: Project Description*

32.3 *Do It!: Questions*

32.4 *Do It!: Project Ideas*

APPENDICES

APPENDICES **319**

APPENDIX I: **Governmental Agencies** • **320**

APPENDIX II: **Selected Private Organizations** • **322**

APPENDIX III: **How to Write for Information** • **323**

APPENDIX IV: **How to Write a Letter to a Governmental Official** • **325**

BIBLIOGRAPHY **329**

unit One

Land Use Issues

- **Surface Mining**
- **Why Recycle?**
- **Soil Compaction**
- **What Price Open Space?**
- **Multiple Use or Multiple Abuse?**

ACTIVITY 1: SURFACE MINING

Activity Summary

Peanuts (or sunflower seeds or other items) are buried in pans of sand to simulate mineral resources. Soil is added to the surface of the sand model to represent topsoil, and plant material is added to represent surface vegetation. As the students mine for their "ore," they observe environmental impacts of surface mining, the production of waste products in the refining process, and resource depletion.

Introduction

Scientists often use "modeling" to simulate events that cannot be easily studied in real life, real time, or on a convenient scale. Modeling could be done with computers, through experiments, or by building models of the situation being investigated. This activity involves models of various environments to simulate areas where mineral resources are being sought, mined, and processed to make useful materials.

Grouping

Teams of 4 to 5 students should be formed. You can use this activity for "cooperative learning" teams, in which each team is balanced according to performance or ability, or you can select teams randomly, or you can let the students choose their own teams. Within each team, students will be given (or choose) various roles as described under **Procedure**.

Time

> **Material preparation:** 15–30 minutes
>
> **Explaining/introducing the activity:** 10–15 minutes
>
> **Actually doing the activity:** 20–25 minutes
>
> **Discussing the activity:** at least 15 minutes

Anticipated Outcomes

The students will:

- increase their understanding of environmental impacts of surface mining.
- increase their understanding of resource depletion.
- increase their understanding of environmental impacts of ore refining.
- increase their willingness to reduce waste of mineral resources.
- utilize models to simulate what happens in the real world.

Materials

—Photocopied student pages:

- 1.1 Surface Mining: Background Information (one per student)
- 1.2 Surface Mining: Instructions and Data (one per team)

> • 1.3 Surface Mining: Questions (one per student)

—One stopwatch or other watch with a second hand

—For each team of students:

- one plastic pan, approximately 12" × 14" × 6" deep (30 cm × 35 cm × 15 cm deep)
- enough clean sand or fine gravel to fill the pan to a depth of about 4" (10 cm)
- enough clean soil to form a layer of (topsoil) about 1 cm thick on top of the sand
- several peanuts (in their shells) (or other items such as sunflower seeds or acorns to represent "ore"—see Teacher Preparation and Modifications sections below). (There are about 200 peanuts in 1 pound of peanuts in the shell.)
- enough small leaves or grass clippings to cover the "topsoil" in the pan
- 1 probe, pencil, or long thin stick
- 1 forceps or tweezers
- 1 small scoop
- 1 teaspoon
- 1 tablespoon
- 1 small kitchen strainer (diameter of the opening about 2–3" [5–8 cm])
- 1 clean cup or other clean container to hold the peanuts
- 1 small broom, preferably with a dustpan, for cleaning up
- 1 nutcracker or pliers

Vocabulary

exponential growth	nonrenewable resource	open pit mine	ore
overburden	reclaim/reclamation	refine	spoil
strip mining	surface mining	tailings	

Teacher Preparation

1. Photocopy the Background Information sheet (1.1), Instructions and Data sheets (1.2), and Questions sheet (1.3).
2. Gather materials and prepare the "mining sites" as described below.
3. The peanuts represent the mineral-bearing ore.
4. You may want all mining sites to have similar "mineral deposits," or you may want different teams to mine sites of different richness in minerals. Some sites may have the minerals spread evenly while others may have them clustered together. For each site, select the peanuts to be deposited. Keep a record of how many peanuts you have deposited in the sand at each site.
5. For each mining site:
   a. Place about 2 inches (5 cm) of sand in the bottom of the plastic pan.
   b. Place the peanuts on top of this layer of sand, either clustered together or spread out.
   c. Add more sand, to a depth of about 4 inches (10 cm).
   d. Cover the top of the sand with about 1 cm of soil.
   e. Cover the top of the soil with small leaves or grass clippings.
6. At the start of the lab, the sites (pans) should look similar. The students should be allowed to select their mining sites (pans).

7. Decide which roles you will have the students assume.

SAFETY CONSIDERATIONS

1. If probes or other sharp objects are used, remind the students to be careful with them.
2. If peanuts, sunflower seeds, or other edible items are used for "ore," be sure that the sand is clean because the students will, in all likelihood, eat some of the nuts even though they have been told not to do so.

Procedure

1. Discuss with the students how scientists can use models to simulate real life and that models can be useful in studying things that cannot be brought into the laboratory. Emphasize that there are limits to the usefulness of models.
2. Discuss the vocabulary terms as needed or as they come up.
3. Form teams of four or five students. Tell them that they are each a mining company and that they will each be given a mining site.
4. Explain that their mining company's job will be to:
   a. locate the "ore."
   b. mine the ore.
   c. separate the mineral from the ore.
   d. safely dispose of the tailings (waste) and reclaim the mining site.
5. Emphasize that this is not a contest and the grade will not be determined by how much mineral is recovered; their job as a mining company is to make a good living for their employees while preserving the environment so that it is a nice place in which to live or for wildlife to live.
6. Have each team select a company name and make a sign to go on their mining site.
7. Describe the following roles and have the students either select who will play each part or select parts by random drawing:
   a. *FIELD GEOLOGIST:* Uses the probe to try to locate where to mine for the minerals.
   b. *MINE OPERATOR:* Uses the forceps or other equipment to remove the ore from the ground.
   c. *PROCESSING PLANT OPERATOR:* Uses pliers or a nutcracker to remove the mineral from the ore (peanut from the shell).
   d. *ACCOUNTANT:* Keeps track of the amount of mineral mined and refined. Uses peanuts to buy new equipment.
   e. *ENVIRONMENTAL ENGINEER:* In charge of cleaning up any spillage, disposing of waste products such as peanut shells, and reclaiming the land.
8. Distribute the Background Information sheet and the Instruction and Data sheets.
9. Give and discuss the instructions. Discuss the roles, timing, and buying of equipment. (You will have to decide on the amounts of "fines" for not cleaning up messes and rewards for reclamation of the site.)
10. Begin the activity. Be aware of the students' progress.
11. After the first round, there may be questions.

12. Depending on the time available, you may want to have several rounds of mining in the same pans. Try not to hurry the students, though.

13. Prior to the last round, announce that this will be the last round.

14. After the last round, have all students return to their seats. Then inspect each site and levy fines for messes and give rewards for reclaimed sites.

15. Have each accountant report to the class the final amount of wealth accumulated.

Discussion

1. Did all mining companies recover the same amount of ore? If not, why not? Do all countries (or states in the United States) have the same mineral wealth? the same technology?

2. If different states in the United States have different mineral wealth, how should it be shared among the various states (people) of the country?

3. If different countries have different mineral wealth, how should it be shared among the different countries (people) of the world?

4. If minerals cannot be mined profitably without harming the environment, should they be mined?

5. Who should pay for environmental damage repair—the company's shareholders? owners? customers? all taxpayers?

6. What happened to the rate of mineral recovery as the mining continued?

7. Is there an infinite amount of any mineral in the Earth?

8. What usually happens to the price of a mineral as its supply diminishes?

9. Discuss the statement: "We do not inherit the Earth from our ancestors. We borrow it from our children."

10. Discuss the impact of technology on mining and the environmental impacts of mining.

Answers to 1.3, Surface Mining Questions

1. This activity is realistic in that the surface of the ground must be disturbed to get at the minerals below. The minerals are not evenly distributed everywhere on Earth. Also, there is waste produced in the mining and processing of the ore. (*Other answers may be acceptable.*)

2. This activity is not realistic because it is much simpler than the actual process. (*Other answers may be acceptable.*)

3. Some options include:

   a. Find new deposits.

   b. Process lower-grade ore.

   c. Close down their operations or switch to mining other materials.

   d. Charge more money per ton of product, or have a governmental subsidy, so that they can still make a profit. (*Other answers may be acceptable.*)

4. *Answers will vary.*

   a. Exploring for minerals may include building roads and digging test holes, sometimes in environmentally sensitive areas. Exploration can be done carefully, with minimal disruption of the environment. It can also be restricted to areas that are not overly sensitive to human impact.

b. Removing the overburden disrupts the vegetation in that area. The topsoil can be saved and carefully taken care of so that it can be placed over the mining area after mining is finished. Saving and replacing the topsoil takes time, space, and money.

c. Removing the ore, especially with huge machines, can disrupt much of the land that does not contain the ore. Care can be taken to minimize disruption of the environment.

d. Processing of ore can produce water and air pollution, as well as tons of rocks and other mineral wastes. Pollution-control equipment can be installed and operated properly. (This, of course, is expensive and we as consumers need to be willing to pay for it.)

e. Transporting minerals to manufacturing plants takes energy. The making of the product may produce air and water pollution, and some of the metal might be wasted. These problems can be reduced by using efficient transportation, installing pollution control equipment, and minimizing waste, possibly recycling scraps.

5. If we don't buy products, they won't be made. As consumers, we need to carefully consider whether we really need a product and whether it is worth not only the money but the environmental impacts of its manufacture. If we buy fewer unnecessary products and take good care of those that we do purchase, we can reduce the need to mine so many minerals. There are, of course, economic impacts of this.

Extensions

(See Activity 32 for suggestions for student projects.)

1. Activity 22 (Fossil Fuel Extraction) is a simpler version of this activity. Consider doing it before this activity.

2. Have the students graph their mining activity. (Production rate [number of peanuts recovered per round of mining] should be on the vertical axis and time [mining round number] on the horizontal axis.)

3. Obtain some printed resources from the 1960s and early 1970s that predict how long various resources will last and compare them to more recent predictions. Discuss the differences. Be sure to note that most predictions are based on "current rate of usage" or some constant growth rate. Also point out that conservation has reduced the use of most energy resources even though the population has increased.

4. Have students investigate the developing industry of mining previously discarded matter.

5. Have the students investigate exponential growth and Thomas Malthus.

6. Have the students investigate mineral rights laws in your state and on federal land.

Modifications

1. Various materials can be used to represent minerals. Peanuts or sunflower seeds are suggested because they are readily available, inexpensive, they require the stage of "refining" before they are useful, and the refining process produces waste that

must be disposed of. As noted earlier, there are about 200 peanuts (in the shell) in a one-pound package. There are about 200 sunflower seeds (in the shell) in an ounce. Acorns will work too. (Different species of oak will produce different numbers of acorns per pound.) Dried beans, corn, gravel, beads, or other items might be used to represent the ore if you want to eliminate the refining stage.

2. If you want to have four students in a team, it is easy for the "Field Geologist" to become the "Accountant." If you have one or two students extra, they can be the Environmental Protection Agency "Inspectors." They can help monitor the clean-up.

3. You might do the activity once with everybody with the same mineral wealth and equal distribution within the mining site. Then discuss the lack of reality in such a setup. The next day the activity could be repeated with unequal distribution of the minerals as described here.

4. You might have more than one mineral present in the sample.

5. Try setting up different types of ground cover. Make a paper "river." Include farmland, deserts, forests, grassland, and possibly even residential areas. Discuss the costs of mining with each scenario.

6. Students can prepare pans for other classes.

References

Christensen, John W., *Global Science Laboratory Manual.* Dubuque, IA: Kendall/Hunt Publishing Company, 1991.

Miller, G. Tyler, *Living in the Environment.* Belmont, CA: Wadsworth Publishing Co., 1990.

Myers, Norman (ed.), *GAIA—An Atlas of Planet Management.* New York, NY: Bantam Doubleday Dell Publishing Group, Inc., 1984.

1.1 Surface Mining: Background Information

We all use mineral resources that are mined with the process called **surface mining, strip mining,** or **open pit mining.** Copper, aluminum, iron, and coal are but a few of the mineral resources that are surface mined. About 90 percent of the minerals mined in the United States are surface mined. As the world's population grows and new uses are found for mineral resources, the demand for minerals often shows exponential growth.

Locating, mining, processing, and using mineral resources have many environmental impacts. Among these are the disturbance of the land and the organisms living on it, erosion, water and air pollution, and the production of waste products.

Mining companies use many different techniques to locate mineral deposits. They study crustal movements of the Earth, use aerial photography and satellite imagery, and samples taken in the field. All of these methods are expensive but necessary if new mineral deposits are to be found. As we use up the easily found and mined mineral deposits, of course, locating new ones becomes increasingly more difficult and expensive.

Mineral deposits found near the Earth's surface are removed either by surface mining or open pit mining. Huge equipment removes the soil, rock, and vegetation that overlies the mineral deposit. This **"overburden"** or **"spoil"** is set aside during the mining operations. This spoil adds about 30 percent to the amount of land disturbed in surface mining. Theoretically, the spoil might be replaced when the deposit is exhausted. This **reclamation** or restoration of the land is expensive, and its feasibility depends on such factors as slope, soil type, precipitation, and other weather factors.

Most minerals occur in combination with oxygen or sulfur. After the **ore** is removed from the ground, it must be transported to a processing plant where the desired mineral is removed from the ore. This **refining** usually requires lots of energy and produces air and water pollution. The **solid waste materials,** or **tailings,** present a disposal problem. Controlling these problems is possible, but costs a lot of money.

As easily recovered resources are used up, mining companies must spend more and more money to locate and mine new deposits. As high-grade ore becomes more scarce, lower-grade ores become economically attractive. These low-grade ores generally produce more solid wastes, require more energy use to extract and process, and result in more air and water pollution.

For these and many other reasons, it is important to reduce our demand for **nonrenewable** resources. Recycling, reduced demand, and substitution of other resources all play a part in efforts to stretch mineral resources and thereby reduce the need for surface mining.

1.2 Surface Mining: Instructions

Congratulations! You have just formed a mining company and have been awarded mining rights to a site that will be given to you by your teacher. Your first task is to learn your jobs. They are described below. Your teacher will tell you how to select who fills each job. As you play this game, you should keep in mind that your goal is to acquire wealth, as represented by peanuts, while preserving an environment that would be a good place to live.

Field Geologist: Your job is to explore the mining site and to probe for mineral deposits. Since mining is expensive, you want to try to find the most minerals that can be recovered with the least movement of the soil (overburden). To find the mineral deposits, you will use a probe as demonstrated by your teacher.

Mine Operator: Your job is to actually remove the mineral "ore" from the ground. At the start you will do this with forceps. After acquiring some of the minerals, though, your company might buy you some more advanced equipment such as a spoon or even a strainer!

Processing Plant Operator: Your job is to remove the mineral from the ore. To do this, you must start with just your fingers, but your company might decide to purchase a nut-cracker or a pair of pliers. *CAUTION:* The shells of the peanuts represent poisonous mining and processing wastes. DO NOT USE YOUR TEETH TO REMOVE THE NUTS FROM THEIR SHELLS!

Accountant: Your job is to keep track of your company's wealth, that is, the peanuts that have been removed from their shells. You will also keep records of the mining operations on the data table. You will be the one who actually deals with the teacher (or a designated student) to buy additional mining or processing equipment (such as a spoon, strainer, or nut-cracker).

Environmental Engineer: Your job has three parts:

1. During the mining process, your job is to keep the mining area neat. You should clean up any spilled sand or other debris. (Put spilled sand back into the pan.)
2. During the processing operation, your jobs are to keep the processing area neat and clean and to remind the processing plant operator not to use his or her teeth to remove the shells. DO NOT PUT THE PEANUT SHELLS INTO THE SAND IN THE PAN.
3. After the mining is complete, your job is to oversee the clean-up and reclamation of the mining site. (See to it that the mess is cleaned up!) Your company will be "fined" for wastes that are not properly disposed of. Your company can earn extra rewards for re-claiming the mining site.

After selecting your jobs, decide on a name for your company.

Each round or "day" of mining will last for 15 seconds. Each round of processing of ore will last 15 seconds. After these two rounds, your company will have 30 seconds to clean up any mess, plot your data, and discuss plans.

Then your teacher will provide an opportunity for mining companies to purchase equipment. The prices are as follows:

teaspoon:	5 peanuts
tablespoon:	10 peanuts
strainer:	15 peanuts
nutcracker:	10 peanuts
pliers:	15 peanuts

As you process your "ore," keep track of it on the data table. Each team member should keep track of the data.

A "round" consists of a complete cycle of mining, processing, cleaning up, and purchasing of equipment (modernizing the plant).

Remember, this is not a contest. Your objective is to acquire "wealth" as represented by peanuts, not to defeat any other team.

Good luck, good mining, and take good care of the Earth!

Name _____ Class _____ Date _____

1.2 Surface Mining: Data

Company name: _____

Other team members: _____

round number	peanuts recovered	price	equipment purchased item and use
1			
2			
3			
4			
5			
6			
7			
8			
9			
10			
11			
12			
13			
14			
15			
16			

1.3 Surface Mining: Questions

1. In what ways was this activity a realistic model of surface mining?

   _____

   _____

2. In what ways was this activity not a realistic model of surface mining?

   _____

   _____

3. As high-grade ore (ore with lots of a mineral in it) is used up, what are some of the options that mining companies have?

   _____

   _____

4. List at least one environmental impact or problem at each of the following stages. For each, tell how the problem can be reduced.

   a. exploration

   _____

   _____

   b. removal and storage of overburden

   _____

   _____

   c. removal of ore

   _____

   _____

   d. processing of ore

   _____

   _____

   e. using the mineral to make a product

   _____

   _____

5. Minerals are mined to make products that we buy. How do our buying habits affect mining? How can you reduce the need to mine so many minerals?

   _____

   _____

ACTIVITY 2: WHY RECYCLE? _____

Activity Summary

A relay-type game is used to demonstrate that resources, such as energy and materials, will last longer if we recycle.

Introduction

Most students probably know about recycling, and many may be avid recyclers. If they are, they may be doing it because it is a "good" thing to do, to make money, or for other reasons. These are good reasons, but it is also important that they understand the benefits of recycling and the global implications of not recycling resources.

One way to introduce this activity is to have a discussion of trash, litter, and wasted resources. This might be started with an examination of the classroom trash can or a school trash can that has discarded cans or bottles in it. A dramatic way to do this is to dump a trash can out on a plastic sheet on the classroom floor and have the students analyze the contents. What can be recycled? What kinds and amounts of foods were wasted? Was the food healthful? What about packaging? Does your school use plastic, cardboard, or Styrofoam plates? What about the cutlery?

Another way to introduce recycling aluminum is as a fund raiser. It is amazing how much money can be raised by collecting aluminum cans.

It is important to emphasize two things when advocating recycling:

- Recycling only postpones the time when we will run out of a resource, whether it is aluminum ore or space in a landfill.
- While recycling is much better for the environment than using new raw materials, even recycling has harmful environmental impacts. Recycling takes energy, materials, money, and time. It produces some air and water pollution, although not nearly as much as using new raw materials does.

Reducing our use of resources should be emphasized. Recycling can help reduce resource use significantly. Reducing demand and reusing can do even more good. One way to do this would be to promote the use of reusable containers.

Grouping

Students are grouped into two teams of equal numbers. Since no special skills or knowledge are required, other than following simple instructions, it is not important to try to balance the teams.

It is possible to demonstrate various scenarios (various percentages of recycling of materials) by having more than two teams and having each team "recycle" at different rates. See "Modifications."

Time

Introducing the Activity: 5–10 minutes

"Playing" the Game: 10–20 minutes

Discussing the Activity: 10–20 minutes

Anticipated Outcomes

The students will:

- better understand how recycling materials can help make our supplies of raw materials and energy last longer.
- understand the importance not only of recycling but of reducing our demand for resources.

Materials

—Photocopied student pages:

- 2.1 Why Recycle?: Background Information (one per student)
- 2.2 Why Recycle?: Instructions and Data (one per team)
- 2.3 Why Recycle?: Questions (one per student)

—1 trash can

—1 recycling container (This could be a box marked "recycling center.")

—1 "aluminum manufacturing plant" (This could be a box so labeled or a space on a table or the floor with a label.)

—40 crushed aluminum cans (Crushed in such a way that there are no jagged edges. Crush them to save space.)

—40 rocks (to represent bauxite ore)

(For other scenarios [different recycling rates], additional cans, rocks, and containers will be needed. Depending on the scenario, you might add more cans and rocks.)

Vocabulary

bauxite   ore   precycle   recycle   refine

Teacher Preparation

1. Make a "recycling center" out of a box with the words "Recycle Here" (or some other appropriate phrase) printed neatly on the outside. The boxes that copy paper comes in work well and can serve as storage for the materials.
2. Label a trash can or other container "City Dump . . . Waste Here!"
3. Make a place to be used as an "aluminum can manufacturing plant." This might be a box (appropriately decorated!) or simply a sign on the table.
4. Obtain 40 (or more) clean rocks, each about 3–5 mm in diameter.
5. Rinse and smash 40 (or more) aluminum cans. When you smash them, be sure to smash them in such a way that there are no jagged sharp edges. (They should be smashed so that they take up less space.)
6. Photocopy the Background Information sheet (2.1), Instructions and Data sheets (2.2), and Questions sheet (2.3).

7. Decide whether to have the students read the Background Information sheet before, during, or after doing the activity.

SAFETY CONSIDERATIONS

Check the smashed cans for sharp edges.

Procedure

1. Divide the class into two teams. This can be done randomly or by allowing the students to choose teams. For fun, they can each choose team names such as "Radical Recyclers" or "Woebegone Wasters."
2. Issue the student activity pages and explain the rules of the game to the teams.
3. The Wasters should select one member of their team to be the "Landfill Operator," and the Recyclers should select a "Recycling Center Operator."
4. The teacher might act as the aluminum-can manufacturing company operator, or a student might be chosen.
5. Each team is given 20 pieces of "bauxite ore" (rocks).
6. The aluminum cans are placed at or in the manufacturing plant.
7. Have the students refer to 2.2, Why Recycle? Data sheet. Have each individual student predict how many rounds of play will occur before each team runs out of ore. Have them record this prediction in the appropriate space on the student data record.
8. Have the students discuss within their teams to predict how many rounds of play they will have until they run out of bauxite ore. Have the students record their team's predictions on their data records.
9. Play the game.

Discussion

1. Discuss the implications of recycling or not recycling. Consider playing another round with various scenarios. (See "Modifications.")
2. Whose aluminum supply ("bauxite ore") lasted longer? Why?
3. What will the society do when it runs out of aluminum?
4. What happens to the aluminum in the dump? Could the dumps be mined?
5. Why were only three cans returned when four were recycled?
6. Do you recycle? Why or why not? How much of your recyclable material do you recycle? Where and when do you recycle?
7. Does your community have a curbside recycling program?
8. What are the advantages and disadvantages of each of the following:
   a. recycling containers
   b. throwing containers away
   c. reusing containers
   d. refusing to buy containers that can't be refilled/reused

9. What materials can be recycled?
10. What alternatives could there be to single-use drink containers?

Answers to 2.3, Why Recycle? Questions

1. Recycling extends the length of time that a resource will last. The higher the rate of recycling, the longer the resource will last.
2. Recycling is not 100 percent effective. There will always be some materials lost or wasted.
3. Recycling cans reduces air and water pollution, preserves landfill space, extends the life of the bauxite supply, and saves the consumer money.
4. Student answers will vary.

Extensions (See Activity 32 for suggestions for student projects.)

1. Visit a recycling center.
2. Visit a plant where recycled materials are used.
3. Calculate the cost of soft drinks in various kinds (sizes, materials) of containers. Be sure to calculate the cost per ounce. Discuss the reasons for the differences. Do these costs include the environmental costs?
4. Start a recycling program in your classroom, school, or community.
5. Investigate the following and report back to the class:

   a. Where does bauxite come from? (What countries are the three leading producers of bauxite ore?)
   b. Where does the bauxite ore go? (What three countries make most of the world's aluminum?)
   c. Why don't the countries with large deposits of bauxite ore make much aluminum?
   d. What percentage of the aluminum cans in your city, county, or state is recycled?
   e. Does your state have a "bottle bill" requiring deposits on beverage containers? Does it work?
   f. What can you do to promote recycling?
   g. What materials can be recycled in your city, county, or state?

6. If your state does not have a bottle bill or does not have a recycling program, contact your state legislators to find out why and what you can do to support such a program.
7. Survey your classmates or neighborhood to determine their recycling habits.
8. Find out how you can support/promote recycling in your area.
9. Visit your local landfill or dump. Talk to local officials about how long the landfill will last and what plans are being made for the future. Find out about the NIMBY (Not In My Back Yard) Syndrome.

Modifications

1. The game described here supposes that the recyclers recycle 100 percent of their cans and that the recycling process is 75 percent efficient. (When they turn their 4 cans in, they get 3 back.) Have the students predict the results if the following parameters are established, then play the game with these conditions:

    a. Only 3/4 of the cans are recycled, and recycling is only 67 percent efficient. (One can "thrown away," 3 "recycled," but only 2 are given back. Two bauxite rocks must be turned in to obtain 2 more cans.)

    b. One hundred percent of the cans are recycled, but recycling is only 50 percent efficient. (Four cans turned in, but only 2 are given back. Two bauxite rocks must be turned in to obtain 2 more cans.)

    c. You can set up any other percentages that you want by varying the number of cans to be held, turned in, and the percentage efficiency of the recycling.

2. A more realistic version of the game would involve having the amount of aluminum needed increase after each round. This would reflect increased demand caused by industrialization and development, and by increased population. Be sure to point out that the world's total supply of bauxite ore is finite. For a quantitatively adept class, discuss exponential growth patterns.

References

Anonymous, *Educator's Waste Management & Activity Guide*. Sacramento, CA: California Department of Conservation, 1991.

Anonymous, *Fifteen Simple Things Californians Can Do to Recycle*. Berkeley, CA: Earth-Works Press, 1991.

Anonymous, *The Green Box*. Eureka, CA: Humboldt County Office of Education, 1989.

Miller, G. Tyler, *Living in the Environment*. Belmont, CA: Wadsworth Publishing Company, 1990.

2.1 Why Recycle? Background Information

One of the basic laws of the universe is the Law of Conservation of Matter. Basically, this law says that matter can neither be destroyed nor created, but it can be changed. The result of this law is that, aside from a few meteors that have survived the trip through the Earth's atmosphere and some cosmic dust, for the foreseeable future, all of the material that we will ever have on Earth is already here. Also, except for a few very costly rockets and spacecraft, all of the matter of Earth will stay here. Our problem is how to wisely use the resources that we have. In some cases nonuse (preservation or saving for the future) is the best use at this time!

In our industrial society, we have become accustomed to using an object once, throwing it away, and buying or making another when we need it. We have become a "throw-away society." We have been able to do this because our environment has been rich in resources, both material and energy. In our country, we have been able to expand our resource base to include countries that are thousands of miles away by obtaining materials from them.

As we continue to use up our resources, it becomes more difficult and more costly to obtain new raw materials. As we use up the resources of other countries, and as they use their own resources, less of their resources are available to us. What we are allowed to buy becomes more expensive.

Recycling is the process of recovering materials from a used object and using that material as raw material for making other objects. Glass from bottles can be crushed, melted, and made into new glass. Paper, oil, and rags can be recycled. Iron, copper, aluminum, and other metals can be recycled.

Aluminum is made from an **ore** called **bauxite.** Most of the bauxite or new aluminum used in the United States has to be imported. Mining, **refining,** and shipping the bauxite or the aluminum all cause damage to the land, air pollution, water pollution, and use a lot of energy. By reusing aluminum we reduce all of these harmful effects.

How important is recycling aluminum cans?

- Making aluminum from recycled cans uses 90–95 percent less energy than making it from raw materials and reduces related air pollution by 95 percent.

- Our nation's consumers and industries throw away enough aluminum every three months to rebuild our entire commercial air fleet.

- Between 50 and 60 percent of the aluminum cans used in America are recycled. That means that about 40–50 percent are still thrown away.

- Recycling a 12-ounce aluminum can saves the energy equivalent of 6 ounces of gasoline.

- Recycling reduces litter and slows the filling of landfills.

For all these reasons, recycling is a wise choice. Why, then, don't more people recycle? The major reason is convenience. While many communities have effective recycling programs, including buy-back programs and curbside recycling, many don't. Only when the citizens insist on effective programs will recycling be easily available to all. Also, it is important to purchase recycled products or the recycling cycle is not complete and does no good.

There are a number of ways to slow down this spiral of materials use. Recycling is one way. We can reduce our use of materials, purchase fewer unnecessary things, make less packaging, and not use material wealth as a measure of our importance or happiness. We can decide not to buy every new product that is offered in the marketplace. We can refuse to buy things that are packaged in wasteful ways. For instance, buying in larger containers and transferring to smaller ones can reduce the number of containers. Some call this **"precycling."**

We can also reuse many things that we now throw away. We can give toys, clothes, and other things that we no longer want to others who can still use them. We can reuse bags, jars, and other containers. (At one time, almost all soda came in "returnable" bottles that were used many times before they needed to be recycled. Lightweight refillable plastic containers, in standardized sizes and shapes, may save both materials and energy in the not-so-distant future.) We can use worn-out clothes for rags rather than using so many paper towels. Our potential for reusing things is limited only by our imagination.

Recycling is treating symptoms (litter, shortages of materials and energy) rather than treating the illness (wasteful habits, overconsumption, and careless attitudes). Recycling is better than discarding. Better still, though, is reusing containers or refusing to buy them in the first place unless they are reusable.

2.2 Why Recycle? Instructions

The object of this game is to produce and have available aluminum cans for as long as you can. For each round of play, your team needs to have 4 cans.

Each team will receive 20 rocks. These represent bauxite ore, from which aluminum is made. Once you have "spent" a piece of ore, you cannot recover it. One piece of ore is "worth" one aluminum can.

Each round of play represents a certain amount of time. So far as the game is concerned, the time represented does not matter. It could be a year, a decade, or a generation. The final results will be the same.

Before playing the game, predict how many rounds it will take until both teams have run out of ore. Record your prediction on the Questions sheet.

For Round One:

- Team "A" (The Wasters, or whatever they call themselves) will spend 4 rocks to make (obtain) 4 aluminum cans. A representative of Team A gives 4 rocks to the aluminum company and obtains 4 cans.
- Then, Team "B" (The Recyclers, or whatever they call themselves) will also spend 4 rocks to make (obtain) 4 aluminum cans. Their representative gives 4 rocks to the aluminum company and obtains 4 cans.

(Now each team has 4 cans and 16 pieces of "bauxite.")

For Round Two:

- The next representative from Team A "throws away" its 4 cans, and spends 4 ore pieces for 4 aluminum cans.
- The next representative from Team B recycles its 4 cans. The representative gets 3 of them back from the recycling company and then spends 1 ore piece to get the fourth can from the aluminum company.

  (Now the Wasters have 4 cans and 12 pieces of ore. The Recyclers have 4 cans and 15 pieces of ore.)

Play continues in this way (like a relay) until one team runs out of ore. Keep track of how many rounds that takes. (Use the data table provided.)

2.2 Why Recycle? Data

Individually and as a team, predict how many rounds it will take each team to run out of ore.

- Record your individual prediction on your Questions sheet.
- Record your team's prediction below.

TEAM PREDICTION

Team A will run out after _____ rounds.   Team B will run out after _____ rounds.

Team A name: _____		
round	**bauxite spent**	**bauxite left**
1.		
2.		
3.		
4.		
5.		
6.		
7.		
8.		
9.		
10.		
11.		
12.		
13.		
14.		
15.		
16.		
17.		
18.		

Team B name: _____		
round	**bauxite spent**	**bauxite left**
1.		
2.		
3.		
4.		
5.		
6.		
7.		
8.		
9.		
10.		
11.		
12.		
13.		
14.		
15.		
16.		
17.		
18.		

Name _____ Class _____ Date _____

2.3 Why Recycle? Questions

My Predictions:

Team A will run out after _____ rounds. Team B will run out after _____ rounds.

1. Explain the effect of recycling on the length of time that a resource will last.

   _____

   _____

2. Explain why the recycling team doesn't get as many cans back as it turns in for recycling.

   _____

   _____

3. What are some ways that recycling aluminum cans helps protect the environment?

   _____

   _____

4. Were your individual predictions close to what actually happened? What about the team's predictions? How can you explain any error?

   _____

   _____

5. What can you as an individual do to support and promote **recycling**?

   _____

   _____

6. If **reusing** beverage containers and other things is better than recycling them, what can you as an individual do to promote reusing?

   _____

   _____

7. **Refusing** to buy wasteful products saves energy and materials. What can you as an individual do to support the idea of refusing to buy wasteful products?

   _____

   _____

ACTIVITY 3: SOIL COMPACTION _____

Activity Summary

In this activity, the students examine the effect of soil compaction on water infiltration.

Introduction

Many of us think of soil erosion as a problem caused by a long drought coupled with either high winds or torrential rains. While these are important causes of much soil erosion, there are other factors that cause soil erosion during periods of less severe weather, and many other factors besides erosion that affect soil's value or productivity. Soil compaction is one of these factors.

Most soils are a complex mixture of inorganic minerals (mostly clay, silt, and sand) and a variety of other components including decaying organic matter, air, water, and many organisms, both microscopic and macroscopic. A healthy soil has all of these components, while unhealthy soils may be without one or more of them.

A healthy mature soil is usually arranged in layers, called horizons. These layers are seen in a soil profile. Soil, as opposed to sand or clay, is a mixture of minerals from the breakdown of the bedrock and other rocks and organic material added from above. The black-line transparency master given with this activity shows these layers or "horizons."

A soil with an almost equal mixture of sand and silt, with some clay, is called a loam soil. Loamy soils are generally the best soils for most crops because they allow for water and air to enter, and they hold water that plants can then utilize.

A very sandy soil has a high permeability to water and air because of the relatively large spaces between particles. Thus, sandy soils do not hold water well and are best for crops that do not have large water requirements or where irrigating is practical.

A soil with much clay is easily compacted. Once compacted, the clay particles do not easily separate from each other and thus do not allow for the easy passage of air and water that is necessary for a healthy soil environment. Even low-clay soils can be compacted.

Soil compaction is a complex issue. When a lot of people walk repeatedly in the same place, such as on a wilderness trail or across the school lawn, compaction generally occurs. Some of the early pioneers' trails, such as the Oregon Trail, are still visible due to the compaction and subsequent erosion.

There are differing viewpoints on how to deal with the problem of compaction. Some people feel that it is better to limit the area affected by the compaction by encouraging or requiring people to use specific well-defined trails. Others feel that the impact should be spread out by not building trails so that no area is compacted as much as it would be if it were a trail. Still others feel that people should not be allowed into sensitive areas because of this and other impacts. These conflicting opinions apply as much to paths on the campus and in the school neighborhood as they do to wilderness trails.

In this activity, students test various sites to determine how rapidly water will enter the soil. There are numerous related activities and extensions to this activity.

Grouping

Students should work in teams of two or three students.

Time

30–50 minutes

Anticipated Outcomes

The students will:

- understand that soil is a complex substance.
- increase their understanding of the effects of compactions on soils.
- increase their willingness to try to protect and improve soils.

Materials

—Photocopied student pages:

- 3.1 Soil Compaction: Background Information (one per student)
- 3.2 Soil Compaction: Instructions and Data (one per team)
- 3.3 Soil Compaction: Questions (one per student)

—For use by the teacher:

- "tin snips" or other tool for cutting the lip or bead off one end of the can
- a fine file, emery cloth, or sandpaper for dulling the sharp edge
- transparency: "A Generalized Soil Profile"

—For each team of 2 or 3 students:

- one tin can prepared as described in "Teacher Preparation" below
- one piece of board slightly larger than the end of the can
- one measuring container (measuring cup, beaker, etc.; the size will depend on the size of the can used)
- one bucket or other container for carrying water
- a supply of water (the amount will be determined by the can size)
- one stopwatch or watch with a second hand
- one ruler
- masking tape or permanent marking pen

Vocabulary

bedrock	compaction	decompose	leach
percolation	porosity	soil horizon	soil profile
subsoil	topsoil		

Teacher Preparation

1. Be sure to check with your principal and groundskeeper or custodian before doing this activity.

2. Photocopy the Background Information sheet (3.1), Instructions and Data sheets (3.2), and Questions sheet (3.3).

3. Prepare the tin cans (percolation cans) as follows: Remove both ends from each tin can. The bead or lip should be cut off one end and the sharp edge somewhat dulled with a fine file, emery cloth, or sandpaper. For safety, the bead should be left on the other end, and the teacher should do the filing of the can. Before doing this activity with the students, you might experiment with various sizes of cans to find out which size is most suitable for your soil type, or you might want to allow the students to do this experimentation.

4. Have the students place a mark on the outside of each can about 2 inches from the sharp end. This can be done with masking tape or with a permanent marking pen. The actual distance from the end will depend on your soil types. (This mark is to ensure that the can is pushed into the soil the same depth each time.) Cans of differing sizes that will "nest" together can be used to save storage space unless you want student teams to compare data with each other.

5. Prepare a couple of extra cans and boards in case some become bent or broken.

SAFETY CONSIDERATIONS

1. The teacher should prepare the cans, being careful when cutting off and "dulling" the sharp end of the can.
2. Be sure to warn the students that the can is sharp on one end, and, possibly, inside where the end was cut out.

Procedure

1. Discuss what soil is, the importance of the organic portion of soils, and how important it is for air and water to be able to enter the soil. Introduce the term "compaction" and discuss the damage that it does to soils.

2. Demonstrate how to use the "percolation can":

   a. This can be done inside if you bring a bucket of soil into the classroom; otherwise, do it outside.

   b. Show the students that the can has a sharp end and discuss safety.

   c. Show the students the mark on the side of the can. This mark indicates how far the can will be pushed into the soil.

   d. Demonstrate pushing the can into the soil, using the wooden block on top of the can to protect your hands and allow you to apply equal pressure all around the end of the can.

   e. Demonstrate pouring the agreed-upon amount of water into the can. Instruct the students that they will time how long it takes the water to completely soak into the ground so that there are no puddles of water at the surface of the ground. (NOTE: You will probably want to do some tests of your own to determine an appropriate depth to push the can to and an amount of water that soaks in in a reasonable time.)

   f. Distribute the student Background sheets, student Instructions and Data sheets, and Questions sheet. Discuss each.

Discussion

1. Discuss the problem of compaction and erosion on heavily used trails. Should people be kept entirely out of sensitive areas? Should trails be eliminated so that people would spread out the damage? (Would they?) Should people be confined to trails so that the damage is limited to that area?

2. Discuss the problem of taking short cuts rather than staying on trails and paths—both in the local community (cutting across lawns) and in the mountains. Consider both environmental impacts and safety.

3. Often rivers and creeks are "channelized" to prevent flooding. Channelizing may be just clearing vegetation from existing stream channels or it may include lining the channel with rocks or concrete. It has many of the same impacts as compaction. Discuss the advantages and disadvantages of channelization.

4. What can be done to reduce compaction on the school campus? in the wilderness?

Answers to 3.3, Soil Compaction Questions

1. Answers will vary.

2. Answers will vary.

3. Answers will vary. There are numerous other factors besides compaction that affect plant health.

4. Soil may be compacted by people (and animals) walking on it, by cars or bicycles traveling on it, or by a variety of other means.

5. Answers will vary.

6. When the soil is compacted, plants cannot grow well. Plants help hold soil in place with their roots and by preventing rain from falling on the soil with its full force. Rain falling on compacted soil does not sink in, so it usually runs off more rapidly. The rapid run-off of the water will carry away more soil than a slow run-off would. In some areas, if the land is level, the water may sit on the surface until it evaporates. (*Other answers are possible.*)

Extensions (See Activity 32 for suggestions for student projects.)

1. If the soil in your area does not have good percolation and water-holding properties, you might prepare a box of "good" soil and allow the students to compare it to your local soil.

2. Contact the local soil conservation service for a speaker on local soil management.

3. Obtain soil maps from the soil conservation service or planning agency. Study them to learn the types and locations of various soils.

4. Invite a speaker from the local planning commission to speak on "planned growth" and zoning in your community.

5. Visit a planning commission meeting.

6. Take a field trip to a natural community and test percolation there.

7. Many communities require "percolation tests" before building is allowed. Invite a guest speaker to demonstrate or explain a "perc test." (Contact your local building department.)

8. Invite the school district's building and groundskeeper to talk to the students about taking care of the plants on the campus.

9. Involve the students in planting grass or other plants on campus.

10. Involve the students in planting or trail-improvement projects at a nearby park or nature preserve.

11. If your students live in areas with different soil types, have the students take the cans home and test their yards' soils.

Modification

Percolation tests can be done by digging a hole, pouring water in, and measuring the time for the water to percolate into the soil.

References

Cheryl, Dr. Charles (Project Director), *Project Learning Tree, Supplementary Activity Guide for Grades 7 through 12.* Washington, DC: American Forest Institute, 1977.

Miller, G. Tyler, *Living in the Environment.* Belmont, CA: Wadsworth Publishing Co., 1990.

A Generalized Soil Profile

Surface Litter:

recently fallen organic matter, beginning to **decompose**

Topsoil (Horizon A):

partially decomposed matter (humus), roots, living organisms, some minerals

Subsoil (Horizon B):

fine particles, material leached from above, some roots

Parent Material (Horizon C):

weathered bedrock and some **leached** material (organic and inorganic)

Bedrock:

underlying solid rock material

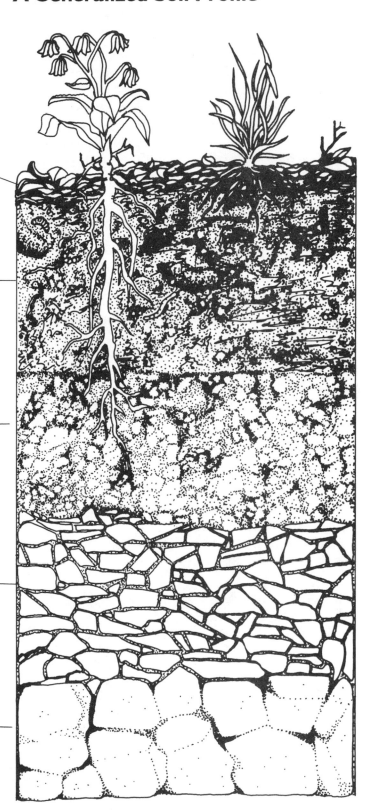

3.1 Soil Compaction: Background Information

That we all depend on a healthy soil should be no surprise to you. Plants require nutrient-rich soil to prosper. We depend on plants for our food. Soil is a complex substance made up not only of pieces of rock, but also of numerous plants and animals as well as air and water.

The organisms that live in the soil, including plants, bacteria, worms, insects, and a variety of other vertebrates and invertebrates, depend not only on the minerals but also on the ability of water and air to penetrate the soil. Spaces between the mineral particles and other soil components allow for this **percolation** of water and the passage of air into and out of the soil. The relative proportion of different types and sizes of soil particles is called soil texture. Soil texture is the main factor in determining soil **porosity,** which is a measure of spaces or openings in the soil.

One of the most common impacts that people have on soil is simple **compaction.** When we walk, ride a bike or horse, or drive on soil, it becomes compacted. The degree of compaction is determined both by the compacting activities and by the soil type. Once compacted, the soil particles do not easily separate from one another and thus do not allow for the easy passage of air and water that is necessary for a healthy soil environment.

Soil compaction has a number of harmful effects. Plant seeds have trouble working their way into the soil to germinate. If a plant does begin to grow, its roots cannot easily penetrate compacted soil. Even if the roots do penetrate the soil, the roots will not survive if air and water are not able to enter the soil. Without air and water, worms, insects, bacteria, and other organisms cannot live in the soil. Without plants and animals living in and on the soil, its fertility will not be built up. If plants cannot live on the soil, it is more easily eroded by water, air, and by such mechanical factors as tire treads, horses' hooves, and treads on shoes and boots.

Soil erosion is an environmental problem of enormous magnitude. You have probably heard of the "dust bowl" in the United States in the 1930s. Even though most erosion in the United States today is not as dramatically visible as the dust bowl, it is still occurring here and elsewhere in the world at alarming rates. Erosion of soils on farmland is especially alarming as we attempt to feed ever-increasing populations and as we cover cropland with roads, houses, and other buildings.

In this activity, we will investigate one common soil problem . . . compaction.

© 1993 by The Center for Applied Research in Education

3.2 Soil Compaction: Instructions and Data

In this activity, you will determine the rate at which water percolates into the soil in two or more locations. This percolation rate is very important for the health of the soil and, therefore, of the plants and animals that depend on it.

Your teacher will demonstrate the use of the "percolation can." To obtain data that is useful, it is important that you follow the same procedure in each percolation test that you do.

CAUTION: One end of the can is sharp! Be careful not to cut yourself!

Also be careful not to damage the can.

Record your data below.

Depth of soil penetration by can (distance from the sharp end of the can to the mark):

_____

Amount of water poured into can: _____

test #	location	description of site/soil	time for the water to percolate into the soil

3.3 Soil Compaction: Questions

1. Of the sites tested, which had the most rapid percolation? Why?

   _____

   _____

2. Of the sites tested, which had the slowest percolation? Why?

   _____

   _____

3. Which site seemed to have the most healthy plant growth?

   _____

   _____

4. List several ways that soil might become compacted.

   _____

   _____

   _____

   _____

5. In what ways might soil compaction increase soil erosion?

   _____

   _____

   _____

6. What should be done to reduce soil compaction?

   a. on the school campus

   _____

   _____

   _____

   b. in wilderness areas

   _____

   _____

   _____

ACTIVITY 4: WHAT PRICE OPEN SPACE? _____

Activity Summary

Students assume the characters of various people in a community that is faced with a decision about what to do with a piece of undeveloped property. Each student is provided with a detailed character description and is given some information about his or her character's position on the use of the property in question. The students present their "sides" of arguments at a role-played public hearing.

Introduction

As our population increases, our cities and suburbs expand. People need places to live. For many years the American Dream has generally included a piece of property with a single family residence on it.

As cities and suburbs expand, though, open space is lost. Many people who moved to a small town to have open space nearby are soon faced with the loss of that open space as others move to the community and as homes and businesses are built on undeveloped land. People often want to lock the gate behind themselves to maintain a small-town atmosphere.

Both individuals and governmental agencies must make difficult decisions about the development of land. The rights of the individual landowner must be weighed against the benefits and problems generated by the development of a piece of property. Private profit must be considered along with the general good. Land-use decisions often have effects on people from neighboring communities. Traffic to and from a new development may affect neighbors. Recreational land is often lost. Property values may increase or decline. Schools and other governmental agencies are impacted. Wildlife, possibly including rare, threatened, or endangered species, may be lost.

Most communities have zoning or planning commissions that make decisions about the use of land in their jurisdiction. There is generally opportunity for public input on major decisions. This activity is a simulation of such a hearing.

Grouping

Character Cards are provided for 13 roles. Individual students assume each role. You can add or delete roles to suit your needs, but if more than 13 or so roles are used, it is difficult for the students to remember what was said.

Time

Three 45- to 55-minute sessions

Anticipated Outcomes

The students will:

- increase their understanding of the complexity of land-use decision making.
- increase their ability to present arguments in public.

• increase their understanding of the public-hearing process that is often used in government.

Materials

—Photocopied student pages:

- 4.1 What Price Open Space?: Background Information (one per student)
- 4.2 What Price Open Space?: Instructions (one per student)
- 4.3 What Price Open Space?: Questions (one per student)
- Character Cards (glued to index cards and laminated) (one per character)

—Props such as podium, microphones, gavel appropriate for a public hearing

—Name plates for each character (made from manila folders that have been cut and folded)

Vocabulary

development   endangered species   open space   zoning

Teacher Preparation

1. Photocopy the Background Information sheet (4.1), Instructions sheet (4.2), Questions sheet (4.3), and Character Cards.
2. Cut the Character Cards apart and glue them to index cards. Laminate the cards.
3. Make name cards for each character. You can use half of a manila tagboard folder, folded in half lengthwise and with the character's name and role printed plainly on it.

Safety Considerations

None

Procedure:

Prior to Day 1: Either select the students for the roles or allow them to volunteer. Consider assigning the students to particular roles so that the discussion is balanced.

DAY I:

1. Provide the students with their Character Cards. Allow them time to read their characters' roles and to jot down some notes to be used in their presentations at the hearings.
2. Explain to the class that a hearing will be held tomorrow and that everybody in the class will participate in one of the following ways:

- Those who have been assigned roles will prepare a short presentation or talk to be given at the hearing.
- Those who have not been assigned roles can either:

    a. make up their own characters and prepare a presentation for the hearing.

    b. assume the role of an expert witness who will prepare a written technical report in support of the other characters.

    c. assume the role of a newspaper reporter who will be covering the hearing.

    d. assume the role of a concerned observer who will subsequently write a letter to the editor of the fictitious town's newspaper.

    e. assume the role of the chairperson of the hearing.

3. Have the students with assigned roles read their Character Cards to the class. This will help the other students to select their roles.

4. Allow time for questions, then allow the class to work on preparing for the hearing. Have the students without Character Cards write down what they are going to do. They should consider this a commitment and class homework. Try to have at least two newspaper reporters and several letter writers, preferably people who will write in support of different sides.

DAY 2:

1. On the day of the hearing, review the rules for the hearing, or, preferably, have the chairperson lead this review.

2. Have each of the students with Character Cards read his or her prepared testimony. Students who don't have Character Cards can ask questions of those who have testified. The chairperson's job is to keep order, and he or she must recognize the other students before they can ask their questions.

DAY 3:

1. Have the students without Character Cards read their letters, newspaper articles, or reports.

2. Allow time for questions from the commissioners.

3. Then, have the commissioners vote and give their reasons for voting as they did.

4. Finally, discuss the hearing and the issues raised.

Discussion

1. What are some of the problems that the commissioners encountered in trying to make their decision?

2. Was this activity realistic?

3. Which was more important:

    a. WHAT a person said, or

    b. HOW he or she said it, or

    c. WHO was saying it?

4. What factors influence voting by commissioners?

5. Did any of the characters change his or her mind as a result of the hearing? Did you?

6. What local governmental agency or agencies is/are responsible for decisions such as this?

7. How can you as a citizen take part in such decision making?

Answers to 4.3, What Price Open Space? Questions

1. Zoning commissioners should consider such things as the effect on traffic, pollution, crowding, jobs, taxes, and the quality of life for the current residents. (*Other factors will probably be mentioned by the students.*)

2. Answers will vary. The students should give their reasons for their choice.

3. Answers will vary, but the students should include such things as getting their facts straight, preparing their speech, practicing it, thinking about their appearance, bringing along some supporters, being on time, and so forth.

4. Once land is developed by paving and building on it, it is extremely difficult to return it to a natural state. If a species becomes extinct in the process, that species is gone forever. Soil quality, water percolation, air quality, and other environmental factors are usually permanently altered. On the other hand, not developing land now still allows for the possibility of future development if the need arises or if conditions change.

5. Answers will vary.

Extensions (See Activity 32 for suggestions for student projects.)

1. Either develop or have the students develop another similar simulation. Students who did not have Character Cards should have the main roles this time.

2. Bring in guest speakers from local planning commissions, builders' or real estate groups, environmental organizations, or other appropriate organizations.

3. Take a field trip to a planning or zoning commission hearing.

4. Visit a local undeveloped area and discuss various potential uses for it. Find out what plans, if any, there are for the site.

Modifications

1. Encourage the students to dress in attire appropriate for their role.

2. Alter the Character Cards and information to reflect a real situation in your community.

3. Provide a map of the area proposed for development.

4. A team of students could videotape the "hearing," then edit their tape and do a "newscast."

5. Class members not participating in the hearing in other ways can play the role of newspaper reporters who are to write articles on the hearing.

References

Cheryl, Dr. Charles (Project Director), *Project Wild, Secondary Activity Guide*. Boulder, CO: Western Regional Environmental Education Council, 1986.

4.1 What Price Open Space?: Background Information

When an individual has a piece of property that he or she would like to **develop** or build on, the person generally needs to get approval from a **zoning** or planning commission. This is because what people do with their property will have impacts on others in the community.

If houses are built, there will be more people traveling the roads, more children in schools, and more need for various services such as police and fire protection. If businesses are built, there will be more traffic, waste to be disposed of, and more pollution. In any case, if undeveloped land is developed, there will be less **open space** and less wildlife habitat. Rare or endangered species may be threatened.

On the other hand, the development of the property will provide jobs for the construction workers. If houses are built, the residents will bring their skills and interests to the community, as well as increase the need for more schools, stores, and other services. If businesses are built, more jobs will be available.

In most communities, there is a general plan that has the land in the community designated or **"zoned"** for different uses such as residential, agricultural, open space, industry, and so forth. If, for example, one has some agricultural land that a person wants to build houses on, he or she would have to apply for a change of zoning from agricultural to residential. To make such a change, a hearing would be needed. The zoning commission hearing usually would involve concerned parties who want to tell the commission what they think of a proposed zoning change. The commissioners would listen to the testimony of various people, including land owners, developers, neighbors, "experts," and others. The commissioners then would make their decision.

The commissioners would have to consider both the rights of individuals and what is best for the general community. Each individual, of course, has his or her own preferences and ideas about what is best. It is hoped that the commissioners would vote for what they think is best for the community as a whole.

In this activity, you will play the part of a resident of the fictitious community of Thoreau. Thoreau has a population of about 10,000 people. The economy is okay, but not thriving. The Bailey Appliance Company is the major employer for the community, currently employing 600 people. They want to expand their operations. This would provide about 200 new jobs. To do this, though, they would have to enlarge their plant and destroy Butterfly Meadow and some adjacent land. In addition, about 180 new homes would need to be built.

There are two related proposals before the zoning commission:

Proposal #1 would change the zoning on Butterfly Meadow from agricultural to industrial.

Proposal #2 would change the zoning of land owned by Tom Olson from agricultural to residential zoning.

4.2 What Price Open Space?: Instructions

In this activity, some students in the class will take on the roles of various people at a zoning commission hearing. Some will be zoning commissioners. Others will be people who speak at the hearing. Others will have roles such as newspaper reporters, "experts" who provide reports, or concerned citizens who write letters to the editor of the local newspaper. Here is the procedure:

Day 1:

The students will be assigned their roles and begin to prepare for the hearing, which will be held tomorrow (Day 2). The roles include:

a. **hearing participants with "Character Cards":** These students will have Character Cards that describe characters that they will play at the hearing. Some will be zoning commissioners and others will be various interested parties from the community.

   Their homework is to prepare their presentations for Day 2.

b. **newspaper reporters:** These students will represent reporters who will write articles for local newspapers. At least one should be in favor of the proposed zoning change and at least one should be against it.

   Their homework is to write their articles after the hearing and be ready to read them on Day 3.

c. **expert witnesses:** These students will prepare reports to support the various viewpoints. They may write about such things as endangered species in the area, the need (or lack of need) for jobs, traffic patterns, whether there is enough water for the development, room in the schools, and so forth.

   Their homework is to write their reports and present summaries of their reports on Day 3.

d. **letter writers:** These students will write "letters to the editor" based on the hearing. They should either support or oppose the proposed development and should make reference to testimony heard in the hearings on Day 2.

   Their homework is to write their letters and present them on Day 3.

Day 2:

The chairperson of the zoning commission presents the proposal and runs the meeting. The various people with Character Cards present their cases. The rest of the class take notes and begin to prepare their letters, articles, or reports.

Day 3:

The newspaper articles, reports, and letters are presented to the commission. After meeting briefly to discuss the proposal and the community input, the commissioners vote for or against the proposal. The class will then discuss the hearing.

4.3 What Price Open Space? Questions

1. What are some factors that zoning commissioners need to take into account when considering a zoning change?

   _____

   _____

   _____

   _____

2. If you were a zoning commissioner in this hearing, how would you have voted? What factor(s) were most important in this decision?

   _____

   _____

   _____

   _____

3. List some things that you would do if you wanted to make a presentation to a zoning or planning commission.

   _____

   _____

   _____

   _____

4. Discuss the statement that "If we don't develop the land now, we can change our mind later. If we develop it now, we can't change our mind later."

   _____

   _____

   _____

   _____

5. Find out when and where your local planning or zoning commission meet.

   _____

   _____

   _____

   _____

Maria or Miguel Martinez, MERCHANT (CHAIRPERSON OF THE ZONING COMMISSION)

You own a store that sells several brands of home appliances, including Bailey's. Business has not been very good lately, and you have not been able to hire any help at the store. As a result, you have little time to enjoy the out of doors.

- ✁ -

Megan or Martin Bailey, VICE PRESIDENT OF THE BAILEY APPLIANCE COMPANY (ZONING COMMISSION MEMBER)

You have lived in the community all your life. You are 45 years old and have two children, ages 13 and 16. Your company is the major employer for the community, and you want to expand your operations. Since you have a vested interest in the proposed zoning change, you will have to abstain from voting.

- ✁ -

Joan or John Elder, REALTOR (ZONING COMMISSION MEMBER)

You have lived in the community for 10 years and are very involved in community affairs. Your company is not developing the property in question, but you generally favor development. At the same time, you are concerned about the quality of life. You like the small-town atmosphere of Thoreau.

- ✁ -

Bonnie or Bob Hubbs, FARMER (ZONING COMMISSION MEMBER)

Your farm is doing well and you have been considering expanding. The parcel under consideration is one of several that you have been considering buying, but you have not yet talked with the current owner. You enjoy working outdoors and try to use environmentally sound farming techniques.

- ✁ -

Mike or Madi Sherron, LOCAL ACTIVIST (ZONING COMMISSION MEMBER)

You have been elected by the liberal faction of the community and almost always vote against development. Like your constituency, you moved to Thoreau because it was a small town and you want it to stay that way. You are also concerned about the impact of 180 new homes on the local sewer system.

- ✁ -

Julie or James Stevens, LOCAL LAND OWNER

Your mother owned the property in question until she died six months ago. You live in a city about 200 miles away and would like to sell the property.

- ✁ -

Helen or Hal Peterson, LOCAL RESIDENT AND HUNTER

You are an avid outdoorsperson and hunter. You have hunted on the property in question all your life, and you enjoy hunting there with your two teenaged children.

- ✁ -

Louise or Lee Chin, DEVELOPER

Your company is the major builder in the Thoreau area. You have a reputation for building good homes at reasonable prices and for attempting to minimize environmental damage done by your developments. You are interested in purchasing the property and building the homes and expansion for Bailey Appliance Company. You would like to build homes that are affordable for working-class people.

- ✂ -

Renee or Ron Stone, BANKER (PRESIDENT OF THE CHAMBER OF COMMERCE)

Your bank is the major real estate financier for the community, and you are interested in making new home loans. You live in a nice neighborhood that overlooks Butterfly Meadow and enjoy the view of the meadow and neighboring woods.

- ✂ -

Alice or Alex Brown, LOCAL RESIDENT AND MEMBER OF THE COMMITTEE TO SAVE BUTTERFLY MEADOW

You moved to Thoreau because you wanted to raise your family in a small town, away from the city in which you were raised. You enjoy hiking and birdwatching in Butterfly Meadow and think that you once spotted an endangered species of bird called Wilson's Spotted Warbler there.

- ✂ -

Cathy or Chris Nelson, LOCAL RESIDENT, RETIRED

You are 85 years old. For the last 15 years you have lived in a small cottage that the former owner of the property in question let you rent very cheaply in exchange for helping maintain the property and general caretaking. You have very little income and cannot afford to buy or rent in Thoreau. If you have to move, you will have to live with your son, who has a family and lives in New York City.

- ✂ -

Fran or Frank Walkingtall, LOCAL RESIDENT

As the leader of the local Native American organization, you are very concerned about the Butterfly Meadow area. It was an important campsite and has several sites that were sacred to your ancestors.

- ✂ -

"J.T." O'Neill, COLLEGE STUDENT

You were raised in the big city and have been attending a college in a town about 50 miles from Thoreau. You are engaged to marry someone who lives in Thoreau and hope to move there to teach school after you graduate.

ACTIVITY 5: MULTIPLE USE OR MULTIPLE ABUSE? _____

Activity Summary

In this activity, the students either select or are assigned to investigate and report on various recreational uses of lands, specifically public lands such as National Forest and National Park lands. They write to appropriate organizations and governmental agencies. After gathering information, they write reports and present both sides of the issue(s) to the class in a debate format.

Introduction

Lands managed by the United States Forest Service and the Bureau of Land Management are supposed to be managed under the principle of "multiple use." These multiple uses include mining, lumber production, livestock grazing, oil and gas production, watershed, soil and wildlife resources, and recreation, including hunting and fishing. It is obvious that balancing these often conflicting uses is a difficult task that requires trade-offs and compromises that seldom completely satisfy any particular special interest group.

Many environmental groups claim that the Forest Service allows excessive cutting of timber, doesn't enforce environmental protection laws, and allows the timber rights to be purchased too cheaply. Similar charges are made with respect to grazing on federal rangeland.

In this activity, we deal with the recreational aspects of multiple use. If you want to expand it to include the commercial uses, you might want to do this activity after doing Activity 7.

As our population has increased, there has been a more than commensurate increase in demands for access to public lands. This is because of changes in attitudes and the development of several "new" outdoor activities such as snowmobiling, off-road vehicle travel, and mountain biking. This increased demand for access often leads to conflicts and disagreement as to what is appropriate use for public lands. It is difficult to enjoy quiet and solitude when there are four-wheel drive vehicles and motorcycles zooming around your campsite. Cross-country skiers often complain of noise and litter from snowmobilers. Hikers worry about hunters during the open season.

Students need to understand these conflicts. It is very important that they understand both sides of the issues. They also need to be willing and able to make their voices heard and to try to influence their governmental agencies. This activity is intended to encourage the students to learn about the various uses of our public lands, to understand both sides of some controversial issues, and to be willing and able to influence other people, including those in appropriate governmental agencies.

Grouping

Groups (teams) of 2 or 4 students per issue.

Time

- 40–50 minutes to introduce the activity and write initial letters
- 2–4 weeks for responses to arrive (during which library research, interviews, etc., can be conducted)

- Two or three 45- to 55-minute periods to prepare and practice presentations
- 15 minutes per team for presentations and discussion
- 30–45 minutes for follow-up, letter writing, etc.

Anticipated Outcomes

The students will:

- increase their understanding of the concept of multiple use.
- increase their understanding of various uses of public lands.
- increase their ability and willingness to write letters to public officials.
- increase their ability to obtain information from public agencies and private organizations.
- increase their ability and willingness to argue orally for or against an issue.

Materials

—Photocopied student pages:
- 5.1 Multiple Use or Multiple Abuse? Background Information (one per student)
- 5.2 Multiple Use or Multiple Abuse? Research Assignment (one per student)
- 5.3 Multiple Use or Multiple Abuse? Questions (one per student)

Vocabulary

multiple use   propaganda   special interest group

Teacher Preparation

1. Photocopy the Background sheet (5.1), Research Assignment sheet with addresses (5.2), and Questions sheet (5.3).
2. Obtain stamps and envelopes for student use. The students should include stamped, self-addressed envelopes with the school's address. You should read and mail their letters. That way you know that the student has actually written for the information.
3. Consider inviting guest speakers from both sides of a locally important multiple-use issue.
4. Obtain the names and addresses of local legislators and governmental agencies such as the U.S. Forest Service, Bureau of Land Management, Park Service, etc. (See Appendix I–IV.)

Safety Considerations

None

Procedure

1. Decide whether to allow the students to select their issues or to assign them.

2. Decide whether to have 2 or 4 students per topic. If your students are self-confident and used to public speaking, one student on a side may be fine. Generally, though, having two students on each side will enable the students to be more secure. Try to balance opposing sides.

3. Decide whether to invite guest speakers to present their opposing sides of a multiple-use issue of interest to your students. This can be an excellent way to introduce this assignment. If you decide to use guest speakers, be sure to:
   - follow your school's guidelines on controversial issues
   - invite speakers from both sides of the issue
   - try to help your speakers understand what is appropriate for students in your class. Consider attention span, maturity, prior knowledge and understandings, and preconceptions.

4. Films and videotapes can also be useful in introducing controversial issues.

5. Provide addresses for the students to use in their research. Some are included with this activity, but you may want to include others. Be sure to provide addresses for both sides of the issue. (Additional addresses are included in Appendix I and II of this book.)

Discussion

1. Who responded faster to your letters—governmental agencies or private organizations?

2. Did the organizations all seem to present both sides of the issue?

3. What are some examples of statements that are used to try to persuade you?

4. Were the governmental agencies objective and neutral in their approach?

5. Which side do you favor? Why? Was your mind changed on any of these issues because of these presentations?

6. If there are uses that are so incompatible that they require an either/or choice, how should the choice be made?

Answers to 5.3, Multiple Use or Multiple Abuse? Questions

1. Answers will vary.

2. Answers will vary.

3. Answers will vary. They should include examples from the materials sent to them. Try to find examples of propaganda techniques used by the environmental organizations as well as by the others. Do governmental agencies use propaganda too? Should they?

4. Answers will vary. Point out that any use by people will have an effect on an environment. In fact, not using it will have an effect. Should we, for example, prevent or put out forest fires? Try to prevent flooding or erosion? Prohibit hiking and camping? There is no free lunch!

5. Answers will vary. If only the users pay the costs, the costs will become prohibitive.

On the other hand, why should people who never use the lands pay for their protection and development? But just because a person doesn't use the land now, that doesn't mean that he or she will never use it, and if it isn't protected, it may not be available for use in the future.

Extensions (See Activity 32 for suggestions for student projects.)

1. Have the students write a short report presenting both (or all) sides of their issue.
2. Invite speakers from both sides on the issues considered.
3. Show films produced by both sides on an issue. Discuss propaganda techniques.
4. Visit a site that has been seriously impacted by use. Discuss options for preventing problems in the future and elsewhere and for restoring the site.
5. Do "values clarification" activities to help the students consider where they stand on the issues.
6. Videotape the "debates" and use the tape to discuss effective presentation and speaking techniques.
7. Have the students present their opinions at a hearing or meeting of an appropriate agency.
8. Contact appropriate conservation agencies to find out what you can do to support them.

Modifications

1. If you do not want to have the students wait for the information, you might write to the organizations and agencies to obtain the information well ahead of time. The ones suggested in this activity are by no means the only ones. Consult local libraries, magazine stores, and agencies.
2. Rather than presenting the issue as a debate, have the students present their findings to the class as reports.
3. Rather than presenting the issue as a debate, have several students in a panel discussion.
4. So that each student will thoroughly understand each side, consider having each student prepare to argue for either side and not telling which side that student will present until just before the debate. To prepare for this, all students on a topic will need to share information. Decide with a coin toss.

References

Anonymous, *Conservation Directory*. Washington, DC: National Wildlife Federation, 1992.

Anonymous, *Group and Key Contact List*. Washington, DC: U.S. Forest Service, 1992.

Causey, Ann S., *Environmental Action Guide*. Redwood City, CA: Benjamin/Cummings Publishing Company, Inc., 1991.

Miller, G. Tyler, *Living in the Environment*. Belmont, CA: Wadsworth Publishing Company, 1990.

Simon, Sidney B. et al., *Values Clarification*. New York, NY: Hart Publishing Company, Inc., 1972.

5.1 Multiple Use or Multiple Abuse?: Background Information

Underdeveloped land such as forests, grasslands, and deserts have many potential uses, and different people look at them differently. To some, a tree-covered hillside represents wood with which to build homes and provides income for families. To others, the same hillside represents a forest where one can camp and hike and enjoy unspoiled nature. To others, it may represent a perfect site to build a ski resort.

Lands owned by the federal government and managed by the United States Forest Service and Bureau of Land Management are supposed to be managed for **"multiple uses."** Sometimes, though, those multiple uses conflict with one another. Making decisions about what will and what will not be allowed in a particular area is not easy. Since we all pay taxes, shouldn't we all have access to federal lands? Once there, shouldn't we be able to enjoy the land in our own way, whether it is birdwatching or motorcycle riding? But what if one person's way of enjoying the land interferes with another person's enjoyment?

Different **"special interest groups"** try to influence the government and its agencies to issue rules and regulations so that the public land will be used in the ways that the groups want it to be used. Since those interests often conflict, each group tries to sway the legislators' opinion.

You may already use federal lands for hunting, camping, or sight-seeing. Even if you don't now use federal lands, you probably will someday. If you want to protect your right to use the land, it is important that you understand both sides of the issues and that you be willing and able to influence your legislators and governmental agencies.

Before making decisions about various uses of public lands, it is important to understand both sides of the issues. Even if you already know a lot about one side, if you are going to argue effectively for your position, you need to understand the other side. Also, if you are going to influence others, you need to know how to present your side effectively, whether it is in an oral presentation or in writing. You will also need to understand the propaganda techniques used by the other side.

There are a number of things that you can do to enhance an oral presentation. If you want to convince others and get them to agree with you, you should:

- Understand your side of the issue thoroughly. Anticipate the arguments that will be put forth by the other side and answer their questions even before they can ask them.

- Understand the other side of the issue thoroughly. Know what claims they will make and address those claims in your presentation.

- Plan your presentation well. Present your information clearly. Consider using visual aids such as large pictures, graphs, slides, and objects. Visual aids must be easily seen and understood.

- Practice your presentation. Notes are okay, but you should know your presentation well enough that you do not need to read your notes word for word. Use notes only as reminders, and for security, not as a text.

- Pay attention to such things as your appearance, tone of voice (vary it so that it is not monotone), and the enthusiasm and conviction that you show in your presentation.

When writing letters, there are a number of things that you can do to make yours more effective.

If you are writing to an individual, agency, or organization company for information, you should:

- Be as clear as possible about what you want and why you want it.

- Be polite. (Remember, you are asking them to assist you.)

- Get to the point. They want to help you because they want to get their side of the story out. They don't need to hear a lot of justification from you.
- Be sure to have your name, address, and telephone number clearly written on the page.
- If you need the information by a certain date, be sure to say that.
- Provide a self-addressed, stamped envelope.

If you are writing to a legislator or agency to try to influence them:

- Write clearly, simply, and legibly. Get to the point, politely.
- Address it properly: For federal legislators:

The Honorable _____	The Honorable _____
U.S. Senate	U.S. House of Representatives
Washington, DC 20510	Washington, DC 20515
Dear Senator _____	Dear Representative _____

- Address only one topic or issue per letter. Be as detailed and specific as you can. If possible, refer to a particular bill, policy, or law.
- Ask for a specific response. What would you like him or her to do?
- Be courteous, factual, and give good reasons for your position. Try to inform as well as influence. Be brief.
- Be positive—don't threaten or attack. It is all right to state your position firmly, but you should do it in a nice way.
- Be sure to include your return address.
- Your teacher may provide samples of letters.

5.2 Multiple Use or Multiple Abuse? Research Assignment

In order to learn more about various recreational uses of public lands, members of the class will learn about those uses and then will present their findings to the class. The presentations may be in a debate, panel, or report format. Whatever way the presentations are done, it is important to present the important information in a clear manner.

You will be assigned or will select one of the following issues to investigate. You will work with one or more other students. Each individual should learn about both the advantages and disadvantages of each issue.

As you prepare your presentation, you will need to do research on your topic. Use your school and public library. You may want to contact local sporting goods stores, clubs, governmental agencies, or individuals for more information. Also check book and magazine stores. Included here are some addresses that may prove useful. If you are writing to an organization for information, do so at once so that there will be time for the information to arrive. Plan your schedule so that you will have time to do your best work!

Begin research on or by: _____ Mail for information on or by: _____

Continue research on:_____, _____, _____, _____, _____, _____

Research Completed by:

Presentation planned by: _____   Visual aids ready by: _____

Practice presentation: _____, _____, _____, _____

Presentation Due:

1. Should recreational 4-wheel drive vehicles be allowed to be driven off the roads in National Forests or on B.L.M land?
2. Should off-road motorcycle riding be allowed in the National Forests or on B.L.M land?
3. Should deer and duck hunting be allowed in the National Forests or on B.L.M land?
4. Should downhill ski runs be built in the National Forests or on B.L.M land?
5. Should snowmobiling be allowed in the National Forests or on B.L.M land?
6. Should R.V. hookups be installed in the National Forests or on B.L.M land?
7. Should mountain bikes be allowed on hiking trails in the National Forests or on B.L.M land?
8. Should horses be allowed on hiking trails in the National Forests or on B.L.M land?
9. Should logging be allowed in the National Forests or on B.L.M land?
10. Should sheep grazing be allowed in the National Forests or on B.L.M land?
11. Should cattle grazing be allowed in the National Forests or on B.L.M land?
12. Should mining be allowed in the National Forests or on B.L.M land?

Note: Addresses of organizations are subject to change. If an address proves to be incorrect, you might try telephoning the organization or contacting the National Wildlife Federation for its current *Conservation Directory.*

U.S. Forest Service
P.O. Box 2417
Washington, DC 20013

U.S. Bureau of Land Management
U.S. Dept. of the Interior
Washington, DC 20240

U.S. Park Service
Interior Building
Washington, DC 20240

(See also your local telephone directory under United States Government.)

American Forestry Association
1516 P Street, NW
Washington, DC 20005

American Mining Congress
1920 N Street, NW
Washington, DC 20036

American Motorcyclist Association
P.O. Box 6114
Westerville, OH 43081

American Sheep Industry Association
6911 Yosemite Street
Englewood, CO 80112

Ducks Unlimited
Suite 800
1155 Connecticut Ave., NW
Washington, DC 20036

Friends of the Earth
218 D Street, SE
Washington, DC 20003

International Mountain Bike Association
Route 2, Box 303
Bishop, CA 93514

International Snowmobile Industry Association
3975 University Drive, #310
Fairfax, VA 22030

League of Conservation Voters
1150 Connecticut Avenue
Washington, DC 20036

National Audubon Society
801 Pennsylvania Ave., SE
Washington, DC 20003

National Cattlemen's Association
Suite 300
1301 Pennsylvania Ave., NW
Washington, DC 20004

National Forest Products Association
Suite 200
1250 Connecticut Ave., NW
Washington, DC 20036

National Forest Recreation Association
Route 3, Box 210
Highway 89 N
Flagstaff, AZ 86001

National Parks and Conservation Association
1015 31st Street, NW
Washington, DC 20007

National Rifle Association
1600 Rhode Island Ave., NW
Washington, DC 20036

National Ski Areas Association
20 Maple Street
P.O. Box 22883
Springfield, MA 01101

National Wildlife Federation
1400 Sixteenth Street, NW
Washington, DC 20036

Recreation Vehicle Industry Association
1896 Preston White Drive
Reston, VA 22090

Safari Club International
5151 East Broadway
Suite 1680
Tucson, AZ 85711

Sierra Club
408 C Street, NE
Washington, DC 20002

Society for Range Management
1839 York Street
Denver, CO 80206

Trust for Public Land
116 New Montgomery Street
4th Floor
San Francisco, CA 94105

United 4-Wheel Drive Associations
105 Highland Avenue
Battle Creek, MI 49017

The Wilderness Society
900 17th Street, NW
Washington, DC 20006

5.3 Multiple Use or Multiple Abuse? Questions

1. What presentation techniques were most effective in swaying your opinion?

_____

_____

_____

_____

2. What presentation techniques were least effective in swaying your opinion?

_____

_____

_____

_____

3. Using the literature that you received, find two examples of statements that were meant to sway your opinion, that is, propaganda. List them and tell why they are propaganda.

_____

_____

_____

_____

4. Discuss the statement that "Public lands must be managed in such a way that they remain unspoiled for future generations. If that means that the current generation's use is restricted, so be it."

_____

_____

_____

_____

5. Who should pay the costs of protecting public lands such as the National Forests—all taxpayers or those who actually use them? Why?

_____

_____

_____

unit

Two

Wildlife Issues

- **Habitats—The Choice Is Yours**
- **Microhabitats**
- **Endangered Species I—What's Happening?**
- **Endangered Species II—Who Cares?**

ACTIVITY 6: HABITATS—THE CHOICE IS YOURS _____

Activity Summary

In this activity, the students assume the roles of land-use planners. They are given a map of an undeveloped area where a new community will be built. As teams they decide how to use the land. Then they present their land-use plan to the class at a "Planning Commission Meeting."

Introduction

Every organism on Earth needs a place to live. A few organisms, like humans and rats, are able to live in a wide variety of habitats. Many organisms, though, have specific requirements for habitats. When their environments are changed, the very survival of many of these organisms is threatened. In fact, habitat destruction is the main threat to the world's wildlife.

Land-use decisions affect us all. The quality of our lives depends directly upon our surroundings. Whether we live in a pleasant neighborhood or an overcrowded unpleasant community depends, to a large degree, on planning decisions. Even if we live in huge apartment buildings, planning and cooperation among the tenants can make our surrounding environment less or more pleasant. Human habitats, including land dedicated to industry, transportation, governmental, and commercial uses, are built on what was formerly natural habitats.

It is easy to be so concerned about protecting the natural environment that we forget that we humans have needs and that by living on the Earth we change our environment. Those of us who are concerned about the environment need to keep in mind that others may have different priorities. Increasing human population, rising expectations, previously made decisions, and changing lifestyles all complicate the issue of land-use choices. In a way, the issue becomes one of quality (of life for humans and other organisms) versus quantity (of people, of "things," of income, of other organisms, of open space, of jobs, etc.). We must not forget, though, that it is very difficult, if not impossible, to undo damage done to a natural ecosystem.

When you introduce this activity, you should try to get the students to develop a feeling of "ownership" of their site so that they will want to develop it in the best (from their perspective) way possible. Don't make value judgments about their use choices. To some of them, it may be very important to have a lot of industry, especially if jobs are scarce in your community. To others, shopping malls, recreational sites, large lots for private residences, or natural sites may be of great importance. Let their planning groups work out the priorities and defend them before the class. Remind them, though, that the job of the planning commission is to make the best plan for everyone in the community, including future generations.

Requiring that the community meet all of its needs within the boundaries of Muir Valley helps make the point that the Earth itself is an ecosystem. What we do in our own communities has impacts elsewhere. In our real world, many of the impacts of our choices are not seen because they occur elsewhere. Examples include mining for minerals, logging, pesticide use, and disposal of sewage. One possible outcome of this activity is that the students might see the need to "think globally and act locally."

This activity works well if the students have already done the previous two activities in this book. It is also easy to tie it to the following activities dealing with timber, endangered animals, and endangered plants.

The color-coding system suggested corresponds fairly closely to the color coding used by most cities and counties. You should feel free to substitute other colors or patterns and to add, subtract, or, especially, subdivide categories.

Grouping

Groups of 4–6 students per planning team

Time

Introducing the activity: about 15 minutes

Student teams working on plans: 30–45 minutes

Presentation of plans to class: 3–10 minutes per team

Possibly another 30–50 minutes if you decide to have the plans revised

Anticipated Outcomes

The students will:

- increase their understanding of the interdependence of the organisms on Earth.
- increase their understandings of the complexity of land-use planning.
- increase their understanding of others' points of view.
- increase their ability to present information and to persuade others.

Materials

—Photocopied student pages:

- 6.1 Habitats—The Choice Is Yours: Background Information (one per student)
- 6.2 Habitats—The Choice Is Yours: Instructions sheet with map (one per student)
- 6.3 Habitats—The Choice Is Yours: Questions (one per student)

—transparency of Muir Valley Planning Map

—butcher paper or other large paper for enlarged student maps

—crayons or colored pens

—masking tape

Vocabulary

agricultural	buffer zone	closed system	commercial
density	endangered species	green belt	habitat
industrial	open space	public facilities	public lands
recreational	residential		

Teacher Preparation

1. Photocopy the Background Information sheet (6.1), Instructions sheet (6.2) and Questions sheet (6.3).
2. Obtain the other materials.
3. Some thought should be given to how to form the planning teams. Some options are:
   a. random selection
   b. let students choose teams
   c. assign teams
      (1) try to balance the teams academically
      (2) try to balance the teams with respect to organization and presentation skills
      (3) try to balance the teams according to apparent concern about the environment
      (4) set up teams so that one is mostly the "environmentalists," one is mostly those who will probably want only to build industries, one is neutral, etc.
4. Decide how the students are to code their maps. You might let each group decide on their own system. This would point out the value of having a standardized system. If you provide a code, the following system is suggested because it corresponds closely to the system used by cities and counties. You should indicate the code either on the student instructions (6.2) before duplicating them or make a large sign to hang at the front of the room.

single family housing:	yellow	*multiple family housing:*	orange
industry/manufacturing:	gray	*raw materials/mining:*	brown
agriculture (food):	dark green	*other crops:*	light green
commercial (stores):	red	*services (banks, doctors, etc.):*	pink
public buildings:	dark blue	*recreational uses:*	light blue
roads and parking lots:	black		

SAFETY CONSIDERATIONS

For reasons of liability, if you encourage the students to attend planning commission, E.I.R., or other hearings, be sure to either provide transportation as if it were a school field trip or be sure that it is understood that the trip is not required.

Procedure

1. Introduce and explain the lesson. Be sure to establish when the presentations are due. (If the students are working well, consider extending the planning time.) Be sure to emphasize that their presentation will determine the future of the area being developed and that the quality of their presentation may be as important as what they say. (*How* they say it may be as important to the outcome as *what* they say.)

2. Let the students use the transparency of Muir Valley to make large maps to use in their presentations. (Project the map onto butcher or other large paper held to the wall with masking tape.) Alternatively, you or a student assistant might make the large maps, or the transparency master can be used to duplicate enlarged maps on a copy machine.

3. At the appointed time, the student planning teams will present their proposals for the use of the land. This is a public "hearing."

4. After each presentation, allow a limited amount of time for questions to clarify their presentation. (This is not the time to debate the pros and cons. This is the time to understand the proposals.)

5. After the proposals have all been presented, allow for (polite) discussion of the relative merits of the various proposals.

6. After this, you may want to allow the student teams to revise their proposals, taking into account the input from the public hearing.

Discussion

1. Did different groups have different priorities for the land use?
2. Is there a simple "right" answer to such questions as land use?
3. Did your group neglect or omit any important types of use?
4. Did the various proposals take into account future generations?
5. Are some types of land use inappropriate for Muir Valley?
6. If all needs of the residents are to be met in the valley, which land use should have the most space allocated for it?
7. Are some uses of land incompatible with others?
8. How should land-use decisions be made? What should be the relative weight given to public input and the opinions of "experts?"
9. Discuss the phrase "Think globally, act locally."
10. Discuss the phrase "All things are interconnected."

Answers to 6.3, Habitats: The Choice Is Yours: Questions

1. Answers will vary.
2. Answers will vary. Many people tend to favor protection of spectacular species of mammals or birds (whales, condors, grizzly bears), but are not so concerned about other organisms such as plants, fungi, insects, reptiles, and amphibians.
3. Answers will vary. Be sure to point out that government money comes from taxes.
4. Answers will vary, but they should realize that people require space and materials that come from the environment.
5. Answers will vary, but they should realize that the more "things" we have and the more energy we use, the more we will impact the environment and other organisms' habitats.
6. Answers will vary.
7. Answers will vary.

Extensions (See Activity 32 for suggestions for student projects.)

1. Invite a member of the local planning commission to talk with the class.

2. Obtain local land use, general plan, or zoning maps. Have the students examine and discuss them.

3. Discuss "variances" from zoning regulations or general plans.

4. Find out about any local undeveloped land that is being considered for development. Find out about the plans and have the students discuss them. Visit the site and study the existing natural communities.

5. Visit a planning (zoning, general plan development) commission meeting.

6. Have the students write letters to the appropriate agencies regarding land-use decisions.

7. Have the students investigate Environmental Impact Reports and Environmental Impact Statements.

8. Visit an Environmental Impact Report public hearing.

9. Invite a speaker from a company that does E.I.R.s.

10. The United States Geological Survey has topographic maps for most locations, including developed areas, in the United States. Obtain the most recent one for your community and have the students calculate what percentage of the land was dedicated to agriculture, natural environments, and built environments when the map was made. (If you live in an urban area, you might want to use the topographic map of a nearby suburban or rural area with which the students are familiar.)
For current maps contact:

> U.S.G.S. Map Sales
> Box 25286
> Denver, CO 80225
> (303)236-7477

Local stores such as sporting goods dealers may have topographic maps.

11. After doing number 10, have the students survey their community to determine what changes have occurred since the map was made.

12. The U.S.G.S. also has older maps available for most locations. Obtain an old topographic map and compare it to the most recent one. (They also have aerial photographs available for most places.)
For older maps or photographs, contact:

> Earth Science Information Center
> U.S. Geological Survey
> Room 3128, Building 3, Mail Stop 533
> 345 Middlefield Road
> Menlo Park, CA 94025
> (415)329-4309

(Inquire about "Historical Maps" for the area[s] of interest.)

13. Obtain old photographs of your community, preferably before it was developed. Discuss why development progressed as it did. Identify the locale shown in an old photograph and have the students find out what is not at the site and take a picture

showing the same perspective now. (Local newspapers are a good source of such photographs.)

14. Invite a speaker from a local environmental organization to speak with the class.

15. Have students investigate endangered species of your state, the United States, or the world. Have them not only find out what species are endangered, but the cause(s) of the endangerment and what can be done to help the species survive.

16. Have the students investigate the Endangered Species Acts of 1966 and 1973.

17. A company called Maxis Software has produced computer planning simulation "games" that students enjoy and learn from. Their programs include Sim City (planning a city), and Sim Earth (planning for development and evolution on Earth). These are available through many software distributors, or write to the publishers at:

> Maxis Software
> 2 Theatre Square, Suite 230
> Orinda, CA 94563-3346
> (510)254-9700

Modifications

1. Allow the students to revise their proposals after receiving public input.

2. Make several maps of different kinds of areas. Some might include more land that is already developed, more or less public land, rivers, ocean front property, waste disposal sites, different proposed populations, and so forth. Provide each group with a different map. This will make their presentation more "safe" since they won't be trying to convince other groups that their plan is better.

3. Provide maps of a real undeveloped area with which the students are familiar. (A local agency might be able to provide such a map.) The students might develop a class proposal and present it to the appropriate agency.

4. If you live in an area with little open space, make this a redevelopment agency. What if the buildings were cleared and we could start with bare ground?

5. Introduce the idea of endangered species to the class. Inform the students that one or more endangered species has been found in the appropriate area of Muir Valley. How does that change their development plan?

References

Anonymous, *The Green Box.* Eureka, CA: Humboldt County Office of Education, 1989.

Clymire, Olga (principal writer), *California Class Project,* Costa Mesa, CA: Orange County Superintendent of Schools and the National Wildlife Federation, 1988.

Miller, G. Tyler, *Living in the Environment.* Belmont, CA: Wadsworth Publishing Co., 1990.

6.1 Habitats—The Choice Is Yours: Background Information

All organisms need space in which to live. Fish need water. Deer, birds, squirrels, and all other land animals, including humans, need land on which to build their "homes" and find or grow their food. There is a limited amount of land available for use by land animals. When people want to build houses, industries, roads, or recreational areas, land is needed. We use land to grow our crops. If undeveloped or natural land is used, communities of organisms are going to be disturbed, and perhaps destroyed.

In this activity, you are part of a land-use planning team. Your task is to plan how to use Muir Valley to support 10,000 people. (At the present time, the valley supports only one family that has a small farm.) At the conclusion of your planning time, you will present your proposal to the other students in the class. For the sake of activity, assume that all 10,000 people must live, work, shop, and have their recreational and other needs met in this valley, that is, that it is a "closed system."

In reality, most, if not all, communities depend on other areas for many things, such as electricity, raw materials for industry, certain foods, and so forth. What we do (or don't do) in one place has an impact on other places. Saving gas and oil helps protect otters and other wildlife. Wasting less wood helps protect forests and the wildlife that depends on forests. Saving energy reduces air pollution and acidic precipitation from coal- and oil-burning power plants. Avoiding the use of tropical hardwoods helps protect rain forests. Recycling aluminum protects areas where aluminum ore is mined. As John Muir said, "When we try to pick out anything by itself, we find it hitched to everything else in the universe."

Many species of plants and animals are either threatened with extinction or endangered. Many species have already become extinct. Many more become extinct every year. Some estimates are that as many as 10,000 species of animals may become extinct each year! Habitat destruction is the main cause of extinction. Hunting for commercial, subsistence, or sport purposes also creates problems for some species. Predator and pest control and pollution threaten others. Use of some species of animals as pets and plants for decoration destroys large numbers of animals and plants.

Aside from aesthetic and recreational reasons, there are many practical reasons why we should be concerned about other species. Many wild species hold great promise as sources of medicines, foods, and fibers. Ecosystems are very complex arrangements of plants and animals, and what affects one species may ultimately affect many others. Finally, there is the ethical question of whether mankind has the right to cause or hasten the extinction of other species. As you develop Muir Valley, keep in mind the many values of the plants and animals that live there.

6.2 Habitats—The Choice Is Yours: Activity Instructions

Your planning team will be given (or will make) a map of an area. Your job is to plan a community in which 10,000 people will live, work, and shop, and will meet their recreational needs. When you have marked your plan on your map, you will present it to the rest of the class. You should be able to explain why you chose to use the land as you did.

The numbers below are not intended to represent actual land-use needs. The actual amount of land needed for a given use varies widely because of differing lifestyles, quality of land, and so forth. For the sake of the activity, use the space requirements given in the table below.

Note that you have several choices to make. For example, what proportion of the population will live in single-family residences as opposed to apartments? How much land will be allowed for such things as stores or roads? Will you allow more industry so that more money will come to Muir Valley?

Use the code provided by your teacher to indicate the various land uses.

USE	LAND NEEDED (acres)	COLOR/ SYMBOL
housing (single-family residences for 1,000)	80 acres/1,000	
housing (multiple-family residences for 1,000)	20 acres/1,000	
industry/manufacturing plants	1,200 acres	
raw materials/mining	6,000 acres	
agriculture (food plants, animals)	6,000 acres	
other crops (fibers, lumber, etc.)	3,200 acres	
commercial		
stores	80 acres	
services (doctors, banks, offices)	40 acres	
public uses such as schools, police, fire, water, public utilities, hospitals, waste disposal, government administration, post offices, etc—at least one of each. (labeled)	400 acres	
public recreational uses (developed areas for sports, parks, camping, etc.)	1,200 acres	
roads and parking	800 acres	

© 1993 by The Center for Applied Research in Education

6.2 Habitats—The Choice Is Yours: Planning Map

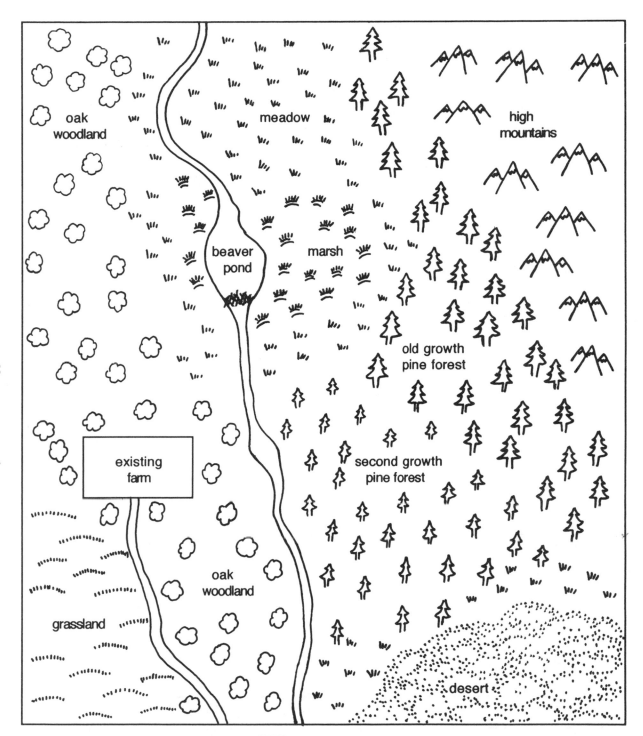

_____
1" = 1 mile

☐ = 40 acres   1 mi² = 640 acres

6.3 Habitats—The Choice Is Yours: Questions

1. How did your protection and use priorities differ from those of other groups? In what ways were they the same? How could such differences be resolved?

   _____

   _____

   _____

2. Should land be protected from development or other uses such as logging or oil drilling if an endangered species is found there? Under what conditions? Even if it is a species of plant or insect? Why or why not?

   _____

   _____

   _____

3. Should the government spend money to protect endangered species? Why or why not?

   _____

   _____

   _____

4. What is the relationship between human population and species endangerment?

   _____

   _____

5. What is the relationship between resource use and species endangerment?

   _____

   _____

6. Discuss the statement that "All things are interrelated."

   _____

   _____

   _____

7. Discuss the idea that we should "Think globally and act locally."

   _____

   _____

   _____

ACTIVITY 7: MICROHABITATS _____

Activity Summary

In this activity, the students collect and compare biological and physical data from various parts of a local habitat—their school campus.

Introduction

Most of us are familiar with threats to various ecosystems or habitats such as the rain forests, deserts, and oceans. Certainly anything that poses problems on a large enough scale to threaten a large part of a forest or ocean should be of concern to us.

Most organisms, however, do not utilize the whole of an ecosystem. Most organisms live in a relatively small portion of their ecosystem—their microhabitat. A type of fern, for example, may live only along streams in the shade in the heart of a forest. A caterpillar may feed only on the leaves of a certain plant. A bird may require dead trees (snags) for its nest. Many parasites are very specific as to the organisms on or in which they live.

It is important to remember that an entire ecosystem need not be destroyed for certain organisms' microhabitats to be destroyed. Sometimes, in fact, the destruction of a certain microhabitat can lead to serious threats to the entire ecosystem. Thus, we need to study not only large ecosystems, but also specific needs of specific organisms and their relationships with other organisms.

Grouping

Teams of 2–4 students.

Time

Training in Data Collection and Equipment Use: 45–55 minutes

Collection of Data: 45–55 minutes

Data Analysis: 30–45 minutes

Anticipated Outcomes

The students will:

- understand that a habitat may be made up of a variety of microhabitats.
- understand that the different microhabitats within a habitat support different kinds of organisms
- understand that organisms can be threatened if their microhabitats are threatened.

Materials

—Photocopied student pages:

- 7.1 Microhabitats: Background Information (one per student)
- 7.2 Microhabitats: Data table (one per team)

- 7.3 Microhabitats: Questions (one per student)

—For each team:

- 1 clipboard
- 1 sling psychrometer (or one dry- and one wet-bulb thermometer)
- 1 relative humidity table
- 1 trowel
- 2 forceps
- 1 magnifying glass or bug box or dissecting microscope
- 1 light-colored towel, approximately 2 x 5
- 1 light meter
- aerial and other collecting nets
- dichotomous keys or field guides for local organisms

Vocabulary

ecosystem	habitat	macrohabitat
microhabitat	relative humidity	

Teacher Preparation

1. Photocopy the Background Information Sheet (7.1), Data table (7.2), and Questions sheet (7.3).
2. Obtain the needed equipment.
3. Locate the various microhabitats on your campus. They might include various types of trees, athletic fields, and areas planted with flowers, hedges, and bushes.
4. Make sure that the principal and custodian or groundskeeper have no objection to your class doing this activity.

SAFETY CONSIDERATIONS

1. Be sure that the students know how to use all equipment safely and properly.
2. Visit the site of investigation to check for any hazards such as trash, dangerous plants or animals, and so forth.
3. Caution the students against damaging plants or animals.

Procedure

1. Discuss the idea of habitats with the students. Draw out the idea that climate is an important factor in determining habitats.
2. Ask whether a given habitat (such as a school campus) might not include a variety of habitats within itself. Introduce the term "microhabitat."
3. Form student teams. Each team should have students assigned to do the following:

   a. collect abiotic data (temperature, light, and relative humidity)

b. describe the soil and count and identify any organisms found in it

c. count and identify plants present at the site

d. count and identify invertebrates

e. count and identify vertebrates

4. Instruct the students in the use of the thermometer, light meter, and sling psychrometer or wet-bulb and dry-bulb thermometers (for determining relative humidity).

5. Instruct the students in the use of field guides and/or dichotomous keys for identifying organisms.

6. Instruct the students in the use of the towel for collecting invertebrates by spreading the towel out on the ground under a bush and shaking a branch to cause the animals to fall onto the towel. (Point out that they should examine the branch carefully before shaking it so that they can observe animals that might fly or run away.)

7. Instruct the students in the use of collecting nets to collect animals.

8. Take the class to the site. Assign each team of students a study site within the habitat. A study site might include an open area 3 meters x 3 meters, or a tree and the ground under its drip line, or a large rock and the area within 0.5 meters of its edge. Have the students approach their site quietly to observe any birds, insects, mammals, or other animals that might be present.

9. Allow the student teams 30–50 minutes to collect their data, using the data table provided.

10. Any animals collected should be returned to their microhabitats.

11. In the field or upon returning to the classroom, have student teams report their findings to the class. List the data on the board or on an overhead projector so that the students can compare the sites.

Discussion

1. What is the relationship between climate and habitat? Discuss adaptations.

2. What are some of the microhabitats found within the habitat of our school campus?

3. What might account for the differences that we found in the various microhabitats? Might the conditions differ on the north and south sides of buildings? in the shade or sun?

4. If an organism lives in a particular part of a forest, on a particular type of bush, for example, does the whole forest need to be destroyed for that organism to be affected or to become extinct?

5. Do aquatic ecosystems such as ponds, rivers, and oceans have microhabitats?

6. Do human ecosystems (towns and cities) have microhabitats?

7. If one microhabitat is affected by some sort of change, is it likely that other microhabitats within that ecosystem will also be affected?

Answers to 7.3, Microhabitats Questions

1. Answers will vary. There may be several reasons for an organism being found in only one microhabitat. Other students may not have noticed individuals in their areas, there may be only a few in any one area, or they may be truly found only in one microhabitat.

2. Answers will vary. Some organisms such as flies can be found in many areas. They

are not very specific in their requirements and tolerate a wide variety of environmental conditions.

3. Generally, organisms that have evolved very specific requirements for survival, such as specific microhabitats, have trouble surviving if their environments change rapidly. Human-caused environmental changes are generally rapid when considered on an evolutionary time scale.

4. If an organism lives in a stable environment, it may be advantageous to specialize to take advantage of specific conditions more efficiently than organisms that do not specialize.

5. Answers will vary. Examples might include:

   - cutting forests (use fewer wood products, find substitutes for wood, recycle wood products)
   - flooding valleys behind dams (reduce water and electrical waste)
   - polluting water (reduce pollution)
   - building in various habitats such as deserts, grasslands, and woods (build up rather than out, build only truly needed buildings, use mass transit so fewer roads are needed)

Extension (See Activity 32 for suggestions for student projects.)

1. After collecting data on the school campus, visit a nearby vacant lot and collect data to compare with that collected on the campus.

2. Soil can be analyzed for water content, temperature, texture, and mineral composition. (Kits are available from science supply companies.)

3. Visit as many "natural" ecosystems as possible. Do microhabitat studies in each.

4. Have the students do similar studies in microhabitats at their homes.

5. After the students have identified various organisms found in their microhabitat studies, have them study about the organisms themselves.

6. Have the students do population density studies for various organisms. Graph the data.

7. Have the students investigate endangered species of plants and animals. They can prepare written and/or oral reports.

8. Have the students make an accurate map of the school's vegetation and other microhabitats.

Modifications

1. Data can be entered into computers and printed out for student analysis.

2. The sites could be various parts of a single tree or large bush (branches and leaves near the top, midway up the trunk, and near the base, for example).

3. If suitable light meters are not available, students might use relative terms such as dark shade, light shade, or open sun.

Reference

Nilsson, Greta, *The Endangered Species Handbook*. Washington, DC: Animal Welfare Institute, 1990.

7.1 Microhabitats—Background Information

If someone were to ask you where you live, what would you say? Your answer would probably depend on where you were at the time and who asked you. For example, if you were talking to a stranger in another state, you might just name your state. On the other hand, if you were talking to a classmate, you might give your address. If you were talking to a visitor at your home, you might point to your bedroom. (Your parents might say that you live in front of the television or in the kitchen!)

If we really want to understand about an organism, we need to know as much as possible about where it lives (its **habitat**) and why it lives there (its needs). Sharks, crabs, and sand worms all live in the ocean, but they all live in different portions of the ocean biome. Woodpeckers, deer, and beavers might all live in the forest, but you wouldn't look for them in the same part of the forest. The specific part of a place where an organism lives is called its **"microhabitat."** To truly understand organisms, we need to understand their microhabitats.

Many people are concerned about threats to large **ecosystems** or habitats such as the rain forests, the deserts, or the oceans. To protect such "macrohabitats," we need to understand their parts, the microhabitats. Certainly the destruction of a <u>**macrohabitat**</u> affects all of the <u>micro</u>habitats within it. Many people do not realize that the destruction of microhabitats can also lead to the destruction of entire ecosystems.

Your school campus is a habitat for a surprising number of creatures besides humans. There are bacteria, insects, and various other kinds of invertebrates. There may be cats, mice, rats, birds, and other vertebrates. In this activity, you and a team of your classmates will be finding out about a certain microhabitat on your campus. You should notice such factors as light, shade, temperature, noise, proximity to human activity, shelter, and sources of food. Other teams of students will be studying other microhabitats on your campus. Then you will compare your findings.

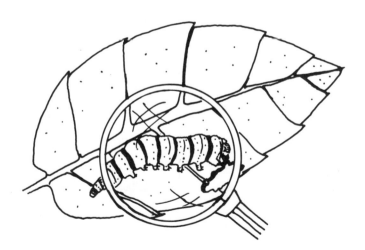

Name _____ Class _____ Date _____
_____
_____
_____

7.2 Microhabitats: Data

Microhabitat: name: _____

description: _____

_____

time of data collection: ____ (A.M.) (P.M.) air temperature: ____°C relative humidity: ____%

weather conditions: current: _____

recent past (last several hours): _____

light conditions: _____ wind conditions: _____

soil data: _____

_____

ORGANISMS OBSERVED OR COLLECTED

type (name)	#	notes	type (name)	#	notes

Other comments, data or observations: _____

_____

_____

_____

7.3 Microhabitats: Questions

1. List the organisms that were found only in your team's microhabitat and tell why you think they were not found in other microhabitats.

organisms	reasons	organisms	reasons

2. List the organisms that were found in several microhabitats and tell why you think that they were found in several microhabitats.

organisms	reasons	organisms	reasons

3. Some organisms are very specific in their habitat requirements. Others are more cosmopolitan. Which type of organism is more likely to become endangered by rapid environmental changes such as those brought about by man? Explain your answer.

_____

_____

_____

4. Why would it be an advantage for an organism living in a relatively stable environment to have specific habitat or food requirements?

_____

_____

_____

5. List three reasons that humans threaten habitats. For each, tell one way that you could lessen the impact.

_____

_____

_____

ACTIVITY 8:
ENDANGERED SPECIES I—WHAT'S HAPPENING? _____

Activity Summary

The students are given data and graph paper and asked to graph the data. At first, they don't know what the data represent. (They show the numbers of species of birds and mammals that have become extinct since 1600 as compared to the human population increase during that same period.) After completing their graphs, they are told what they show and discuss the implications.

Introduction

Most high school students have heard of endangered species and know what "extinct" means. Many, however, have little understanding of the causes, the extent of the problem, or of the role that humans have in both species endangerment and protection. Nor do many appreciate the importance of protecting the diversity of life on Earth.

In this activity we examine the relationship between human population increases and the numbers of birds and mammals that have become extinct. This should indicate to the students that humans have assumed a major role in determining the fate of numerous species on the planet.

Biologists have specific meanings for the terms *extinct, endangered,* and *threatened*. The distinction between endangered and threatened is often a fine one, but it is an important one because of the way that some laws work.

Threatened species are those that have sizable populations in nature, but are declining and are likely to become endangered if current conditions continue to cause their decline. Often their status will improve if people stop doing whatever is causing the problem.

Endangered species are those that are in immediate danger of becoming extinct. To save these species, we need to do more than just stop doing something. We need to take measures to protect them and to help them to survive.

Extinction is not a new phenomenon on Earth. Species of plants and animals have evolved and died out for as long as life has been here. It is a necessary part of natural selection. Millions of species, ranging from bacteria to dinosaurs, have evolved, flourished, and become extinct. We cannot halt extinction any more than we can halt evolution.

What has accelerated in the last few hundred years is the *rate* of extinction. Some scientists estimate that the number of species lost forever may soon exceed 40,000 per year! Most of these extinctions are due to human impacts on their environments. As human populations increase, we destroy natural environments to grow food, to clear land on which to build, and to obtain raw materials.

There are ways to grow food, build, and obtain raw materials that reduce our need to destroy natural environments. Eating plants rather than meat enables us to grow more food per acre of farm land. Living in multiple-family units of more than one story can enable us to house more people per acre, leaving more land available for open space. Recycling and reducing waste enables us to reduce the amount of raw materials that we need to remove from the Earth.

All these alternatives, however, treat the secondary problems. The primary cause is the growth in the human population. Before we are willing to address the problems of human overpopulation, we will need to feel a need to do so. This activity is intended to point out one reason to control human population. It should be done in conjunction with the next activity in this book, Endangered Species II—Who Cares?, which addresses the importance of saving endangered species.

Grouping

Individual students

Time

45–55 minutes

Anticipated Outcomes

The students will:

- increase their understanding of the terms extinct, endangered, and threatened.
- increase their ability to make and understand graphs.
- understand the relationship between human population and extinctions.

Materials

—Photocopied student pages:

- 8.1 Graphing Data Activity (one per student)
- 8.2. Endangered Species I—What's Happening? Information sheet (one per student)
- 8.3 Endangered Species I—What's Happening? Questions (one per student)

Vocabulary

endangered species   extinct   threatened species

Teacher Preparation

1. Photocopy the Graphing Data Activity sheet (8.1), Information sheet (8.2), and Questions sheet (8.3).
2. Make a transparency of the data table and graph sheet (8.1).

Safety Considerations

None

Procedure

1. Give the students the data table and graph page (8.1) without explaining what the lesson is about.
2. Have them complete the graph per the instructions on the page.

3. After they have completed their graphs, either show a graph that you have done or graph the data during class on the overhead projector.

4. Elicit from them the idea that there seems to be a correlation between the factors graphed.

5. Ask them to guess what the data represent. Many will probably guess the human population portion.

6. THEN tell them what the data are and discuss the implications. The human population data (Table 8-A, left axis) are in millions. The bird and mammal extinction data (Table 8-B, right axis) are numbers of species.

7. Distribute and discuss the Information sheet (8.2).

8. Distribute the Questions sheet (8.3).

Discussion

1. What did you think was being graphed? What made you think that the graphs might represent that?

2. Does there seem to be a correlation between human population and extinctions?

3. How might an increase in human population lead to extinction of other species?

4. Did species become extinct before there were people?

5. Do people cause all extinctions now?

6. Why should we care about other species?

7. What can be done to reduce human-caused extinctions?

Answers to 8.3, Endangered Species I—What's Happening? Questions

1. The mere fact that both graphs have the same shape does not prove that the increase in human population caused the increase in extinctions. It does, however, suggest a relationship. Examining the specific examples of extinctions and their causes indicates that humans were a major factor in most of these extinctions. Since habitat loss and hunting are major factors, increases in human populations logically have been a major cause.

2. For many people, birds and mammals are the most interesting and noticeable organisms. Consequently, we have records of bird and mammal populations for many years. Additionally, since birds and mammals are relatively large organisms and tend to require more space than insects, for example, they may tend to feel the impact of human encroachment first. Finally, most of the organisms that have been hunted to extinction were birds and mammals.

3. Humans alter habitats in many ways. Clearing land for building, flooding canyons behind dams, cutting trees for lumber, extracting energy resources, burning forests to clear land for agriculture, and simple encroaching with roads are all ways of altering habitats. (*The students will think of other ways.*)

4. a. *habitat alteration:* With more people, we need more land for building, growing crops, and obtaining raw materials. (See also the answer to question 3.)

   b. *commercial hunting:* More people means more food is needed. Commercial hunting provides food and a few other products that people need or want.

c. *competition with introduced species:* As human populations spread into wild areas, they bring other species with them, either intentionally or unintentionally.

d. *sport hunting:* As more people take up the sport of hunting, there is more pressure on the wild populations that they hunt.

e. *pest control:* "Pests" are generally controlled because they either impact human health or food supplies. As human populations grow, there is more pressure to reduce the losses to pests.

f. *subsistence hunting for food:* More people need more food.

g. *pollution:* As the human population increases, there is also an increase in demands for materials and for "things." Much pollution is caused by obtaining raw materials and making the things that people want.

5. Individuals can help reduce extinctions in numerous ways. One way is to make a commitment to not have more than one or two children, perhaps none. Recycling reduces the need to mine for new mineral resources. Saving energy reduces pollution. Influencing governmental officials to support laws to protect and help other species is an important way. They can be influenced by voting, letter writing, speaking at public meetings, and by writing letters to the editor. Supporting the many wildlife protection organizations is a way that even nonvoting students can help.

Extensions (See Activity 32 for suggestions for student projects.)

1. Have the students do reports on various endangered species. Be sure to include plant species and less glamorous species such as insects, reptiles, and amphibians. (The paucity of information on such species indicates part of the problem. In many ways we are more dependent on plants and "lower" animals than we are on mammals and birds, but we seem less interested in protecting them.)

2. See Activity 9.

3. Participate in an "Adopt-a-species" program. (See the *California Endangered Species Resource Guide.*)

4. Make a bulletin-board-size graph of the data. Surround it with pictures of endangered species, either cut from magazines or drawn by the students.

5. Investigate local endangered or threatened species. If it can be done without causing problems for the organism, visit a site where they can be seen.

6. In the United States, we have laws that require environmental impact reports before major environmental changes such as building or logging can take place. These require *consideration* of threats to threatened or endangered species, but don't necessarily protect the species. Have the students investigate examples of a threatened or endangered species slowing or stopping a project such as a dam, building project, or logging operation. Have them present both sides to the class in a debate or panel discussion.

7. Have students investigate the role of zoos in protecting (or threatening!) endangered species.

8. Have the students investigate "Germ Banks," where genetic material such as seeds are stored for future use.

9. Invite guest speakers from environmental and animal protection groups to speak to your class. (See Appendices II and III.)

10. Find out about some of the "success stories" of species that have been saved, at least for now, from extinction. These include the American bison, whooping crane, and trumpeter swan.

11. Obtain a free copy of *The Endangered Species Handbook* (see References). Have teams of students prepare reports based on the information therein.

12. The students could make a pie graph of the data in Table 8-C.

Modifications

1. Rather than simply graphing the data, have the students develop a three-dimensional representation of the data. They might use wooden or styrofoam blocks, beans in graduated cylinders, or other methods.

2. Let the students know what the data represent before they graph them.

3. Obtain similar data for a particular species and do a graph of them.

References

Anonymous, *California Endangered Species Resource Guide*. Sacramento, CA: California Department of Education, 1991.

Anonymous, *Endangered and Threatened Wildlife and Plants* (50 CFR 17.11 & 17.12). Washington, DC: U.S. Fish and Wildlife Service, Department of the Interior, 1991.

Braus, Judy (editor), *NatureScope: Endangered Species: Wild and Rare*. Washington, DC: National Wildlife Federation, 1989.

Enger, Eldon, and Bradley Smith, *Environmental Science: A Study of Interrelationships*. Dubuque, IA: Wm. C. Brown, Publishers, 1992.

McNeely, Jeffrey et al., *Conserving the World's Biological Diversity*. Washington, DC: World Resources Institute, et al., 1990.

Miller, G. Tyler, *Living in the Environment*. Belmont, CA: Wadsworth Publishing Company, 1990.

Myers, Norman (editor), *GAIA, An Atlas of Planet Management*. New York, NY: Bantam Doubleday Dell Publishing Group, 1984.

Nilsson, Greta, *The Endangered Species Handbook*. Washington, DC: Animal Welfare Institute, 1990.

Name _____ Class _____ Date _____

8.1 Data Graphing Activity

Two sets of data are given in tables A and B below. Use the axes given below to make line graphs of the data.

- Use a blue pen or pencil to graph the data from Table 8-A, using the left axis.
- Use a red pen or pencil to graph the data from Table 8-B, using the right axis.

Table 8-A		**Table 8-B**	
1650	550	1650	5
1700	610	1700	9
1750	760	1750	7
1800	950	1800	12
1850	1210	1850	27
1900	1630	1900	70
1950	2520	1950	124
2000	6000	2000	??

GRAPH OF ???

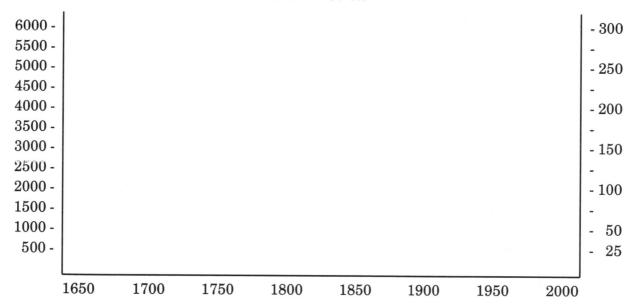

1. How are the two graphs similar? _____

_____

2. Can you guess what the data from tables A and B might represent?

Table 8-A might represent: _____

Table 8-B might represent: _____

3. If the trend continues, what will happen to each graph after 2000?

_____

8.2 Endangered Species 1—What's Happening?: Information

The data in Table A represent the human population of the world, in millions. The data in Table B represent the numbers of birds and mammals that became **extinct** during each 50-year period. It is important to note that these are only the species known to have become extinct during that time. There may have been others that we do not know about. It is also very important to keep in mind that these are only the birds and mammals. Reptiles, fish, amphibians, insects, and plants are not included in the data. Loss of plants and insects can be especially important to ecosystems and, most likely, to mankind.

No doubt you noticed that the rate of species loss has accelerated along with the growth in human population. This makes sense, because as human populations grow they will have more and more impact on their environment.

Species have been becoming extinct for as long as organisms have been evolving on the earth. Some scientists estimate that the average rate of vertebrate extinctions over the last 200 million years has been about 90 species per century or less than 1 per year. The data in the table show that in the 50 years between 1900 and 1950, about 124 species of birds and mammals became extinct. When other vertebrates are included, it is easy to see that the rate of vertebrate extinctions has nearly tripled the historical average!

The data are even more alarming when one considers plants and invertebrates. Some scientists estimate that we are losing at least one species per day! The loss of plants is especially important partly because many animals are dependent on specific species of plants, so if the plant becomes extinct so will some species of animals. There are even estimates that the annual rate of loss may accelerate to 50,000 species per year by the year 2000. This would be a loss of about 130 species per day!

There are several reasons for this alarming loss of species. Even today, some species undoubtedly become extinct due to "natural causes," but most are due to human activities. The following table lists some of these human activities and the percentage of extinctions caused by each.

Table 8-C: Causes of Extinction

habitat alteration	30%	pest control	7%
commercial hunting	21%	subsistence food hunting	6%
competition with introduced species	16%	captured to serve as pets	5%
sport hunting	12%	superstitious beliefs	2%
		pollution	1%

It is important to realize that many extinctions are caused by combinations of these factors. Also, the percentages and causes may change with time. For example, extinctions caused by pollution may increase while those caused by superstitious beliefs may decrease.

8.3 Endangered Species 1—What's Happening?: Questions

1. Do the data provided in Tables 8A and 8B prove that the increase in extinctions is due to the increase in human population? Explain your answer.

_____

_____

_____

2. Why do you think statistics were given for birds and mammals, rather than some other kind of organism?

_____

_____

_____

3. Habitat alteration is a very important part of the species endangerment and extinction problem. List several ways that humans alter the natural habitat.

_____

_____

_____

4. For each of the following causes of extinction, discuss how increases in human population make the problem worse.

a. habitat alteration _____

b. commercial hunting _____

c. competition _____

d. sport hunting _____

e. pest control _____

f. hunting for food _____

g. pollution _____

5. List some ways that you as an individual can help protect endangered species.

_____

_____

_____

ACTIVITY 9: ENDANGERED SPECIES II—WHO CARES? ___

Activity Summary

Students first survey their classmates to determine which of several endangered or threatened species they would protect or save if they had to choose. They then do research and design posters or other advertisements to show how some relatively unglamorous organisms are very important. Finally, the students complete and present research projects on endangered species.

Introduction

Protection of the diversity of life on Earth is of great importance to mankind for many reasons. Some are purely practical: medicines, foods, and other products can be obtained from plants and animals, and many uses have yet to be discovered. Other reasons are aesthetic or ethical. Do we as humans have the right to knowingly cause the extinction of other species?

Many of us are aware of the plight of such famous species as the giant panda, the California condor, or the black rhinoceros. While it is important to save large birds and mammals, there are literally thousands of other species that are threatened with extinction. Many of them have not yet even been discovered!

Even common species can become extinct, as evidenced by the extinction of the passenger pigeon and the near extinction of the American buffalo. Just because a species is common does not mean that it is without value or that it is not potentially threatened.

It is important that students realize that there are thousands of threatened and endangered species. It is important that they realize that most species are neither big, pretty, cuddly, nor famous. It is also important that they learn that there are ways to influence public and governmental opinions about protecting species of life on Earth.

It would be desirable to do Activity 8 either just before or just after doing this activity.

Grouping

Individual students and teams of 4–6 students.

Time

Introduction of Activity: 15–30 minutes

Students Complete Hard Choices Questionnaire Individually and in Teams: 30 minutes

Research and Making Advertisements (Aardvark Ads): as long as you want to allow

Presentation of advertisements: 50 minutes or more

Research on Endangered Species: as long as you want to allow

Anticipated Outcomes

The students will:

• increase their understanding of the importance of all organisms.

- increase their understanding of the diversity of organisms that are endangered.
- learn more about specific endangered or threatened species.
- increase their ability to influence others.
- increase their ability to present ideas clearly, simply, and with impact.

Materials

—Photocopied student pages:

- 9.1 Endangered Species II—Who Cares? Background Information (one per student)
- 9.2 Endangered Species II—Assignments (one per student)
- 9.3 Endangered Species II—Questions (one per student)

Vocabulary

biodiversity   consensus   endangered species   extinct

Teacher Preparation

1. Photocopy the Background Information Sheet (9.1), Assignments sheet (9.2), and Questions sheet (9.3).

2. Obtain descriptions, pictures, and/or lists of endangered species. Most libraries have books that have pictures and other information. You might obtain a copy of the *Endangered Species Handbook,* by Nilsson (free) or the *NatureScope Endangered Species: Wild and Rare* book.

3. Obtain examples of advertisements from magazines, posters, and, if possible, from tapes of local television stations.

4. Decide which medium or media will be used. Obtain the necessary materials such as paper, colored felt-tip pens, crayons, video-taping equipment, and/or audio-taping equipment.

Safety Considerations

None

Procedure

1. Ask the students to name the endangered species that they have heard of. As they list them, write them on the chalkboard, overhead projector, or on large paper. Group the organisms into taxonomic groups—mammals, birds, plants, and so forth.

2. Give the assignment sheet to the students. Give a brief description of each organism in the "Hard Choices" portion. If possible, show a photograph of each. (Consider substituting other species if you wish, but be sure to include little-known species and plants and invertebrates.)

3. Have the students complete the Hard Choices priority list individually.

4. Have the students form teams of 4–6 students. Each student should then each tell

his or her priority sequence and explain his or her reasons to the others in the team. The team is then to come up with a consensus priority list.

5. Have a representative of each team tell his or her team's priority list to the class. Tally the class results on the board. (Record the top three and the bottom three for each team.)

6. The students will probably select large mammals as the ones that they would save. Discuss our tendency to favor cuddly, large, beautiful, or famous species. (See Discussion, following.)

7. Explain the "Aardvark Ads" assignment.

8. When the "Aardvark Ads" are complete, have the students present their ads to the class.

9. Explain the "Endangered Species Research Assignment."

10. When the Endangered Species Research Assignments are complete, have each student give a 3-minute presentation on his or her species.

Discussion

1. Why do most of us tend to care more about mammals than invertebrates?

2. Which are more important to most ecosystems—mammals or insects? plants or animals?

3. Could we live without other mammals? without plants?

4. Which endangered species have gotten the most publicity? Why?

Answers to 9.3, Endangered Species II—Who Cares? Questions

1. There are many reasons to save plants, but two of the most important practical ones are that they provide many medicines and foods that we want or need. To destroy a species of plant may be to destroy a yet-to-be-discovered source of much-needed medicine or food. (*Students will have other answers.*) See the student information sheet (9.3).

2. There are many reasons to save species of animals. Many are useful as food sources or as sources of recreation. They are also important parts of their various ecosystems. (*Students will have other answers. Remind them of ethical considerations.*) See the student information sheet (9.3).

3. See answers to questions 1 and 2. Other answers are acceptable.

4. Biodiversity includes both the variety of species and the genetic diversity within a species. It is important to the survival of a species because the genetic diversity of the species helps protect it from becoming extinct. Diversity of species types in an ecosystem helps to stabilize the ecosystem.

5. Student answers will vary, but controlling the size of human populations, making and enforcing protective laws, controlling development, establishing preserves, and reducing pollution are all important actions.

Extensions (See Activity 32 for suggestions for student projects.)

1. Invite speakers from animal or animal protection groups to speak to the class.
2. Have the class raise funds to support an animal- or plant-protection program or group.
3. Write letters supporting animal and plant protection.
4. Participate in an "Adopt-a-species Program." (See References.)
5. Find out about locally endangered species and invite a local expert to speak to the class.
6. Visit a site where students can observe a local threatened or endangered species (if this can be done without causing problems to the organisms).
7. Visit a zoo or wildlife park. Try to arrange for a "behind the scenes" visit.
8. Have the students produce ads for endangered or threatened species and have them put up in the community, shown on local television, or played on local radio. Emphasize local species and why and how the public can support endangered species.
9. Show the film *The Lorax,* which is based on a Dr. Seuss book with the same title. Discuss the meaning of the film. It is available for purchase or rent in 16-mm film or video-tape formats from Phoenix Films, 468 Park Avenue South, New York, NY 10016; 800-221-1274.

Modifications

1. Change the species list on the Hard Choices and Aardvark Ads assignments.
2. Consider how you want the written reports to be done, including citations.
3. Obtain pictures of various endangered species listed in the questionnaire.
4. Obtain pictures of various organisms listed in the Aardvark Ads assignment.
5. Obtain pictures of as many endangered or threatened species as possible.

References

Anonymous, *California Endangered Species Resource Guide.* Sacramento, CA: California Department of Education, 1991.

Anonymous, *Endangered and Threatened Wildlife and Plants.* Washington, DC: U.S. Fish and Wildlife Service, 1991.

Braus, Judy (editor), *NatureScope: Endangered Species: Wild and Rare.* Washington, DC: National Wildlife Federation, 1989.

Miller, G. Tyler, *Living in the Environment.* Belmont, CA: Wadsworth Publishing Company, 1990.

Nilsson, Greta, *The Endangered Species Handbook.* Washington, DC: Animal Welfare Institute, 1990.

9.1 Endangered Species II—Who Cares?: Background Information

Many people have heard about **endangered** species such as the wolf, bald eagle, elephant, and giant panda. Most people would agree that it would be nice to help protect these species. But what about small species, or plants, or animals such as fish, snails, or insect? What about species that you will never actually see? Are there reasons why we should care about them and take actions to help protect them?

Species have been becoming **extinct** since life first formed on Earth four billion years ago. Most species that have ever lived are now extinct. But that does not mean that extinction is nothing to be concerned about. The rate of extinction has vastly accelerated in the last few decades, and most extinctions today are due to the activities of one species—*Homo sapiens*—humans.

One reason to preserve species is because they may have **economic or medical importance** to us. Many of the products that we use every day are made from plant and animal products. New uses for plants and animals are found daily. Many medications are made from plants. Some of the species that people have utilized for years are endangered. A species that has not even been discovered yet may yield an important new product, food, or medicine.

Wild species of plants and animals also provide us with a genetic insurance policy. For example, there are over a hundred varieties of corn, but almost all of the corn grown for human consumption comes from less than ten varieties. If a disease or some other problem reduces the ability of those few varieties to produce food, we will need to have the **genetic diversity** provided by the other varieties. **Biodiversity** is becoming increasingly important to us.

Wild plants and animals provide a source of beauty, wonder, and joy for millions of people. To lose the great diversity of life on Earth impoverishes all of us for **aesthetic** reasons as well as practical ones. In addition to the purely aesthetic values of wildlife, many species have **recreational value.** Hunting, fishing, bird watching, photography, and other recreational uses of wildlife are enjoyed by millions of people.

As scientists try to learn more about life on Earth, about ecology and evolution, about botany and zoology, they study the organisms living in various ecosystems. Every species in an ecosystem has a particular role or niche, and the loss of a species reduces our ability to learn from it. Every species of life on Earth has purely **scientific and ecological value** in addition to whatever other value it may have. Biodiversity is important to all organisms.

Perhaps the most important reason to care about other life forms is simply because **it is the right thing to do.** What right do we as humans have to hasten the extinction of other species of life, especially if they are of no threat to us? The ability of humans to think, reason, and make value judgments is one of the characteristics that, supposedly, sets us apart from most other species. Is it ethical for us to use our awesome power to destroy entire species of life?

9.2 Endangered Species II—Who Cares?: Assignments

Part I: Hard Choices

Assume that you are a wealthy philanthropist who has money that you want to use to save endangered species. You have only enough money to save one of the species listed below. Number the plants and animals in the order that you would select them for saving. Use #1 for the species that you would save first.

After each member of the class has selected his or her personal choices, the class will form teams to come up with a priority list that the team agrees upon. This team list needs to be a **consensus** agreement. Everybody needs to agree on the sequence, rather than just voting.

ENDANGERED SPECIES	MY PRIORITIES*	TEAM PRIORITIES*
Apache Trout	_____	_____
Arizona Cliff Rose	_____	_____
Blunt-Nosed Leopard Lizard	_____	_____
California Condor	_____	_____
Giant Carrion Beetle	_____	_____
Giant Panda	_____	_____
Hawaiian Crow	_____	_____
Oahu Tree Snail	_____	_____
Pitcher's Thistle	_____	_____
Red-Footed Tortoise	_____	_____
Salt Marsh Harvest Mouse	_____	_____
Schaus Swallowtail Butterfly	_____	_____
Texas Blind Salamander	_____	_____
Wyoming Toad	_____	_____

*#1 is the first to be saved.

Part II: Aardvark Ads

Your job is to design an advertisement for one of the following organisms. While these are not endangered species, they play an important role in their environments. Your teacher may add to or subtract from the list. Your advertisement might be a poster, a magazine ad, a television ad (acted out for the class or video-taped), or a radio (audio-tape) commercial.

With your partner(s), learn as much as you can about the organism, plan your advertisement, produce the ad, and present it to the class on the due date.

Remember: Your goal is to convince the class that this organism is wonderful!

Our advertisement data is due: _____

bread mold	yeast	moss	rhinovirus
dandelion	crabgrass	garden snail	liver fluke
starling	crow	gopher	house mouse
rattlesnake	fence lizard	housefly	mosquito
puffball mushroom	poison oak/ivy	sucker fish	tapeworm
black widow spider	head louse	tarantula	garden slug
garden toad	striped skunk	coyote	centipede

Part III: Endangered Species Research Assignment

On the due date given by your teacher, you are to submit a research report on an endangered species. You are also to give a short oral report to the class about your organism.

Due dates: written report: _____ oral presentation: _____

In your written report, be sure to give the source(s) of your information. Use the format suggested by your teacher. Your report should include the following information:

- organism name (common, scientific)
- picture or drawing of the organism
- range: where originally lived, where it now lives
- population: how many are still alive in the wild
- any special or unique things of interest
- what caused it to become threatened or endangered
- what is currently being done to help the species
- what students can do to help
- sources of information (author, title, date, publisher, date, page[s])
- other: _____

9.3 Endangered Species II—Who Cares?: Questions

1. Why is it important to save plant species?

   _____

   _____

   _____

   _____

2. Why is it important to save invertebrate species?

   _____

   _____

   _____

   _____

3. List three reasons to protect species that you as an individual may never see.

   a. _____

   b. _____

   c. _____

4. What is "biodiversity" and why is it important?

   _____

   _____

   _____

   _____

5. What are some ways that you can help protect species of plants and animals?

   _____

   _____

   _____

   _____

unit Three

Water Issues

- Oil Spill!
- Water Treatment
- "Water" We Going to Do?

ACTIVITY 10: OIL SPILL! _____

Activity Summary

Students first build "island habitats" using rocks, feathers, pieces of fur, and plastic animals. Oil is "spilled" on the habitat, then the students have to try to clean it up. They are provided with a variety of materials and are directed to test the effectiveness of them. Activity follow-up will lead to better understanding of the risks to the environment caused by energy use.

Introduction

This activity can be incorporated into a number of studies. In Earth Science courses, it could be part of units on energy, oceanography, water, pollution, or Earth resources. In Biology or Life Science courses, it could be part of units on water pollution, conservation, vertebrates (especially birds, fish, or mammals), invertebrates, or organic chemistry. In Physical Science or Chemistry courses, it could be part of units on organic chemistry, pollution, or energy.

One excellent way to introduce the activity would be to utilize a current news article on a recent oil spill. Articles on wildlife problems or other water pollution types are also common in news magazines and newspapers.

You could have the students spend time building a coastal or island "habitat" using rocks, sticks, plastic animals, and so forth. After they have built their habitats, an oil spill could occur. While some high school students might think that they are "too sophisticated" to build habitats with rocks and plastic animals, if you can get them past that block, they will usually develop some ownership of their habitat, and this can lead to a very powerful lesson.

Grouping

Students build their habitats in teams of 3–5 students, depending on materials available.

Time

Habitat building: 5–15 minutes

Testing of cleaning methods: 10–30 minutes

Discussion: 20–40 minutes

Anticipated Outcomes

The students will:

- design and conduct experiments to test the effectiveness of various methods of cleaning oil off feathers, fur, and inanimate objects.
- increase their understanding of problems resulting from oil spills.
- increase their understanding of the relationship between energy use and oil spills.

Materials (for each team)

—Photocopied student pages:

- 10.1 Oil Spill! Background Information sheet (one per student)
- 10.2 Oil Spill! Data Table (one per student)
- 10.3 Oil Spill! Questions (one per student)

—One pan in which to build the habitat; it might be:

- a "disposable" aluminum cooking pan approximately 10" × 14" (not to be disposed of, though—clean it and save it for next year!)
- a metal cooking pan (If you don't want to have to clean it up enough to use it for cooking, consider picking up some used ones at garage sales or flea markets.)
- half-gallon cardboard milk cartons cut lengthwise, yielding two pans
- gallon milk cartons, cut to be about 3 inches deep

—Enough water to fill the habitat to a depth of about 1–2 inches (2–5 cm)

—Oil: 4–8 ml per team; cooking or other light oil will work; if you use motor oil, consider what to do with the residue

—Small containers for the oil to serve as "tankers"; small paper cups work well (You might even purchase some small plastic boats such as those used for cake decorations at children's birthdays, or small toy boats from a toy store.)

—Items with which to form a "habitat":

- rocks
- sticks
- plastic animals (from toy or party-supply stores, or garage sales)
- feathers (preferably waterfowl, untreated): at least one 5 cm length per team. This may be a section cut from a larger feather. You might obtain them from students or parents who hunt ducks or geese (one duck will supply you for years!), local farms, students who are in 4-H or Future Farmers of America (contact your local farm bureau or agricultural extension office), or biological supply houses.
- pieces of animal skin with fur attached. These might be available from the same sources as the feathers. Contact leatherworking or hobby shops or local taxidermists. You might also find a fur coat, stole, or hat of some sort at a flea market or a thrift shop. Wool (untreated) or other animal hair such as from a dog or cat work too.

—Cleaning materials such as:

- dishwashing detergents or soaps (try a variety of brands)
- laundry detergents or soaps

• baking soda	• borax	• mineral oil
• sponges	• gauze	• paper towels
• pieces of cloth	• cotton balls	• cotton swabs

—Hand lens, or compound or binocular microscope with which to examine feathers and fur

—"Medicine" droppers

—Plastic bags for "oil-spill clean-up kits"

—Newspapers for "tablecloths"

Vocabulary

blowout	crude oil	insulation
runoff	supertanker	toxic

Teacher Preparation

1. Photocopy Background Information sheet (10.1), Data Table (10.2), and Questions (10.3).

2. Place the habitat building materials in sets for each team.

3. Either prepare "oil-spill clean-up kits" for each team or set up a clean-up supply station to which the students will go to select their cleaning materials. The latter is usually less wasteful but results in more commotion in the class. You will need to limit the amounts of materials that the students can use.

4. If you are using the following supertanker accident scenario as described, prepare your "fleet" of cups of oil ahead of time.

SAFETY CONSIDERATIONS

1. Be sure to provide clean-up materials for the students.

2. If you do not have aprons or lab coats available, you might warn the students the day before doing this lab that it might be messy and that they should not wear good clothes.

3. Proper disposal of motor oil is a consideration. If you have an auto shop at your school, you might use that facility. If not, seek a recycling center, garage, or public agency garage such as a fire or police station.

Procedure

1. Provide the materials with which the students are to build their island habitats.

2. Add water to surround the "islands."

3. Have the students examine (sketch?) the feather and fur with the hand lens or microscope. They should look at the shape, color, texture, symmetry, cleanliness, and other characteristics.

4. Have the students use medicine droppers and water to test the feathers and fur for water-repellant properties. Have them record their data.

5. Explain that there is a shipping lane that passes near the island. Then explain that oil supertankers use the shipping lane.

6. Either give them the container of oil (the supertanker) or you bring it to their station. Explain that there is an oil spill that affects the island and its inhabitants. Spill oil on the water and the plastic animals, feathers, and fur.

7. Have them examine the fur and feathers, comparing to the first and second examinations. They should record their observations. (Sketch?)

8. Discuss possible approaches to cleaning up the spill. You might have them present

a written clean-up proposal, or have them predict the relative effectiveness of various methods and materials.

9. Provide clean-up materials and allow them to work on cleaning up the oil. They should record their results on the data table provided. You can have them try to clean up the feathers, the animals, the water, and/or the rocks.

10. Have the students examine (sketch?) the fur and the feather again.

11. Have them test the feather and fur for water repellance. Record the observations.

12. Have them compare the feather and fur before and after exposure to oil, and before and after cleaning. Discuss the effects of oil spills, AND ways that we can reduce the need to transport oil. It is very important to be sure that the students understand that so much oil wouldn't need to be shipped if we weren't using and wasting so much of it.

Discussion

1. Which clean-up method(s) worked best for removing the oil?

2. What would be the effect of the various clean-up methods on wildlife?

3. What things need to be considered when selecting from various clean-up options? (Include expense, time, material availability, environmental effects, stress on organisms, etc.)

4. How can the likelihood of oil spills be reduced by the following? Give pros and cons of each.
   a. better tanker construction
   b. better methods of transferring oil to and from tankers
   c. better drilling methods
   d. better training of crews
   e. better laws
   f. reducing oil consumption

5. Who should pay the costs of oil-spill clean ups?

6. What are you willing to do to help prevent spills?

7. Would you take a day off from school to try to help clean up an oil spill?

8. What are you willing to do to save energy?

9. To do this activity, we used some oil and created some waste. Was the environment helped or hurt by this activity?

10. How else might birds and other animals be affected by an oil spill?

Answers to 10.3, Oilspill! Questions

1. a. Spilled oil harms water fowl in many ways. Birds become stuck in the oil as they try to swim or dive through it. It can stick their eyes and beaks shut and clog their nostrils. The oil destroys the insulating ability of their feathers, resulting in death from the cold water or air. Birds may be poisoned when they ingest the oil, or it may clog up their throats. Additionally, the oil kills food or makes it poisonous for the birds to eat. Chemicals from the oil may be carcinogenic.

b. Oil has much the same effect on marine mammals as it does on birds. (See question 1a.)

c. Fish gills can be stuck or clogged with oil. Chemicals from the oil can be poisonous to fish. As bacteria decompose the oil, the oxygen may be depleted. Fish eggs can be poisoned or covered with oil.

d. Invertebrates can be covered with oil, be poisoned by the oil in the water, and can have their eggs killed.

e. Some kinds of bacteria and other microorganisms can be killed by the oil. Others might thrive by feeding on the oil. Photosynthetic organisms (plants such as diatoms and algae) are generally harmed by the oil if it remains at the surface and cuts off the light supply for a long time, or if they are coated with the oil.

f. The water itself becomes poisonous to many organisms. Additionally, oil floating on the surface of the water reduces mixing of the water. Efforts to clean up the oil spill often add chemicals to the water, many of which can be dangerous to marine life.

2. If we save energy, less oil will need to be shipped, thereby reducing the risk of oil spills.

3. Anything that one does to save energy or oil will help reduce the need for shipping oil and thereby reduce the risk of oil spills. Driving less, using our home heaters and air conditioners less, and recycling are a few ways to save energy. Additionally, putting pressure on the legislature to pass and, especially, to enforce strict shipping regulations will help to reduce oil spills. We can do this by writing letters and by asking questions and making suggestions when legislators come to town to talk with their constituents.

Extensions (See Activity 32 for suggestions for student projects.)

1. Design an experiment to determine whether oil can pass through an eggshell. If it does, what might the effects be on developing bird embryos? What about animals that don't produce shells?

2. Try similar experiments with a variety of different oils—crude oil, diesel oil, and so forth.

3. What is the effect of the oil on aquatic plants?

4. What happens to run-off from driveways, streets, and parking lots? Is there oil in that water?

5. Visit a local sewage treatment plant, oil refining or recycling plant, gas station, or other place that must deal with waste oil.

6. Visit a local wildlife rescue center, or invite a speaker to the class.

7. Design oil clean-up apparatus—skimmers, booms, absorbers, and so forth.

8. Do research to find out about various oil spills.

9. Do research to find out about oil-spill clean-up techniques.

10. Do research to find out about laws pertaining to oil spills.

11. Do research to find out about the controversy that waged before the oil fields in Alaska were opened up to drilling.

Modifications

1. Some students may not be willing to create environments with toy animals. The activity can be done without the island habitat. Just have them examine the feathers and fur and then dip them into water, examine, then dip into oil and examine again.
2. Include hard-boiled eggs in the experimental environment.
3. Design and carry out experiments to find out the effects of turbulence or mixing of the water.
4. Is there a difference between the effects of oil in saltwater and fresh water?

References

Cheryl, Dr. Charles (project director), *Project Wild—Secondary Activity Guide*. Boulder, CO: Western Regional Environmental Education Council, 1986.

Drutman, Ava, and Susan Zuckerman, *Protecting Our Planet*. Carthage, IL: Good Apple, 1991.

Miller, G. Tyler, *Living in the Environment*. Belmont, CA: Wadsworth Publishing Co., 1990.

Schwartz, Linda, *Earth Book for Kids*. Santa Barbara, CA: The Learning Works, Inc., 1990.

Sly, Carolie (Project Coordinator), *The California State Environmental Education Guide*. Hayward, CA: Alameda County Office of Education, 1988.

10.1 Oil Spill! Background Information

Every year, millions of gallons of oil are released into the environment, either accidentally or intentionally. This oil comes from tanker accidents, **blowouts** or spills at offshore drilling rigs, and from **runoff** and dumping of waste oil from cities and industries.

In 1979, a huge blowout occurred at the Ixtoc I oil well in the southern Gulf of Mexico. Over 184 million gallons of oil leaked into the environment. It took eight months to cap the well. As horrendous as that seems, releases from offshore wells during normal operations and during transportation of the oil add much more oil to the environment than such occasional accidents.

Oil tanker and **supertanker** accidents account for about 10 to 15 percent of the annual input of oil into the world's oceans, but they can be disastrous when they occur. Most of the rest comes from leaks at wells, purging of tanks, seepage from natural sources, and so forth. The largest tanker accident to date was in 1983, when the tanker Castillow de Bellver caught fire and released 78.5 million gallons into the ocean off the coast of Capetown, South Africa.

In March of 1989, the tanker *Exxon Valdez* hit a reef and released about 11 million gallons of oil into the Prince William Sound of Alaska. More than 33,000 seabirds, nearly 1,000 sea otters, and more than 100 bald eagles were killed.

The type and amount of damage from an oil spill depend on a number of factors such as the type of oil, weather conditions, what kinds of organisms are in the area, the season, and other conditions.

Crude (unrefined) **oil** is actually a mixture of hundreds of different substances. Some are very **toxic;** some are relatively innocuous. Some evaporate into the air, some dissolve in water, some float, and some sink. Some are very sticky and tend to coat whatever they contact.

The effects of an oil spill are many and varied. The most obvious effect is the waste of an increasingly rare and valuable resource, the oil itself. While attempts to recover the spilled oil are made, much is lost and much of what is recovered is not usable because of contamination from the clean-up process or the environment.

Some of the components of crude oil, such as benzene and toluene, are extremely toxic (poisonous). Sticky oil coatings smother many organisms. Oil destroys the **insulation** and buoyancy of marine birds and mammals, so that many drown or die of exposure to cold water and air. Fish gills are clogged. Animals that ingest the oil or eat other organisms contaminated by the oil may be poisoned or have their digestive systems clogged by the oil.

Oil companies, governmental agencies, and people who are concerned about the environment have tried a number of ways to clean up spilled oil. It is always a difficult, expensive effort. Even as recently as the 1989 *Exxon Valdez* spill, many of the methods used were still in the experimental stage, and some of the experiments didn't work well. Sometimes people's efforts to clean up after a spill may do more damage than good.

10.2 Oil Spill! Data Table

1. Sketch and describe the dry feather and the dry fur.

sketches

feather   **fur**

descriptions

2. Sketch and describe the feather and the fur after they are coated with oil.

sketches

feather   **fur**

descriptions

3. Sketch and describe the feather and fur after cleaning.

sketches

feather   **fur**

descriptions

4. Create a table to record the effectiveness of the methods that you use to clean up the oil.

10.3 Oil Spill!: Questions

1. What would be the effects of an oil spill on:

   a. water fowl _____

   _____

   _____

   b. marine mammals _____

   _____

   _____

   c. fish _____

   _____

   _____

   d. invertebrates such as clams, crabs, starfish, sea urchins, and larvae of various animals

   _____

   _____

   e. bacteria and other microorganisms _____

   _____

   _____

   f. the water itself _____

   _____

   _____

2. How can saving energy reduce the likelihood of oil spills?

   _____

   _____

3. List some things that you can do NOW to reduce the likelihood of oil spills.

   _____

   _____

   _____

ACTIVITY 11: WATER TREATMENT _____

Activity Summary

Students investigate primary sewage treatment, learning that it is basically filtering and settling of polluted water. They then find that many pollutants are not removed by this process. In addition, they learn about secondary and tertiary sewage treatment.

Introduction

Pollutants are removed from water in several ways. Percolation through many feet of soil provides a sort of natural water purification system, but it is not effective for all pollutants. Larger particulates and many bacteria are removed by passing through soil, but many dissolved chemicals and viruses are not removed by percolation alone.

Sewage treatment plants take advantage of natural processes of settling and filtration in primary sewage treatment plants. In primary treatment plants, large objects are physically removed by passing the water through a series of grates and screens. Smaller particles are removed in grit chambers and settling tanks. Primary treatment removes about 60 percent of the solids and 30 percent of the organic wastes. Chlorine is usually added to the water before it is released into the environment in an attempt to kill bacteria. Many dissolved chemicals remain in water that has received only primary treatment.

Eutrophication can result if such water is released into water systems such as lakes. When water containing organic matter and such fertilizers as nitrates and phosphates enters a lake, an algal bloom may result in the production of millions of algae plants. When these plants die, bacteria begin to decompose them. As the bacteria decompose the algae, they use most of the oxygen in the water. Without enough oxygen, fish and other organisms soon die. This often results in the death of thousands of fish.

Secondary treatment uses the activity of bacteria, protozoa, and other small organisms to remove much of the organic matter. In secondary treatment, water that has received primary treatment may be passed through a large tank where the activity of the microorganisms is supported by aeration. It may also be passed over and through a bed of stones by a trickle filter or sprinkler system. In either case, up to 90 percent of the solids and organic wastes are usually removed. Phosphates, nitrates, and other chemicals are also removed to some extent. Other chemicals such as heavy metals, salts, and pesticides are largely untouched by secondary treatment. Secondarily treated water is usually chlorinated before release.

Tertiary treatment plants use a variety of chemical processes to remove the remaining impurities. These processes are generally quite costly. Some plants use algae or other aquatic plants to help remove the chemicals.

It is important for students to realize that not all potentially harmful chemicals are removed by primary or secondary sewage treatment. Water that looks clear and clean may have many dissolved and dangerous chemicals in it. They also need to realize that the treatment of water is an expensive process that will require them to be willing to pay taxes. Finally, they need to realize that their personal actions can help sewage treatment plants work properly and can reduce the need for such costly plants.

In rural and suburban areas, septic tanks may be used for the disposal of domestic waste water and sewage. Basically a septic-tank system includes a tank in which large solids settle to the bottom. This tank is periodically emptied by pumping. The liquid is distributed to a drain field of gravel or crushed stone where bacteria and microorganisms remove the organic chemicals.

Grouping

Teams of 2–3 students.

Time

45–55 minutes

Anticipated Outcomes

The students will:

- understand what primary sewage treatment is.
- understand that primary sewage treatment does not remove all pollutants.
- understand what secondary and tertiary sewage treatment are.

Materials

—Photocopied student pages:

- 11.1 Water Treatment: Background Information (one per student)
- 11.2 Water Treatment: Instructions and Data (one per team)
- 11.3 Water Treatment: Questions (one per student)

—For each team of students:

- balance
- two 250 ml beakers
- Bunsen burner, hot plate, or other method for evaporating water
- (optional): ring stand and ring to support the filter bottle
- filter materials (see list below)

—For the class: a supply of materials to use in making their filters, including:

- 2 L plastic bottles with the bottoms cut out (invert to use as filter container)
- screen material to push into the opening (mouth) of the bottle to keep gravel in
- a variety of filtering materials, including, but not limited to:

gravel	sand	soil
cotton balls	cloth scraps	styrofoam pellets
charcoal briquettes	charcoal from a fish or pet store	

—A supply of "polluted" water (approximately 300 ml per team), made by mixing mud, clay, sand, and salt to tap water. Consider adding food coloring.

Vocabulary

chlorination	effluent	potable	primary treatment
secondary treatment	septic tank	settling tank	sewage
sludge	tertiary treatment		

Teacher Preparation

1. Photocopy the Background Information sheet (11.1), Instructions and Data sheet (11.2), and Questions sheet (11.3).
2. Obtain and prepare the materials listed here.
3. Make a sample filter to show to the students.
4. Consider having the students bring in the 2L bottles and having them cut out the bottoms.

SAFETY CONSIDERATION

Remind the students to wash their hands after completing this activity.

Procedure

1. Show the students two samples of water: one that is clear (sample A) and one that is muddy (sample B). Ask which one is safe to drink. Most will probably say that the clear one is safe to drink (potable). Then ask whether all pollutants can be seen.
2. Point out that water purification involves the removal of both visible and invisible pollutants.
3. Ask how visible pollutants might be removed from a water sample.
4. Distribute the Background Information sheet (11.1) and the Information and Data sheet (11.2).
5. Show a sample of a filter system and how to use it.
6. Have the students do the activity and clean up.
7. Discuss the activity (see the discussion questions below).
8. Distribute the Questions sheet (11.3) and discuss the questions.

Discussion

1. Which filtration system worked best? Why?
2. Did the filters remove all of the pollutants?
3. What other processes are used in primary sewage treatment? in secondary? in tertiary?

4. What are some of the sources or causes of water pollution?

5. What are some pollutants that cannot be seen in water?

6. What could be done to improve the filters?

7. What else is done in primary treatment?

8. Primary, secondary, and tertiary treatment all generate sludge or waste. What could be done with it?

9. The Law of Conservation of Matter (Mass) tells us that matter can neither be created nor destroyed. How does this relate to sewage-treatment plants?

10. Industrial processes produce many water pollutants. What are some of the options for paying to remove them from the water?

11. What is the relationship between population and the need for water-treatment plants?

12. How is water purified in nature? Is the water in a mountain stream really pure water? Are naturally occurring impurities such as algae, silt, and dissolved minerals any more or less of a concern than are toxic chemicals?

Answers to 11.3, Water Treatment: Questions

1. Primary sewage treatment involves removing the large particles by a series of screens, then allowing the solids to settle out, possibly with a filter system. The water is chlorinated before release. Secondary treatment adds bacterial and microorganisms that remove much of the organic matter. Tertiary treatment involves a variety of chemical reactions to remove various additional pollutants.

2. The Law of Conservation of Matter or Mass says that matter can neither be created nor destroyed. Pollutants, whether in the water, in the air, or on land, will not just "go away." The atoms and molecules will still be around. We need to find ways to reduce the production of harmful molecules and to alter, remove, or store those that are produced.

3. In the home, one can reduce the amount of chemicals such as cleaners, pesticides, fertilizers, paints, and so forth, that are added to the water system by not buying them in the first place, by minimizing their use, and by disposing of containers properly. If on a septic tank system, the homeowner should be sure that it is functioning properly. Voters need to be willing to vote for (and pay for) good sewage treatment facilities and water pollution control laws (and officials who will enact and enforce them).

4. Industries produce what we purchase. By becoming informed about products, we can make intelligent choices in our purchases. We also need to be willing to pay for increased production costs caused by pollution control at the manufacturing site. As voters, we need to be willing to support pollution-control laws and to insist that our governmental agencies enforce them. We also need to support (and participate in!) the development of ways of living that pollute less.

Extensions (See Activity 32 for suggestions for student projects.)

1. Have the students devise methods to further purify the water. Include granulated activated charcoal.

2. Have the students devise methods to measure the turbidity (cloudiness) of the water.

3. Use commercially available test kits to test locally collected waters for various chemicals.

4. Visit a sewage treatment facility (or invite a guest speaker).

5. Visit a water pumping and delivery facility.

6. Find out where your community's water comes from. On a map, have the students trace the water from its source to their homes or the school.

7. Have the students prepare detailed diagrams of the water cycle.

8. Find out about local industries that produce water pollutants and what they are doing about them.

9. Discuss the process of eutrophication, including "biological oxygen demand." Test samples for dissolved oxygen.

10. Have the students learn about biological magnification (biological concentration) of pollutants.

Modifications

1. Add soap to the water. Test for its presence by shaking a sample in a jar or a test tube and looking for suds.

2. Add alum to the water to increase settling.

3. Rather than making "polluted" water, obtain some water from a local stream or lake.

References

Anonymous, *The Green Box*. Eureka, CA: Humboldt County Office of Education, 1989.

Blaustein, Elliott, *Antipollution Lab*. New York, NY: Sentinel Books Publishers, Inc., 1972.

Chiras, Daniel, *Environmental Science*. Redwood City, CA: Benjamin/Cummings Publishing Co., Inc., 1990.

Drutman, Ava, and Susan Zuckerman, *Protecting Our Planet*. Carthage, IL: Good Apple Publications, 1991.

Miller, G. Tyler, *Living in the Environment*. Belmont, CA: Wadsworth Publishing Company, 1990.

Weaver, Elbert (editor), *Scientific Experiments in Environmental Pollution*. New York, NY: Holt, Rinehart and Winston, Inc., 1968.

11.1 Water Treatment: Background Information

Water pollution comes in many forms. It may be as simple as sand or mud suspended in water, or as complex as radioactive isotopes or viruses. It includes chemicals such as nitrates, phosphates, pesticides, and salts. It includes organic wastes such as feces and garbage disposal effluent. Some sources of pollution, such as mud slides or minerals from the earth, are natural. Others are caused by human activities.

People need clean water to be healthy, to grow crops, and for many industrial purposes. Plants and animals need unpolluted water, too. To reduce the possibility of polluting the water with household or industrial waste, most communities have **sewage** treatment plants. Individual homes may have **septic tank** systems. Many industrial plants have their own water treatment facilities.

Most water-treatment processes start with a simple filtration process. A series of screens is used to filter out large items such as sticks, stones, and rags. The water is then held in a **settling tank** for a period of time to allow suspended solids to sink to the bottom. The settled solids are called **sludge**.

After the sludge has settled out, the water is usually treated with chlorine to kill bacteria, and then it is discharged into a river, lake, or the ocean. This mechanical separation coupled with the addition of chlorine to kill bacteria **(chlorination)** is called **primary sewage treatment**.

A similar process is used in household septic tanks. In septic-tank systems, the water flows to a tank in which the solids settle to the bottom and the greases and oils float to the top. The water is carried through pipes to perforated pipes in a drain field where it flows out over and through gravel. The gravel and microorganisms living in the soil remove many contaminants from the water.

Many communities have a more advanced sewage treatment system called **secondary sewage treatment.** In secondary treatment, the water from the settling tank is aerated by one of several ways. This aeration encourages the growth of bacteria and other microorganisms that remove many organic chemicals and suspended solids from the water. After additional time in a settling tank or pond, the water is chlorinated and released.

Even secondary treatment does not remove all pollutants. Many salts, pesticides, phosphates, and other pollutants remain in secondarily treated water. To remove the remaining chemicals is an expensive proposition, but a few communities have invested in tertiary treatment facilities. **Tertiary water treatment** involves different processes, many of them chemical, to remove different pollutants. Many tertiary treatment plants claim that the water they release is **potable,** or safe to drink.

Without clean water, our communities and industries cannot survive. As more people compete for the finite amount of water on Earth, it becomes increasingly important for us to take care of our water systems. It is important for us to understand how we can protect and improve our water supplies.

Name _____ Class _____ Date _____

11.2 Water Treatment: Instructions

In this activity, you will design and test the effectiveness of various methods of filtering water, which is the first step in primary sewage treatment. Your teacher will supply you with some "polluted" water. You will make visual observations of the water that has passed through your filter (the filtrate), and then you will evaporate the water to see whether there were dissolved or suspended materials that you did not see.

Follow your teacher's instructions for building your filter or filters. Sketch your filter system(s) in the space provided below, labeling each part.

Then follow these steps to test your sample(s):

1. Find the mass of a 250 ml beaker as precisely as possible. Record the mass on the table below.

2. Obtain 250 ml of the "polluted" water. Record its appearance.

3. Pour the water carefully through your filter, collecting the filtrate in the massed 250 ml beaker, which should be placed under the filter.

4. Observe and record the appearance of the filtered water.

5. Follow your teacher's instructions to evaporate the filtered water (filtrate).

6. Find the mass of the beaker and residue remaining after all of the water has evaporated.

7. Find the mass of the residue by subtracting the mass of the beaker alone (step 1) from the mass of the beaker plus residue (step 6).

FILTER SYSTEM DESIGN(S)

System A   **System B**

DATA

	System A	System B
a. mass of clean beaker		
b. appearance of polluted water		
c. appearance of filtered water		
d. mass of residue		

11.3 Water Treatment: Questions

1. Briefly describe primary, secondary, and tertiary sewage treatment systems.

_____

_____

_____

_____

_____

_____

2. With regard to water pollution, discuss the Law of Conservation of Matter.

_____

_____

_____

3. What are some ways that you as an individual can help reduce water pollution produced at your home?

_____

_____

_____

_____

_____

4. Industries are important producers of water pollutants. How can individuals influence industries to reduce water pollution?

_____

_____

_____

_____

ACTIVITY 12: "WATER" WE GOING TO DO? _____

Activity Summary

Students first guess how much water they think they use in their daily activities. Then they record their actual water use in a day. They learn that our water use at home is only a small part of the water used for each of us. Water wasted by a slow leak from a faucet is measured and extrapolated to show how much is wasted from a small leak over a period of a year. The students then learn some water-conservation methods, including how to change a faucet washer.

Introduction

Water is an absolute necessity for life and for most of our industrial processes. The amount of water on Earth is finite, yet our demand keeps increasing as our population and industrial needs increase. Some investigators estimate that 30 to 50 percent of the water used in the United States is wasted. Many experts consider water conservation to be the quickest and cheapest way to increase our water supply.

One reason that so much water is wasted is that it is generally inexpensive. Federal and state funds are usually used to build dams and water-delivery systems to farms, industries, and communities. If the users had to pay directly for the costs of this water, they would waste much less. These subsidized water projects enable farmers to grow crops that demand lots of water, like cotton, alfalfa, and rice, in naturally dry areas such as Arizona and California. This artificially inexpensive water also enables farmers and industries to use wasteful methods and still make profits. Typical amounts of water use for various products is shown in Table 12-A on the student Background Information sheet (12.1).

Inexpensive water also fails to encourage water conservation at the home. People think little of a toilet that uses 6 or 7 gallons of water per flush even though 1.5-gallon-per-flush toilets are available. Lawns are often kept green and lush all year long in areas where there is no rainfall for much of the year. We wash our sidewalks and driveways with the most precious fluid on Earth! Table 12-C shows how we use water at home.

Most of us forget that the water that we use at our homes is only a fraction of the water use for which we are responsible. Water use in the United States is shown in table 12-B. It is important to realize that our purchasing habits determine what industry does. Driving cars for longer periods of time before replacing them, recycling aluminum, and saving energy all reduce water consumption by industry. Growing only crops for which the climate is suitable and adopting water-conserving agricultural practices could save huge amounts of water.

Another reason to conserve water is because the collection and movement of water have environmental effects. Damming rivers flood the valleys behind the reservoir. Canals and pipelines alter the environments through which they pass. Channelizing rivers destroys the natural riparian ecosystems. Diverting water from one area to supply another area is harmful to the ecosystems from which the water is taken.

Even if we have adequate water to meet our current domestic needs, we need to conserve water because shortages can occur at any time. It is predicted that many metropolitan areas of the United States, including those with adequate water supplies now, will have serious water shortages in the next ten years. Developing water-conserving habits today can help forestall the problem and make it easier to deal with when water shortages occur.

Grouping

Individuals and teams of two.

Time

Introduce the personal water use activity: 15 minutes

Teach how to change the faucet washer: 15 minutes

Assign and explain the home conservation survey: 15 minutes

Discuss the results of the home conservation survey: 15 minutes

Anticipated Outcomes

The students will:

- list several ways that we each use water in addition to our personal at-home use.
- demonstrate how to change a faucet washer.
- do a home water-waste survey.
- list several ways to conserve water at home.

Materials

—Photocopied student pages:

- 12.1 "Water" We Going to Do?: Background Information sheet (one per student)
- 12.2 "Water" We Going to Do?: Personal Water Use Data table (one per student)
- 12.3 "Water" We Going to Do?: Home Water Conservation Survey (one per student)
- 12.4 "Water" We Going to Do?: Questions (one per student)

—For each team of 2 or 3 students:

- one typical faucet (see "Teacher Preparation")
- one screwdriver (see "Teacher Preparation")
- several extra faucet washers of an appropriate size

—One 250 ml–500 ml graduated cylinder

—one funnel

Vocabulary

channelization   drought   riparian

Teacher Preparation

1. Photocopy the Background Information sheet (12.1), Personal Water Use Data table (12.2), Home Water Conservation Survey (12.3), and Questions sheet (12.4).
2. Obtain faucets, faucet washers, and screwdrivers of an appropriate size and type (flat-head or phillips). Ideally, all would be of a similar style. You can probably ob-

tain these free from local plumbing suppliers, hardware stores, plumbers, or kitchen and bath fixture stores. Your school district may have some. *NOTE:* To make it less awkward to hold the faucet, you may want to use screws to mount the faucet on a piece of wood.

3. Consider asking your school maintenance person or a local plumber to teach the students how to change the washer. This might be a good idea even if you already know how to do it.

4. Practice setting the "leaky faucet" so that it leaks at a rate that seems realistic for an unfixed leak. A reasonable amount is about 250 ml in 15 minutes.

SAFETY CONSIDERATIONS

1. Caution the students to be careful with screwdrivers.
2. Before asking students to undo the screws, test them to make sure they are not too tight.

Procedure

1. Discuss the ways that we use water in our daily lives. List on the board common uses suggested by the students.

2. Issue the Personal Water Use Data sheet to each student. Ask them to write down how many gallons of water they think they use in a typical day, including drinking, cooking, showering, dish and clothes washing, flushing the toilet, and so forth. Point out that some items may not be done daily.

3. Assign them to keep track of the amount that they actually use in the next 24 hours.

4. The next day, have the students tell you their totals as you record them on the board or on an overhead projector.

5. Discuss other uses that may not have been recorded. These might include watering flowers or a garden, bathing pets, washing the car, cleaning windows, swimming-pool evaporation, or others.

6. Issue the Background Information sheet and assign the students to read it.

7. The next day, turn on a faucet so that it drips slowly. Ask the students to predict how much water would be wasted by such a leak in a 24-hour period.

8. Place the graduated cylinder and funnel under the leak to catch the water.

9. Discuss the importance of water conservation.

10. During the period, introduce the Home Water Conservation Survey form and assignment.

11. Near the end of the period, read the graduated cylinder. Use that data to calculate how much water would have been wasted in a 24-hour period, a week, and a month, and a year.

12. The next day, ask the students what were the most common types of water waste and what could be done to eliminate or reduce water loss from those sources.

13. Teach the students how to change a faucet washer.

14. Assign sheet 12.4, "Water" We Going to Do? Questions.

Discussion

1. How much water would be wasted in a year if everybody in this class had a faucet leak similar to the one we simulated in class?

2. How much water would be saved per year if all of those leaky faucets were fixed?

3. In what ways does saving water save energy?

4. What accounted for most of the water used in the home?

5. What were the most common places where water was being wasted in the home?

6. How can water be conserved in the yard?

7. What are some ways that water is used by others to produce products or services for us?

8. How can we influence others to save water?

Answers to 12.4, "Water" We Going to Do?: Questions

1. Agriculture is the major water user in the United States.

2. Flushing toilets is the major water use in most homes.

3. a. Water can be conserved in agriculture by planting crops in areas where the rainfall or naturally available water is adequate to grow them and by using drip irrigation, mulching and other methods. (*Other answers are acceptable.*)

   b. Water can be conserved in manufacturing by recycling water that is used and by developing less wasteful processes. (*Other answers are acceptable.*)

   c. We can reduce the water needed for electrical generation by reducing our demand for electricity. There are many ways to reduce electrical consumption. (*Other answers are acceptable.*)

4. Answers will vary. Point out that governmental subsidies make such practices possible. Also discuss the demand created by both lifestyle and population.

5. Saving water at home saves money and energy as well as water. It helps develop a conservation ethic or conserving attitude. It makes water available for other uses. (*Other answers are acceptable.*)

6. See the Home Water Conservation checklist. Other answers are acceptable.

7. Building reservoirs to supply water floods valleys and changes water flow downstream. Taking water from one area to another via pipes or canals deprives one area of its water as well as affects the area through which the pipes and canals pass.

Extensions (See Activity 32 for suggestions for student projects.)

1. If the students do not know the water cycle, teach it.

2. Include a variety of types of faucets and valves when you teach how to change a washer.

3. Teach the students how to install flow reducers, low-flow shower heads, and other water-conserving devices.

4. Do cost analyses on the water-saving devices. What is the "pay back" time?

5. Teach the students how to read a water meter and water bill.

6. Visit a water company. Find out about sources, pumping methods, purification, costs, and so forth.

7. Have the students draw maps showing how water gets to their community.

8. Have the students make "pie graphs" of the data in Tables 12-B and 12-C

Modifications

1. If only one faucet is available, demonstrate how to change the washer, then leave a station set up where the students can practice changing the washer any time during the next several days. Have the students demonstrate their ability to change the washer to another student, after which the students will both sign a sheet verifying that the task has been done.

2. Collect the water from faucets leaking at various rates.

3. Have the students measure the amount of water used in various situations such as:

   a. shower vs. bath

   b. shower in which one leaves the water on all the time vs. turning the water off except to wet, wash, and rinse.

   c. leaving the water on while brushing teeth vs. turning it off after wetting the brush

   d. leaving dish rinse water running vs. collecting rinse water in a pan.

   e. using a dishwasher vs. washing dishes in a pan

   f. leaving water running while rinsing vegetables vs. rinsing in a bowl

   g. washing a car with the hose running vs. using a bucket

4. Modify the Home Water Conservation Survey (12.3) to include additional questions generated by the class.

References

Anonymous, *Parent/Student Water Conservation Checklist*. Sacramento, CA: California Department of Water Resources, 1991.

Johnson, Bob, *The Official Captain Hydro Water Conservation Workbook*. Oakland, CA: East Bay Municipal Utility District, 1982.

Miller, G. Tyler, *Living in the Environment*. Belmont, CA: Wadsworth Publishing Company, 1990.

Schwartz, Linda, *Earth Book for Kids*. Santa Barbara, CA: The Learning Works, Inc., 1990.

Sly, Carolie (project coordinator), *Water Wisdom*. Hayward, CA: Alameda County Office of Education, 1990.

12.1 "Water" We Going to Do?: Background Information

Water is a precious resource. Without water, life itself would be impossible. All plants and animals need water. Most of us, however, take an abundant supply of clean fresh water for granted.

While most of us are aware of the water that we use in our homes, the amount of water used by industry is enormous. Table 12-A shows the amount of water used to produce various products in the United States. Table 12-B shows the percentage of water consumed by different uses in the United States. When studying Table 12-B, note that it is for water "consumed." This is the water that is not returned to the surface water or underground water system. Water used to cool electricity-generating plants accounts for 38 percent of the water used in the United States, but it is not consumed.

TABLE 12-A

Gallons of water typically used to produce various products in the United States:

1 automobile	100,000	1 pound of grain-fed beef	800
1 ton of brown paper for bags	82,000	1 pound of rice	560
1 pound of cotton	2,000	1 pound of steel	25
1 pound of aluminum	1,000	1 gallon of gasoline	70

TABLE 12-B

Percentage of water consumed by various uses in the United States:

irrigation	60%	industry	13%
rural domestic use	59%	power plant cooling	2%
urban domestic and business	29%		

It has been estimated that between 30 percent and 50 percent of the water used in the United States is wasted. Many water experts believe that conservation is our cheapest, quickest, and best source of water in the near future.

As our demand for water increases due to population increases and additional demand for various products, our water problems will increase. Even many areas that currently seem to have abundant water may well experience water shortages in the coming decades. **Droughts** are always a possibility, and even without droughts, there is not an infinite amount of water available.

Since most of the water used in the United States is not used in our homes, it may seem that we can do nothing about its use. We must keep in mind that industries use the water to produce the products we purchase. If we don't demand a new car every two years, if we recycle as much as possible, and if we don't waste food and other materials, water will be saved.

We can also encourage conservation of water by industries by legislative action. Laws can be passed to require water conservation equipment and methods. Federal and state subsidies that encourage waste of water can be eliminated or reduced.

Learning where we use water in our homes can help us learn where we can best conserve water. Table 12-C shows the percentage of water used for various uses in a typical home in the United States.

TABLE 12-C

Domestic uses of water in the United States:

toilet flushing	40%	laundry	4%
washing and bathing	37%	household cleaning	3%
kitchen use	7%	garden	3%
drinking	5%	cleaning car	1%

Notice that reducing the amount of water used in toilet flushing by only 10 percent would save as much water as is used for laundry and save almost as much as is used for drinking. Using a water-saving toilet cuts water used for flushing from about 6 gallons per flush to about 1.5 gallons—a savings of 75 percent!

Water pollution is a problem even in communities that have adequate supplies of water. This makes the wise use of the available clean fresh water even more important.

Aside from concerns about shortages of water for human consumption, we should be concerned about water use because of the impact it has on the environment. When reservoirs are built, valleys are flooded and downstream rivers are changed. **Channelizing** of streams destroys the **riparian** communities along their banks. Diverting water from one area to another via canals or pipes damages the environment from which the water was taken as well as the areas through which the canals and pipes pass.

Conserving water makes sense—environmentally, financially, and ethically!

12.2 "Water" We Going to Do?: Personal Water Use

Predicted Water Use

Your class has listed various ways that water is used in the home. Before actually recording how much water you use in a day and a week, record how much you think you use.

I think I use about _____ gallons per day and _____ gallons per week.

Actual Water Use

For the next 24 hours, keep track of the actual ways that you use water and the number of times you use water each way. You can use the estimated amounts per use or you can actually measure the amount of water used.

WATER USE	TIMES PER DAY	AMOUNT USED		TOTAL USED	
		estimated gallons*	measured gallons	per day	per week
bathing		30[1]			
showering		50[2]			
flushing toilet		6[3]			
washing face/hands		5[4]			
getting a drink		0.25[5]			
brushing teeth		2[6]			
cooking		10[7]			
washing clothes		60[8]			
washing dishes		30[9]			
other					

TOTALS (should include things that don't happen every week): _____ _____

*notes on estimates:
(1) depends on how full the tub is (2) 25 gal with low-flow head
(3) 1.5 gal with water-saver toilet (4) 2 gallons if you turn the water off
(5) includes running water to cool it (6) 0.25 if you turn water off
(7) per supper, includes rinsing (8) large load
(9) 10 gallons with dishwasher or if you use two 5-gallon pans

12.3 "Water" We Going to Do?: Home Water Conservation Survey

Use this form to survey your home for water use. Use the space provided to add an additional question in each category. If the answer is sometimes yes and sometimes no, mark the one that is usually true.

INDOORS

Bathrooms

____ yes   **Have toilet tanks been checked for leaks?**
____ no   (Place a few drops of food coloring or dye tablets in the toilet tank. If coloring is seen in the bowl without flushing, there is a leak that needs to be repaired.)

____ yes   **Are tissues disposed of in the toilet?**
____ no   (Use a waste basket for tissues! Each flush uses up to 7 gallons of water, depending on the type of toilet!)

____ yes   **Is there a plastic bottle, bag, or "dam" in the toilet tank, or do you have a low-flush toilet?**
____ no   (Put a little clean sand or some pebbles in the bottom of a plastic bottle or bag and fill it with water. Cap the bottle or tie the bag. Place it in the toilet tank, SAFELY AWAY FROM ALL MOVING PARTS. Better yet, consider installing a low-flush toilet, which uses only 1–5 gallons per flush, rather than 5–7 gallons per flush!)

____ yes   **Is there a leaky faucet in the sink or shower?**
____ no   (You can fix it either by tightening the fixture or replacing the faucet washer.)

____ yes   **Are family members taking short showers (5 minutes or less?)**
no   (Taking shorter showers can save up to 8 gallons of water per minute!)

____ yes   **Do you have low-flow shower heads and flow restrictors?**
____ no   (Low-flow shower heads and flow restrictors significantly reduce water use and save money and hot water too!)

____ yes   **Make up your own question:**
____ no

Kitchen and Laundry

____ yes   **Are there leaky faucets?**
____ no   (Tighten the faucet or replace the washer.)

____ yes   **Are there flow restrictors on the faucets?**
____ no   (Flow restrictors are easy to install and save water, energy, and money!)

____ yes   **Are dishwashers and washing machines turned on only when full?**
____ no   (Wait until you have a full load. Use water and energy-saving cycles.)

____ yes   **Do you rinse vegetables with the water running?**
____ no   (Rinsing vegetables in a bowl or stoppered sink saves water. The rinse water can be used to water plants!)

____ yes   **Make up your own question:**
____ no

OUTDOORS

____ yes   **Have all faucets been checked for leaks?**
____ no   (Small leaks add up to large losses! Replace leaky washers.)

____ yes   **Are lawns and plants watered only when they really need it?**
____ no   (Check lawns and shrubs to see if they need water. A lawn that springs back after being stepped on doesn't need water. Devices can be purchased to test for soil moisture. Turn automatic sprinklers off in rainy weather.)

____ yes   **Do you use drought-tolerant plants in your landscaping?**
____ no   (Landscaping with drought-tolerant plants can reduce both water use and maintentance in your yard. Consult a local nursery.)

____ yes   **Do you water plants and lawns early in the morning or late in the evening?**
____ no   (Watering in the hot part of the day wastes water because of evaporation.)

____ yes   **Do you use a hose to clean driveways and sidewalks?**
____ no   (Use a broom. It does the job just as well!)

____ yes   **Do you use a bucket when you wash the car?**
____ no   (Using a hose wastes water. At least turn the water off when not actually spraying the car. Wash the car while it is on the lawn.)

____ yes   **Make up your own question:**
____ no

12.4 "Water" We Going to Do?: Questions

1. What is the major use of water in the United States? _____

2. What is the major use of water in the home? _____

3. In your daily life, how can you reduce water used in the following areas?

   a. agriculture _____

   _____

   _____

   b. manufacturing _____

   _____

   _____

   c. electrical generation _____

   _____

   _____

4. Should we be growing crops such as alfalfa, cotton, and rice in areas such as California and Arizona where there is not enough naturally available water for them? Why or why not?

   _____

   _____

5. Why is it important to conserve water at home?

   _____

   _____

   _____

6. List several ways to conserve water at home.

   _____

   _____

7. List several ways that conserving water benefits the environment.

   _____

   _____

unit Four

Atmospheric Issues

- **Detecting Air Pollution**
- **Acidic Precipitation**
- **Global Warming**

ACTIVITY 13: DETECTING AIR POLLUTION _____

Activity Summary

Various methods are used to demonstrate the presence of particulates and carbon dioxide in the air. Quantities of particulates collected from various locations in the community are compared.

Introduction

"Air pollution" is of great importance to us all, but it is also something that most of us feel helpless to do much about. Many people feel that factories cause most of air pollution and that there is nothing that we as individuals can do about that. Some think of air pollution as being a problem in places such as Los Angeles, New York, or Detroit, but not in small towns.

It is important that students realize that there are a great many different sources of air pollutants, and that there are hundreds of different substances found in the air. Some naturally occurring substances can be considered pollutants, and some man-made pollutants are also produced by natural processes. Some are produced directly as a result of natural events or human activities, while others are formed in the air as a result of chemical reactions among the pollutants and other components of the air. Some pollutants are bothersome but not very harmful or dangerous, while others are extremely toxic and harmful.

Detecting and measuring air pollution can be a very complex process. In this activity, the students observe the production of water, soot, and carbon dioxide in the process of combustion. They then collect particulate pollution in their community.

Grouping

Teams of 2 or more students.

Time

Demonstrations and Instructions: 45–50 minutes

Students Preparing Particulate Collectors: 30–45 minutes

Particulate Collectors Remain in Place: 1–14 days

Examination of Particulate Collectors Data Analysis: 45–50 minutes

Anticipated Outcomes

The students will:

- construct simple particulate detectors.
- collect particulate samples from various parts of their community.
- compare the quantities of particulates found in various locations.
- understand that combustion produces both visible and invisible products.
- increase their willingness to reduce air pollution.

Materials

—Photocopied student pages:
   • 13.1 Detecting Air Pollution: Background Information (one per student)
   • 13.2 Detecting Air Pollution: Instructions and Data (one per student)
   • 13.3 Detecting Air Pollution: Questions (one per student)

—Pencils

—Candle and matches

—White (preferably) or clear Pyrex® dish cover or other heat resistant glass such as Pyrex® Petri dish or beaker

—3" × 5" index cards, cut in half to make 3" × 2.5" cards (1 of the small cards per student)

—Paper punch

—String (approximately 12" per student)

—Petroleum jelly

—Hand lens or microscope

—Push pins or thumb tacks

—Masking tape

—One L beaker or 1 quart canning jar

—Two manila folders

—Several balloons

—Limewater solution or Bromothymol Blue solution

—Several "twist-ties"

Vocabulary

Oxide   particulate   petrochemical

Teacher Preparation

1. Photocopy the Background Information sheet (13.1), Instructions and Data table sheets (13.2), and Questions sheet (13.3).
2. Obtain required materials.
3. Make at least two funnels for collecting automobile exhaust gases. Make one end large enough to fit over the exhaust pipe end. The other end should be small enough to fit into the opening of the balloons.

SAFETY CONSIDERATIONS

1. When collecting the automobile exhaust, have the students stand well back from the exhaust pipe so as not to breathe the fumes and not touch the hot exhaust pipe, and do this in a well-ventilated area.
2. Caution the students to be careful when installing their particulate collectors.

Procedure

1. Discuss the topic of "air pollution" with the students. Point out that some is visible and some is invisible.

2. To demonstrate one of the invisible components of automobile exhaust, hold a 1 L beaker or quart canning jar near the exhaust pipe to collect exhaust coming from an automobile. (Water should condense in the jar from the water vapor in the exhaust.)

3. (Consider having students do this activity.) To demonstrate another invisible component, carbon dioxide, use the cardboard funnel to fill several balloons with exhaust gas. Use a twist-tie to close each balloon. Carefully insert a plastic straw into the balloon's open end and tape the balloon's open end so that the straw is securely attached to the balloon. Insert the end of the straw in some limewater or Bromothymol Blue (BTB) solution. If the limewater turns milky white or the BTB turns green or blue-green, the presence of CO_2 is indicated.

4. To demonstrate the presence of tiny particulates in the air above a fire, hold a Pyrex® dish or beaker in a candle flame. "Soot" should accumulate, showing the presence of particulate matter.

5. Ask the students where in their community they would expect to find large amounts and small amounts of particulate air pollution. Consider having them design particulate sampling devices. (See the Modifications suggested below.)

6. Tell the students that they are going to make particulate collectors and place them in the community to sample the air for particulate matter. Decide who will place their collectors in what areas. Try to get volunteers to place the collectors throughout the community. It might be interesting to place collectors upwind and downwind from stationary polluters such as factories or major highways. It is a good idea to place more than one in the same general area to help protect from vandalism or so that one can be left longer if neither has been disturbed.

7. With the students, decide how long to leave the collectors out. At least 24 hours is recommended.

8. Have the students make the collectors as instructed on the Instructions sheet (13.2).

9. Collectors should be set out in the classroom and one should be put in a box as a control.

10. On the agreed upon day(s), have the students bring in the particulate collectors. Being careful not to get petroleum jelly or dirt on the microscopes or lenses, examine the collectors for particulates. Have the students report the relative amounts of particulates according to the scale provided on the Data table (13.2).

11. Discuss possible sources of particulates in each sampled area.

Discussion

1. What areas of your community had the most particulate pollution in the air? Why do you think this was so?

2. If a factory's smokestack produces little visible pollution, does that mean that the factory is not polluting the air?

3. Besides proximity to pollution sites, what other variables might have affected the amount of particulates collected on a collector?

4. Who should pay for cleaning up air pollution?

5. What are some of the health hazards of air pollution?

6. Besides health problems, what other problems does air pollution cause?

Answers to 13.3, Detecting Air Pollution Questions

1. Particulates are particles or pieces of matter suspended in the air. Examples include smoke, dust, salts, pollen, and other solids and liquids.

2. Transportation is the major single source of air pollution in the United States.

3. Answers will vary. Things that students can do might include talking to the plant owners, helping pass laws, changing buying habits, and the like.

4. Transportation-caused air pollution can be reduced in many ways, including keeping cars tuned properly, utilizing carpools and mass transit, walking, bike riding, eliminating unnecessary trips or combining short trips, purchasing more efficient vehicles, and working for the passage and enforcement of laws to reduce pollution.

5. Answers will vary. Students must realize that industries and governments respond to the will, be it real or perceived, of the people. If we don't demand certain products, they won't make them. If we demand that laws and regulations be created and enforced, they will. Organizations, governments, and companies are made up of individuals. It may not be easy, but individuals, especially when they organize with other individuals, can (and do) bring about change!

Extensions (See Activity 32 for suggestions for student projects.)

1. Relate this activity to Activity 15 on Global Warming.

2. Invite a representative of the local air-pollution-control agency to speak to the class, or obtain data from them about local air pollution.

3. Take the class to the auto shop and have the auto shop teacher demonstrate the use of an exhaust-emissions analyzer on a well-tuned car and on an untuned one.

4. Contact your local highway patrol or other agency regarding automobile emissions standards and testing.

5. Have students investigate air-pollution-control devices such as those used on automobiles and wood stoves and factories.

6. Rubber bands and many synthetic fibers deteriorate in the presence of ozone and other air pollutants. Have the students design experiments testing rubber bands and synthetic fibers for their rate of deterioration in various places in the community. (See *Environmental Science Activities Handbook for Teachers* by Del Giotto.)

7. Take a field trip to a local industry or other potential air-pollution source. Find out about air-pollution-control devices or other measures being used.

8. The students can design, build, test, and compare different methods of collecting particulate pollution. (See the following "Modifications.")

Modifications

1. Use a map of your community to plot the data collected. Have the students devise a system of symbols to attach to push pins to indicate the amount of particulates found.
2. Rather than cards, microscope slides can be used. They can be taped to cards for hanging or can be taped in place with masking tape. Tape or self-adhesive labels can be used on the slides.
3. Clear double-sided tape can be used rather than petroleum jelly.
4. Single-sided clear tape can also be used. Use a hole punch to make holes in the card and apply the tape to the back of the card so that the sticky side is exposed by the hole.
5. Light cooking oil can be used by drawing a square or circle on a glass slide and placing one or two drops of oil in the center of the square.

References

Blaustein, Elliott, *Anti-Pollution Lab*. New York, NY: Sentinel Books, Inc., 1972.

Del Giotto, Bette, and Millicent Tissair, *Environmental Science Activities Handbook for Teachers*. West Nyack, NY: Parker Publishing Co., Inc., 1975 (out of print).

Hocking, Colin et al., *Global Warming & the Greenhouse Effect*. Berkeley, CA: Lawrence Hall of Science, University of California at Berkeley, 1990.

Miller, G. Tyler, *Living in the Environment*. Belmont, CA: Wadsworth Publishing Company, 1990.

Seidel, Patricia, *Ecology Action Pack*. Chalfont, PA: Symmetry Promotions Publishing, 1990.

13.1 Detecting Air Pollution: Background Information

Clean, dry air near the surface of the earth consists primarily of nitrogen (78 percent) and oxygen (21 percent). The remaining 1 percent is mostly argon and carbon dioxide. Naturally occurring air also contains water vapor, dust, pollen, smoke, and a variety of chemicals such as carbon monoxide, sulfur dioxide, nitrogen oxides, salt, ozone, and many other chemicals. What, then, is "air pollution"?

Generally, a chemical in the air would be called a pollutant when it is present in quantities that are large enough to cause harm to humans, other animals, plants, metals, stone, or other materials. There are nine major classes of pollutants:

1. **oxides** of carbon: carbon monoxide (CO) and carbon dioxide (CO_2)
2. oxides of sulfur: sulfur dioxide (SO_2) and sulfur trioxide (SO_3)
3. oxides of nitrogen: nitric oxide (NO), nitrogen dioxide (NO_2), and nitrous oxide (N_2O)
4. volatile organic compounds such as methane (CH_4) and chlorofluorocarbons
5. suspended **particulate** matter including *solids* such as dust, soot, salts, and pollen and *liquids* such as sulfuric acid, oils, and pesticides
6. **petrochemical** oxidants formed in the atmosphere by the reactions of various chemicals found in the atmosphere
7. radioactive substances
8. heat
9. noise

There is little that we can do to prevent or reduce naturally occurring pollutants. Many pollutants, though, are produced by human activities, and we <u>can</u> do something about these. Nearly half of the major outdoor air pollutants in the United States comes from transportation. Thus, when we use mass transit, carpool, walk, or ride our bikes, we reduce air pollution. Using more fuel-efficient vehicles and keeping them tuned properly is important, too. Burning fuels, for example, to produce electricity and heat, produces another 28 percent of the outdoor air pollution in the United States. Thus, anything we can do to save energy will help reduce air pollution. Most of the rest of the air pollution comes from various industrial processes. When we make our material goods last by taking care of them and when we refuse to buy unnecessary products we help reduce air pollution.

Many important pollutants such as CO_2, CO, and radiation are invisible. Water vapor, smoke, and dust are often visible when viewed from a distance or when they are especially abundant. When particulates are not especially abundant, though, they must be concentrated to be seen. In this activity, you will be collecting particulate matter from the air in your community.

© 1993 by The Center for Applied Research in Education

13.2 Detecting Air Pollution: Instructions

In this activity, you will be making particulate collectors to test for the presence of particulates in various areas of your community. Each student should make at least one particulate collector. When you place your detector(s), be sure to record the information on the top part of the data page.

To make your particulate collector:

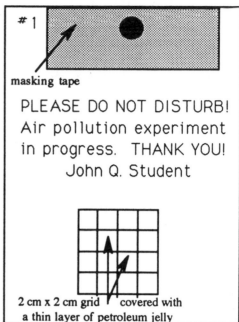

masking tape

PLEASE DO NOT DISTURB!
Air pollution experiment
in progress. THANK YOU!
John Q. Student

2 cm x 2 cm grid covered with a thin layer of petroleum jelly

1. Attach a 1" (2–3 cm) piece of masking tape to the narrow side of a 2.5" × 3" card provided by your teacher. Use a hole punch to make a hole in the masking tape. The hole is for attaching a string with which to hang the card if it is not attached with push pins or tape. The masking tape will reinforce the hole.

2. Use a PENCIL to write the following on both sides of your card(s):
   "Please do not disturb. Air pollution experiment in progress. Thank you!"

3. Use the pencil to write your name on the card. If you are placing more than one card, number each one so that you do not get them mixed up.

4. Use the pencil to draw a 2 cm × 2 cm square on one side of the card. Use the pencil to divide the square into a grid of squares with 0.5 cm sides.

5. EITHER:
   a. Place a small amount of petroleum jelly in the middle of the square. Use your (clean) finger, a clean toothpick, or the edge of a card to spread the petroleum so that it forms a thin, even layer over the square. Carry your pollution detector in a small box so that the petroleum doesn't get smeared or contaminated before you place it in the community.

   or

   b. Obtain a small amount of petroleum jelly in a piece of foil or plastic. Apply the jelly as above when you place the card in the community.

6. Obtain push pins, masking tape, and/or string to use to place the pollution detector(s) in the community.

7. On the assigned day, place your collector(s), recording the appropriate data.

8. On the assigned day, bring your collector(s) to class, again recording the appropriate data.

9. Use magnifying lenses or microscopes to examine the particulates collected.

10. Record your observations on the data table.

Name _____ Class _____ Date _____

13.2 Detecting Air Pollution: Data

collector #_____

SITE OF PLACEMENT: address or location: _____

description of site/area: _____

_____

prevailing winds from: _____   wind condition today: _____

sticky side facing (direction): _____   height above ground: _____

possible pollution sources in the area (what and where?): _____

_____

COLLECTOR SET OUT: date: _____ day of week: _____ time: _____

position (horizontal, vertical, or ?): _____

notes:

_____

COLLECTOR PICKED UP: date: _____ day of week: _____ time: _____

notes:

_____

The particulates on my collector look most like:

mine   **none**   **light**   **moderate**   **heavy**

Can you identify any of the particles?

Other notes:

Name _____ Class _____ Date _____

13.3 Detecting Air Pollution: Questions

1. What are "particulates"? (Define and give several examples.)

   _____

   _____

2. What is the major single source of outdoor air pollution in the United States?

   _____

   _____

3. List the major stationary sources of air pollution in your community. For each one, list one thing that you could do to reduce its air pollution.

   source   **something that I can do**

   _____   _____

   _____   _____

   _____   _____

4. Describe several things that you as an individual can do to reduce air pollution from transportation. Circle those that you are now doing or are willing to do.

   _____

   _____

   _____

5. Some people feel that what they as individuals do is not important, that they cannot do much to address major problems such as air pollution. Others say that the problems are caused by individuals and that individuals can work together to address the problems. Individuals can change buying habits, which will then change the habits of industries; they can drive more fuel-efficient cars that pollute less; they can save energy; and they can enact and enforce laws. What do you think—can the individual make a difference? Why do you think as you do?

   _____

   _____

   _____

ACTIVITY 14: ACIDIC PRECIPITATION _____

Activity Summary

By applying vinegar to a variety of rock types, the student will test for reaction with an acid. Bubbling or fizzing indicates a chemical reaction. This bubbling can be observed visually and by listening for a fizzing sound.

Introduction

The topic of acidic precipitation can be introduced as part of many units. It is important in studies of air pollution, water pollution, soils, forestry, wildlife, and energy. It can also be introduced as part of units on aquatic biology, geology (fossil fuels, soil building, soil types), chemistry, and forestry. In social studies, it is important to consider economic aspects, health aspects, and the international relations implications of acidic precipitation.

Before beginning the following investigation, students should be introduced to the concept of acids and bases. They should be familiar with the use of pH measuring techniques and materials such as indicator papers, liquids, or meters. The pH papers should include both litmus paper and pH indicator paper that changes to different colors in solutions of different pH values.

One way to introduce acids and bases is to start with common litmus paper. Be sure to demonstrate or, better, have the students experiment to find out the reaction of litmus paper in acids, bases, and a neutral substance such as distilled water.

After learning about litmus paper and the use of pH indicator papers, students can test many of the substances listed on the accompanying table, which can be made into an overhead transparency. For these tests, they should use the pH indicator paper that changes to different colors in solutions of different pH.

Litmus paper is made with paper impregnated with a powder made from certain lichens. This dye turns red in acids and blue in bases. It is unchanged in neutral solutions.

A memory aid is:

Bases are **B**lue, aci**D**s are re**D**.

Lichens are important in the formation of soils because they release acids that help break down rocks into smaller particles, and in the process also add organic material to the soil. Thus, acidic precipitation acts on rocks and buildings in much the same way as naturally occurring lichens do, but it has a much stronger and more rapid effect. Students find it interesting that we use a chemical from a natural acid producer to test for too much acid. This use of a seemingly useless (to humans) organism such as a lichen is also an example of the dangers of losing an organism by extinction.

While the vinegar used in this activity is more acidic than most acidic precipitation, the students will be observing it for only a short period of time. If a piece of marble reacts enough to form noticeable bubbles in a few minutes, the students should understand that a somewhat weaker acid in precipitation would affect the rock when the rock is exposed for long periods of time.

Grouping

Students can be grouped in teams of two or three students, or they may do the experiments individually.

Time

The tests do not take very long to do. Time for the lab will depend on how many rock types you have the students test. Each additional rock type will require more time for testing and for cleaning up. To test four rock types will take about 20 minutes, including instructions and cleanup.

Anticipated Outcomes

The students will:

- demonstrate an understanding of the meaning of the term "pH value."
- describe the effects of acidic precipitation on marble, limestone, granite, and concrete.
- make careful observations and record them in a clear manner.

Materials

—Photocopied student pages:

- 14.1 Acidic Precipitation: Background Information (one per student)
- 14.2 Acidic Precipitation: Instructions and Data Table (one per student or one per team)
- 14.3 Acidic Precipitation: Questions (one per student)

—Vinegar (preferably clear/white vinegar): about 100 ml per team, in a beaker or small jar such as a baby-food jar

—Medicine droppers (eyedroppers)

—One container for each rock sample (or plan to have the students rinse the container between tests). Petrie dishes work well. You might consider using rinsed out 8-oz milk cartons from the cafeteria—they make the fizzing sound easier to hear.

—Rock samples such as granite, sandstone, shale, marble (reacts with vinegar), limestone (reacts with vinegar), concrete/cement (reacts with vinegar). Rock samples can be purchased from science supply companies at surprisingly inexpensive prices. Rocks can be gathered locally, and this is desirable because the students can "identify with" local rocks. You can probably obtain some wonderful marble, granite, and limestone samples from local companies who make countertops, tables, mantles, and/or cemetery markers. (Check your telephone book under "marble," "granite," and "monuments.")

—Transparency of pH table

Vocabulary

acid, acidity	alkaline	base, basic
neutral	pH	precipitation

Teacher Preparation

1. Prepare the accompanying overhead transparency (pH values).
2. Photocopy the Background Information sheet (14.1), Activity Instruction and Data

Table sheet (14.2)—or have them prepare their own tables; this can be a good way to introduce the important skill of making data tables—and Questions sheet (14.3).

3. Organize "sets" of rocks and testing materials for each team.

4. Prepare an overhead transparency of the following pH values table.

SAFETY CONSIDERATIONS

1. Students should be reminded to avoid getting any chemicals in their eyes. (Wear safety goggles or glasses.)
2. Be aware of any sharp edges on rock samples.

Procedure

1. Introduce the topic of acidity and pH.
2. Demonstrate the use of litmus paper and pH paper as described earlier.
3. Demonstrate the method for testing for reaction with acids, that is, apply about 1 ml of the vinegar to the rock sample and observe closely for bubbles or fizzing (look <u>and</u> listen).
4. Demonstrate how to record data on the table (or have students figure out and agree upon a good way to record and report their data).

Discussion

1. What effect do you think acidic precipitation might have on the following:
   a. plants
   b. paints on homes and cars
   c. brick buildings
   d. fresh water plants and animals
   e. human health
2. What are some acidic substances found in nature?
3. What are some things that YOU could do to reduce acidic precipitation?
4. What are some things that OTHERS could do to reduce acidic precipitation?
5. What are advantages and disadvantages of each of the measures you listed for reducing acidic precipitation? Be sure to include aesthetic, economic, wildlife/natural, and health issues.
6. How do acids help build soils? If a weak acid helps build soils by breaking rocks down, will a stronger acid be good for the environment? Discuss.

Answer to 14.3, Acidic Precipitation Questions

1. Many kinds of rock, including marble, sandstone, granite, and concrete are used in building. Concrete is used in sidewalks, roads, and other structures. Cement is used to hold bricks and other rocks together in buildings. Marble, granite, and limestone are used for statues and monuments.

2. If acidic precipitation is dissolving the building materials, the structures will be weakened.

3. Answers will vary. In most homes, the main energy users—and therefore the most important places to save energy—are space heating and cooling, refrigeration, and hot water use. At schools, lighting is often the main energy user in mild climates.

4. The disadvantages of installing the equipment are the purchase, installation, and maintenance costs. The advantages include better health, less damage to paints, rubber, plastics, and other materials. Avoidance of suits is an important factor for industries to consider. International relations, such as with Canada, should also be considered and have economic aspects.

5. Any industry that burns fossil fuels such as coal and oil is a potential source of acidic precipitation. The steel industry also burns a lot of fossil fuels. Automobiles are main polluters in most urban areas.

6. Besides saving energy, we can insist on effective legislation and enforcement of the laws that we already have in effect. We can communicate our willingness to pay for air-pollution-control equipment. We can buy fewer unnecessary things, thereby reducing the need for making so much steel and other materials. We can recycle used materials.

Extensions (See Activity 32 for suggestions for student projects.)

1. Contact your local soil conservation service, air pollution, and/or water pollution agencies to find out about local acidic precipitation or problems with acids in streams.

2. Visit a cemetery with monuments over 100 years old and examine marble monuments, noting their condition and dates. Devise a scale for recording your observations. Does the deterioration seem to have accelerated in recent years?

3. Have the students collect rain samples and test for acidity. Keep records during the rainy season or during a long series of storms. Are the first rains more acidic than those that fall later in the season or in the storm series? Are the rain samples collected in various locales (for example, downwind from industrial plants or power stations or along busy roads) different from those collected elsewhere?

4. Have the students find out about air pollution control devices used in industry and on automobiles. What alternatives do we have to the private automobile?

5. Have the students design and perform experiments to test the effects of acids on other kinds of rocks, plants, automobile and house paints, and different synthetic materials such as tires, lawn furniture, plastics, and the like.

6. Have the students test the acidity of your local soil. Have them design an experiment to find out what happens when an acid percolates through 5 mm, 10 mm, and 20 mm of your local soil.

7. Some students will probably want to see if a piece of marble or limestone will completely dissolve in the vinegar. This can lead to many different ways of learning, including investigations of:

   a. What is the chemical reaction involved? What is actually happening? Is the acid in the vinegar eventually "used up"?

   b. How much vinegar will it take to completely dissolve one gram of marble? One gram of limestone?

    c. What happens if you dissolve a gram (or more) of marble in vinegar and then allow the vinegar to evaporate? What is the mass of the precipitate/residue left behind or crystals formed?

    d. What effect does grinding up one gram of marble have on the time required to dissolve the rock completely? (This will lead to investigations of the relationship of surface area to volume and reaction time.)

    e. After several pieces of limestone or marble are dissolved completely, let the vinegar evaporate and examine the crystals formed.

8. If you are using polished specimens of marble or granite, what is the effect of roughing up the polished surface with sandpaper?

9. What is the effect of different coatings on the reaction with rocks?

10. What are the pH values of various fruit and vegetable juices and other liquids found around the home?

Modifications

1. Baking soda reacts quite actively with vinegar. You can use this to demonstrate the sort of reaction that the students are looking for in their experiments, but be sure to forewarn them that the rocks won't react as noticeably as the baking soda does.

2. You can make some artificial "rocks" that will react very actively by mixing some clay (or other soil that is sticky when wet), some water, and baking soda, forming "rocks" by compressing about a teaspoon of the mud. This mudball can be dried in an oven or air-dried. You should experiment with different ratios of baking soda, mud, sand, and water until you find a combination that makes fairly hard rocks that have enough baking soda to react actively. (I find that a ratio of 1 part baking soda: 1 part sand: 2 parts of our local clay makes a good "rock.")

Reference

Miller, G. Tyler, *Living in the Environment.* Belmont, CA: Wadsworth Publishing Company; 1988.

Approximate pH Values of Some Common Solutions

pH	solution
0	
1	battery acid
2	stomach acid (1.0–3.0)
	lemon juice (2.3)
	acid fog (2–3.5)
3	vinegar, wine, beer, soft drinks
	orange juice
4	tomatoes
5	black coffee
	pH-balanced shampoo (4.0–6.0)
6	
	milk (6.6)
	saliva (6.3–7.5)
7	pure water
8	sea water (7.8–8.3)
	non-pH-balanced shampoo
9	baking soda
	phosphate detergents
	antacids
10	milk of magnesia (9.9–10.1)
11	household ammonia (10.5–11.9)
	nonphosphate detergents
12	
	hair remover
13	
	oven cleaner
14	

increasing acidity

neutral

increasing alkalinity (less acidic)

14.1 Acidic Precipitation: Background Information

When air pollutants such as sulfur dioxide (SO_2) and nitric oxides (NO_x) are released into the air, they do not just "go away." They are carried by air currents and can chemically react with one another and with other chemicals in the air. They can form nitrogen dioxide (NO_2), sulfuric acid (H_2SO_4), nitric acid (HNO_3), and solid particles of sulfates and nitrates.

Many of these chemicals can be dissolved in rain water, snow, sleet, fog, and dew. When this polluted water falls to Earth, it is called "acidic precipitation" or, more commonly, "acid rain."

Acidity is measured in terms of **pH**. A low pH value indicates a high acid content in the substance. Each whole number on the pH scale represents an increase or decrease by a factor of 10. Thus, a substance with a pH of 5 is ten times as acidic as one with a pH of 6.

Acidic substances have a pH less than 7. **Basic or alkaline** substances have a pH of between 7 and 14. A pH of 7 is **neutral,** neither acidic nor basic. Pure water has a pH of 7. The accompanying table gives some approximate pH values of common substances.

Natural **precipitation** has an average pH of about 5.1 due to the presence of carbon dioxide and other naturally occurring atmospheric chemicals. This slight acidity is useful because it helps dissolve soil minerals that plants need.

Even precipitation with a pH of less than 5.0 can be harmful. It can cause too many chemicals to dissolve from the soil, thereby polluting water. The precipitation itself may be acidic enough to cause damage. It damages trees, crops, paints, buildings and other structures such as monuments (especially those made from marble), artwork, tires, and it may even be dangerous to health.

The SO_2 emissions and NO_x emissions come from a variety of sources. In the United States, coal-and oil-burning power plants are major sources. So are industries that burn coal and oil. The northeastern United States and southeastern Canada have very high acidity in the precipitation, in the range of a pH of 4.2 to 4.4. Much of the Canadian acidic precipitation probably originates in the United States and is carried into Canada by the prevailing winds. This is a cause of some animosity between the United States and Canada. In some areas where coal and oil are not heavily used, automobile exhaust is a major source. This seems to be the case in southern California.

The type of soil upon which the acidic precipitation falls is an important factor in determining how much damage will be done. Some soils, such as those with limestone or other basic substances, can react with the acids to partially neutralize them. Other soils, such as granitic and some types of sandstone, do not have this neutralizing capability. Such soils are very susceptible to damage by acidic precipitation.

While a pH of 4.2 or 4.3 may not seem very harmful, it is important to consider the effects of exposure over extended periods of time. Even slight changes in pH can have disastrous results, especially in aquatic ecosystems.

© 1993 by The Center for Applied Research in Education

14.2 Acidic Precipitation: Instructions and Data Table

When a chemical is applied to a sample of another chemical and bubbles are given off, there is a chemical reaction occurring. Acids react chemically with some kinds of rocks. In this activity, you will find out whether an acid (vinegar) reacts with various kinds of rock.

When you apply the vinegar:

1. **Be sure to avoid getting any in your eyes!**
2. Look closely for any bubbles that might form. Listen for any fizzing noises that you might hear.
3. Record your observations on the data below.

DATA TABLE FOR ACIDIC PRECIPITATION

OBSERVATIONS

rock type	visual observations	sounds	other
1. _____			
2. _____			
3. _____			
4. _____			
5. _____			

14.3 Acidic Precipitation: Questions

1. How are the types of rocks that you tested used by people?

   _____

   _____

   _____

2. What implications do your observations have for builders?

   _____

   _____

   _____

3. Many of the chemicals that form acidic precipitation are produced at power plants. If we save energy, less coal or oil needs to be burned, so there will be less of these acid-producing chemicals discharged into the air. List several ways that you can save energy.

   _____

   _____

   _____

4. List several economic advantages and disadvantages of reducing acidic precipitation by installing equipment on power plants.

   _____

   _____

   _____

5. List several other causes of acidic precipitation besides power plants.

   _____

   _____

   _____

6. In addition to saving energy wherever possible, what can you do to reduce acidic precipitation?

   _____

   _____

   _____

   _____

ACTIVITY 15: GLOBAL WARMING _____

Activity Summary

Students use plastic two-liter bottles to model the "greenhouse effect" or global warming.

Introduction

The "greenhouse effect" results from changes in sunlight as it passes through the atmosphere, is absorbed by the earth and molecules in the atmosphere, and is radiated back toward space. As the light is changed to infrared energy wavelengths (heat), it is absorbed by water vapor and a variety of "greenhouse gases." Many scientists fear that if these greenhouse gases increase, less heat will be radiated into space, and Earth will become warmer. This warming of Earth could have a variety of harmful results, as discussed in the Student Background Information sheet (15.1).

The topic of global warming is one about which many students have heard, but about which there is great uncertainty in the scientific community. Some scientists point to measured increases in average annual temperatures as indicators of a general warming trend that is caused largely by human activities. Others say that the evidence is inconclusive for a variety of reasons. It may be a normal fluctuation that is not significantly affected by human activities and about which humans can do little. The validity of the temperature measurements themselves is sometimes questioned because of changes in the local areas where the data have been collected for many years.

This uncertainty within the scientific community affords us a chance to make decisions based on judgment. Is it better to continue spewing carbon dioxide and other greenhouse gases into the atmosphere and hope that those who are concerned about a "greenhouse effect" are wrong, or is it better to take steps to reduce the production of greenhouse gases and hope that we are not too late? Should we not err on the side of safety?

This activity allows students to use a model to simulate what happens in a greenhouse and may be happening in our environment. The sides of the 2-liter bottle and the plastic "lid" prevent the heated air from escaping into the environment, thus causing the air inside the bottle to become warmer faster than that in the "control," which has shorter sides and no lid. It is important for students to understand that this is a model of what may be happening. Scientists use models to try to understand phenomena that are difficult to test in the laboratory or in nature because they are too small, too far away, too large, or take too long to happen. While models, including computer models, are not perfect, they can be useful in understanding a variety of phenomena.

Grouping

Teams of 2 students.

Time

45–55 minutes

Anticipated Outcomes

The students will:

- increase their understanding of the conversion of light energy to heat energy.
- increase their understanding of the "greenhouse effect."
- increase their willingness to make choices that might help reduce air pollution.
- increase their understanding of the use of models, hypotheses, and controls in science.

Materials

—Photocopied student pages:

- 15.1 Global Warming: Background Information (one per student)
- 15.2 Global Warming: Instructions and Data (one per team)
- 15.3 Global Warming: Questions (one per student)

—Per team of 2 students:

- 2 clear plastic 2-liter bottles
- 1 plastic wrap or plastic bag with which to cover the "greenhouses"
- string, tape, or rubber bands with which to hold the plastic in place
- 2 thermometers (preferably the 6" long metal, plastic, or cardboard-backed type)
- 2 pieces of thin cardboard, about 2" × 2" (tagboard or halves of a 3" × 5" card)
- plastic ruler
- 2 rocks, approximately 2" in diameter, clean, dry, and of the same type
- 1 utility knife or single-edged razor blade (if you are having them cut the top off the bottles)
- masking tape

—If doing Extension activity 1:

- ice
- soil
- sand
- water
- grass/sod

—If doing the activity indoors, per team of 2 students:

- a light source such as a 100-watt (or more) bulb in a clip-on socket attached to a 2" × 4" × 12" board
- extension cords as needed

Vocabulary

chlorofluorocarbons	control	global warming
greenhouse effect	model	photosynthesis

Teacher Preparation

1. Photocopy the Background Information sheet (15.1), Instructions and Data sheets (15.2), and Questions sheet (15.3).

2. Obtain the required materials.

3. Decide whether to have the students cut their own bottles. (After the activity, save the bottles for use next year or in other activities.) Half of the bottles should be cut near where they narrow for the neck. The other half should be cut about 4" from the bottom.

4. If the activity is to be done outside, locate a place in the sun where the bottles will not be disturbed. Be aware of shadows caused by buildings or trees at the time of day when the activity will be done.

5. Prepare a sample of the "greenhouse" setup to help the students set up theirs.

6. See Activity 13, Detecting Air Pollution.

7. Consider obtaining *Global Warming & the Greenhouse Effect* by Hocking, et al.

SAFETY CONSIDERATIONS

1. If this activity is done inside using a light bulb, caution the students that the light bulb may become hot.
2. Plastic two-liter bottles are difficult to cut. Be careful!

Procedure

1. Using masking tape, attach (or have the students attach) the thermometers to the inside of the bottles.

2. Tape the small cardboard pieces over the thermometer's bulb so that it is not exposed directly to the rays of the sun, or not exposed to the light if the activity is to be done inside. The bottom of the thermometer should be about 2" above the bottom of the bottle. If there are portions of the bottle's label remaining, the thermometer should be attached next to the remaining label so that the label does not interfere with incoming light.

3. A dry, clean rock (or other weight) should be placed in the bottom of each bottle to keep it from tipping or being blown over.

4. The taller bottle should be covered with clear plastic held in place with string or a rubber band. This is the "greenhouse." The short bottle should remain uncovered. This is a control. (Since we are testing the effect of the plastic cover and sides, both the sides and cover need to be absent in the control.)

5. On the data table (15.2), have the students record the starting air temperature in each bottle.

6. Have the students set their bottles in open sunlight, with the thermometers facing away from the sun.

7. The students should record the temperature inside of the bottles every two minutes for 20–30 minutes.

8. The temperatures should then be graphed.

9. After discussing the results of this experiment, have the students read the Background Information sheet (15.1) and discuss global warming.

10. Extension 1 is highly recommended as it provides good practice in setting up experimental controls, hypothesizing, and collecting and interpreting data.

Discussion

1. How is this model like and unlike the real atmosphere and global warming?

2. What was the purpose of the short bottle without the plastic cover?

3. Since not all scientists agree that we have evidence for global warming, should anything be done now to reduce the so-called "greenhouse gases"?

4. What can be done to reduce the production of greenhouse gases?

Answers to 15.3, Global Warming Questions

1. The bottle that is covered should get warmer than the control. The light energy is changed to heat energy in the bottle. In the greenhouse bottle, the warm air cannot escape. In the control, the warm air can escape.

2. Carbon dioxide is produced primarily by burning fossil fuels. It can be reduced by using alternative energy sources, conserving energy, and growing more plants. Chlorofluorocarbons (CFCs) are man-made chemicals used in refrigerators, air conditioners, as solvents, and in aerosols. They can be reduced by stopping their production and use and by finding and using alternatives. Methane is produced by various organisms and in some petro-chemical processes. More efficient use of waste products and controlling leaks from wells and pipelines would reduce methane in the atmosphere. Nitrous oxide is produced by burning biomass and from the breakdown of livestock wastes and fertilizers. It can be reduced by more efficient use of wastes and fertilizers and by controlling burning.

3. If global warming is occurring and we do not take steps to halt it, there will probably be severe weather and climate changes resulting in flooding, droughts, and crop failures. Oceans will rise and flood coastal areas.

4. If we take the recommended steps to stop global warming that is not actually occurring, millions of dollars will be spent. However, most of the things that would be done to prevent global warming are good things to do anyway because they help reduce air pollution.

5. Answers will vary.

6. Scientists use models to investigate things that are too small, too large, too distant, or would take too long to investigate in the field or directly in the laboratory.

7. The control bottle provides temperatures with which to compare the greenhouse bottle's temperatures. It allows us to see the effect of the sides and top of the bottle, which represent the greenhouse gases.

Extensions (See Activity 32 for suggestions for student projects.)

1. The students can test a variety of variables for their effect on the temperature changes. When testing the variables, have them be sure to set up a control and to make a hypothesis predicting what the effect on temperature change will be. Some possible things to check are:

a. What would happen if the control bottle were as tall as the experimental bottle?

b. What would happen if the thermometers faced the sun?

c. What effect would dry soil have?

d. What effect would moist soil have?

e. What effect would water have?

f. What effect would grass or other plants have?

g. What effect would ice cubes have?

h. Do ice cubes melt faster in the bottle with a closed top?

i. Does the color of the bottle affect the results?

j. Does the size of the bottle affect the results?

k. Are the same results achieved if the bottles are in shade?

l. Do different types of light bulbs produce different results?

m. What is the effect of placing the bottles different distances from the light bulb?

n. Does wind have an effect?

o. Do different sizes, colors, or types of rocks have an effect?

2. See Activity 13, Detecting Air Pollution.

3. This activity can lead to or follow from investigations of carbon dioxide and other gases, alternative energy sources, and air pollution.

4. Students could debate a proposal to stop CFC production entirely.

Modification

Consider giving the students the graph (15.2) with unlabeled axes. Have them decide on the scale and units and mark the axes on their graphs.

References

Blaustein, Elliott, *Anti-Pollution Lab.* New York, NY: Sentinel Books, Inc., 1972.

Hocking, Colin, et al., *Global Warming & the Greenhouse Effect.* Berkeley, CA: Lawrence Hall of Science, University of California at Berkeley, 1990.

Miller, G. Tyler, *Living in the Environment.* Belmont, CA: Wadsworth Publishing Company, 1990.

Tomera, Audrey, *Understanding Basic Ecological Concepts.* Portland, ME: J. Weston Walch, 1989.

15.1 GLOBAL WARMING: BACKGROUND INFORMATION

Have you ever gotten into a car that had been left in the sun on a hot day with its windows rolled up and found it very hot? If so, you have experienced the **"greenhouse effect"**! When sunlight is absorbed by the car seats, it is converted to heat energy. The glass of the car blocks much of this heat energy from being radiated back out into the air. Carbon dioxide, water vapor, and other gases in the atmosphere act somewhat like the glass of the car when they absorb and hold the heat that the Earth normally radiates back out into space. Thus, "greenhouse gases" trap heat and, theoretically, could cause a warming of the Earth.

Some scientists are concerned that the Earth's atmosphere may be increasing due to the greenhouse effect. Since the late 1800s, we have been putting large amounts of carbon dioxide (CO_2), methane, and nitrous oxide (N_2O) into the atmosphere. All of these act as greenhouse gases. At the same time, we have cut down forests that would normally remove CO_2 from the air by the process of **photosynthesis.**

The average global temperatures have also been rising since the late 1800s. While there have been fluctuations, the general trend has been toward increasing temperatures. Since 1880, average global temperatures have increased about 0.7°C (1.2°F). The decade of the 1980s was the warmest decade on record. (The data for the 1990s are not in yet.)

To many people, warmer temperatures may seem desirable. Most scientists agree, though, that significant warming would have many harmful effects. Lower heating costs might be offset by higher air-conditioning costs. Areas that now grow most of the world's crops might become too warm or too dry to grow foods. Areas that would become warmer, such as much of Canada, often don't have soils that are suitable for most crops. Lower water levels in fresh-water lakes would concentrate pollutants. Weather patterns would change, and hurricanes would probably hit the coast farther north and with greater ferocity. Warmer temperatures would expand the volume of the oceans and melt much of the ice in glaciers and arctic and antarctic ice caps. This would raise the level of the oceans, flooding many of the coastal cities, where about a third of the world's population lives. Entire (populated) island chains would disappear under the sea! Barrier islands and reefs would disappear, exposing the coast to increased erosion. For these and many other reasons, **global warming** is something that many scientists are very concerned about.

Some scientists, though, are not convinced that global warming is occurring at this time, or if it is, that it is due to human activities. They point out that the Earth's average temperature, so far as we can tell, has fluctuated since the Earth was formed. Some say that the observed temperature increase may just be due to natural causes and that there is nothing that we can do about those causes. Others question the validity of the temperature measurements themselves. Many of the data collecting sites are in or near large cities where colleges and universities are found. These areas have changed significantly over the last 100 years, and many of these changes, such as asphalt streets, industrialization, and taller buildings that interfere with cooling winds, could result in local warming that does not necessarily reflect increased global temperatures.

Carbon dioxide is thought to be responsible for about 55 to 60 percent of the global warming trend. Increased carbon dioxide from fossil fuel burning coupled with reduced carbon dioxide removal from deforestation have resulted in an increase in CO_2 levels in the atmosphere from about 314 parts per million in 1958 to about 348 in 1988.

Chlorofluorocarbons (CFC's) are thought to be responsible for about 25 percent of the global warming trend. CFC's are used in air conditioners and refrigerators, in the production of plastic foams, in various industrial processes, and in aerosol propellants.

Methane (CH_4) is thought to be responsible for about 12 percent of the global warming trend. It is produced by anaerobic bacterial decay of decomposing matter and in the digestive tracts of cattle, sheep, termites, and other organisms. Some escapes from industries and other man-made sources.

Nitrous oxide (N_2O) is responsible for about 6 percent of the global warming trend. It is produced by the breakdown of nitrogen fertilizers, livestock wastes, and by burning of various fuels.

Even though not all scientists believe that global warming is occurring, most would agree that we should take steps to reduce the release of the air pollutants that are thought to cause it. Regardless of whether global warming is occurring or not, those steps would help reduce air pollution and save energy. Some things that are recommended are:

- stop producing CFC's, or at least greatly reduce their production.
- reduce the use of fossil fuels such as coal, oil, and natural gas by increasing the use of renewable alternative energy sources and conservation.
- increase the use of air-pollution-control devices.
- stop the clearing and burning of tropical forests.
- plant trees and other plants.
- reduce water pollution, which poisons aquatic plants that remove CO_2.
- slow human population growth, stop it, and perhaps even reduce the human population to a sustainable level.

While the debate over global warming continues, time passes. Should we do nothing now, wait for more data and hope that the concerns about global warming are without merit? Should we act now and hope that it is not too late?

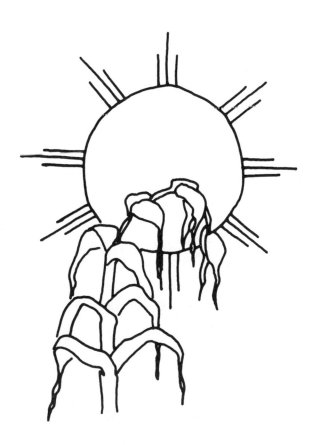

15.2 Global Warming: Instructions

In this activity, you will use a model to learn about the "greenhouse effect." First prepare a "greenhouse" and a **"control"** as instructed by your teacher. (See the diagram below.)

You will either set your greenhouse and the control in the sun or will place a light bulb between them as a source of light energy. As the light passes through the plastic and is absorbed by the contents of the bottles (air and a rock), it is changed to heat energy. Heat energy does not easily pass through the bottle, so it is trapped inside. The plastic bottle is a **model** of the greenhouse gases that some scientists fear are causing the earth to get warmer.

CONTROL BOTTLE   **"GREENHOUSE" BOTTLE**

clear plastic held in place with a rubber band, tape, or string

thermometer taped on inside of the bottle

the thermometer and any remaining label should be on the side away from the light source

thin cardboard guard over the bulb

When you set up your experiment, be sure to do the following:

1. Use a piece of cardboard to shield the thermometer bulb from the light.

2. Be sure that both the thermometer and any of the label that has not been removed are on the side away from the light source.

3. Be sure to place your bottles where they will not be disturbed and where they will not be shaded before the data have been collected.

4. If you are using a bulb as a light source, be sure that the bottles are both the same distance (about 2 cm) from the light bulb and that the thermometers are oriented in the same position relative to the light bulb.

5. Read the thermometers every two minutes. Try to take your readings as close to the same time as possible. Always read the same thermometer first.

6. Accurately record your data on the data table.

7. Graph your data. Be sure to use the "key" on the graph to show which graph is the control data and which is the "greenhouse" bottle data.

15.2 Global Warming: Data

Use the table below to record the temperatures of both thermometers every two minutes. Be sure to record them as close to the same time as possible. Be careful not to shade the bottles when reading the thermometers.

TIME	BOTTLE #1 (control)	BOTTLE #2 ("greenhouse")	TIME	BOTTLE #1	BOTTLE #2
			10 min.	_____°C	_____°C
0 (start)	_____°C	_____°C	12 min.	_____°C	_____°C
2 min.	_____°C	_____°C	14 min.	_____°C	_____°C
4 min.	_____°C	_____°C	16 min.	_____°C	_____°C
6 min.	_____°C	_____°C	18 min.	_____°C	_____°C
8 min.	_____°C	_____°C	20 min.	_____°C	_____°C

Record the temperatures from both bottles on the graph below, connecting the points with lines. Either use different colors to record the temperatures from the different bottles, or use a solid line for the control and a dashed line for the "greenhouse" bottle. Identify the colors or symbols on the "KEY" box.

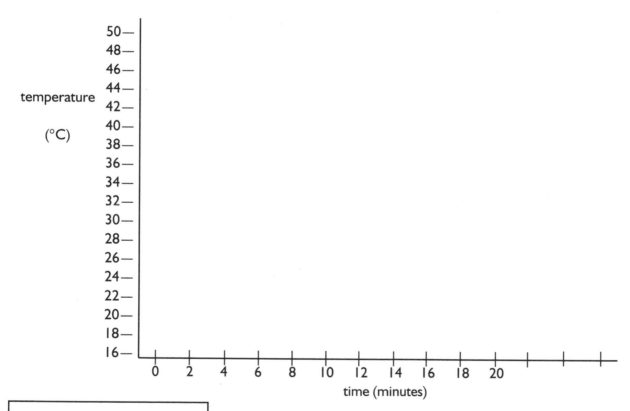

15.3 Global Warming: Questions

1. Was there a difference in the warming rate of the control bottle and the greenhouse bottle? If so, describe the process that took place.

   _____

   _____

2. List three "greenhouse gases," their sources, and at least one way that they could be reduced.

   _____

   _____

   _____

3. What would be some likely consequences if the scientists who say that humans <u>are</u> significantly increasing global warming are correct and we do <u>not</u> take steps to halt it?

   _____

   _____

   _____

4. What would be some likely consequences if the scientists who say that humans are <u>not</u> significantly increasing global warming are correct and we <u>do</u> take steps to halt it?

   _____

   _____

   _____

5. Which do you think we should do: Take immediate action to stop any possible human-caused greenhouse effect or wait another 5–10 years while more studies are done? Why?

   _____

   _____

6. Why do scientists sometimes use "models"?

   _____

   _____

7. What is the purpose of the "control" bottle in the model?

   _____

   _____

   _____

unit Five

Energy Issues

- **Food Chains**
- **Hidden Energy Uses**
- **"Watts" the Cost?**
- **Conserve a Watt**
- **Keep the Heat!**
- **Catch the Sun!**
- **Fossil Fuel Extraction**
- **The Nuclear Power Puzzle**
- **Biogas**
- **Energy Alternatives**

ACTIVITY 16: FOOD CHAINS _____

Activity Summary

Students are given cards with pictures of organisms in a food chain. They are to arrange the cards in a "food chain" and be able to explain their arrangement.

Introduction

While many students have heard of "food chains," this activity will help them to visualize the sequence of organisms that forms a food chain. They will see that different ecosystems and biomes have different organisms, but that food chains are similar in each place. The same niches (producer, herbivore, carnivore, scavenger, decomposer) are filled by different organisms. Since some animals may feed on a variety of organisms, the food chain can be more difficult to form than one might expect. This leads to the concept of the "food web." In addition to the basic set of organisms, additional optional ones, including humans, are provided.

One way to introduce this activity is to begin a discussion of vegetarianism with the students. Another way would be to pose the following problem:

The crew of a space shuttle bound for Neptune is able to grow wheat and corn in its spacecraft. Would the crew be able to support more crew members by:

1. eating the wheat and corn;
2. feeding the wheat and corn to chickens, then eating the chickens;
3. feeding the wheat and corn to chickens, then eating the chickens' eggs?

Grouping

Teams of 5 students.

Time

30–45 minutes, including discussion

Anticipated Outcomes

The students will:

- be able to place five given pictures of organisms in a typical food chain in a logical sequence and be able to explain that sequence, orally or in writing.
- be able to define the following terms listed under "vocabulary" and use them appropriately when discussing the concept of energy in an ecosystem.

Materials

—Photocopied student pages:

- 16.1 Food Chains: Background Information sheet (one per student)
- 16.2 Food Chains: Questions (one per student)

—Transparencies of food chains and a food web (made from masters provided)

—One set of laminated food chain cards for each team of students

Vocabulary

abiotic	biomass	carnivore	consumer
decomposer	ecosystem	food chain	food web
herbivore	omnivore	photosynthesis	producer

Teacher Preparation

1. Prepare food chain cards, either from the drawings on the following pages or from pictures cut from magazines, calendars, and so forth. You might consider having the students color the drawings before laminating. Consider simplifying the students' task of forming chains by color coding the cards, either by coloring the margins differently or by mounting each chain on a different color of paper or tagboard.

2. Familiarize yourself with the sequences. If you don't have even teams of five students, you might leave off the "abiotic" cards from some or all of the teams after explaining that the abiotic part of the environment is the basis upon which the food chains are built. You might also add organisms to one or more chains (for example, humans can be added to many chains, as can parasites such as mosquitoes).

3. Use the masters provided to make transparencies of food chains and a food web.

4. Photocopy the student Background Information sheet (16.1) and student Questions sheet (16.2).

SAFETY CONSIDERATION

Remind the students to avoid pushing or shoving as they arrange themselves.

Procedure

1. Discuss food chains with the students. Use transparencies made from the black line master to explain the concept.

2. Divide the class into teams of 4 or 5 students each.

3. Explain that this activity is to be done without talking.

4. Explain that their team's task is to arrange themselves into a logical food chain by lining up in order, from the abiotic to the last member of the food chain. (This might be a race.)

5. Issue the food chain cards to the students.

6. Have them arrange themselves silently.

7. When all the students have formed their food chains, have each student explain why he or she placed himself or herself at that point in the food chain.

Discussion

1. Discuss the benefits of eating lower on the food chain. Include both health benefits to the individual, benefits to other people, and environmental benefits.
2. When considering food chains, discuss the role of scavengers, parasites, and omnivores.
3. Where do humans fit into most food chains?
4. Discuss the effect of removing a link in the food chain. (What would happen if an organism became extinct, especially to the organisms above it on the food pyramid and those immediately below it?) Discuss the interconnectedness of organisms.
5. What is the effect of polluting the abiotic environment?
6. What would happen if decomposers were removed from a food chain, for example, with agricultural bactericides and fungicides?

Answers to 16.2, Food Chains Questions

1. A food chain is a simplified sequence that shows a series of organisms each eating or decomposing the preceding one. A food web is a more realistic representation of what actually happens in an ecosystem. It is a complex network of many interconnected food chains.
2. a. Abiotic factors are the nonliving part of an ecosystem. Examples include air, water, temperature, and minerals. All living things depend on abiotic factors in order to live.

   b. Producers are organisms, usually green plants, that convert light energy into stored chemical energy. It is this stored chemical energy that most organisms depend upon for their energy source. Producers build up complex organic compounds from simpler molecules.

   c. Consumers are organisms that feed upon other organisms to obtain the energy and materials that they need in order to live. All animals are consumers.

   d. Decomposers are organisms that get their nutrients by breaking down organic matter from dead bodies and the waste products of other organisms. Examples include fungi and some bacteria.

   e. Scavengers are animals, such as many crabs, some kinds of sharks, and other organisms that obtain their food mostly by feeding on dead bodies of other animals (as opposed to hunting and killing their prey).
3. If producers were eliminated from a food chain, all of the other organisms (consumers and decomposers) that depend upon them would be unable to live.
4. Man is usually considered to be at the top of a food chain. There are few animals that consume us, even though there are many human parasites. As the top organism in our food chain or pyramid, we are absolutely dependent upon the other organisms in our food chain.
5. Answers will vary.

Extensions (See Activity 32 for suggestions for student projects.)

1. Have the students investigate and report on other food chains.
2. Have the students make bulletin boards illustrating food chains, food webs, or pyramids of numbers (biomass).

3. Have the students build a three-dimensional model of a pyramid of numbers.

4. Trace the path of a bit of energy or matter through a food chain.

5. Form a food web with students representing the parts and showing the linkages with string or yarn. Have the students hold the string taut. What happens when a part of the web is removed? Are other parts affected? (Have them drop the string when they feel the effect of removing part of the food web, that is, when their string goes slack.)

6. Have the students investigate the effect of pesticides on food chains, including "biological magnification/concentration."

7. Invite a vegetarian to talk with the class. Plan vegetarian menus; eat a vegetarian "dinner" in class.

8. Write vegetarian cookbooks, duplicate, and send home.

9. This activity leads nicely into Activity 27, Food? What Food?

Modifications

1. Leave out top carnivores to shorten the chain.

2. Leave out decomposers. What happens to the materials stored in the organisms' bodies?

3. Remove an organism from the middle of the food chain. What happens to all those that follow?

4. Give food chain cards that are not color coded. The students will form a variety of food chains. Have them justify their choices.

5. Give the students magazines with nature pictures. Have them create food chain cards of their own.

6. Use the supplemental food chain cards (or pictures that you find) to add to the food chains.

Reference

Tourtillot, Leeann, *Conserve & Renew*. Sacramento, CA: California Energy Extension Service; 1990.

Food Chains

A TYPICAL FRESH-WATER FOOD CHAIN

A TYPICAL GRASSLAND FOOD CHAIN

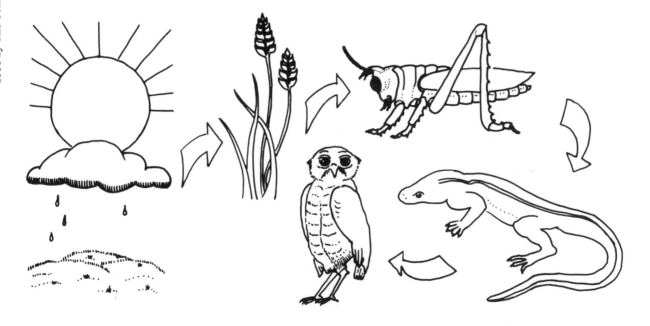

A Food Web

16.1 Food Chains: Background Information

Energy is one of the basic requirements for all living things. Indeed, much of what we call "living" centers around obtaining food. We use food as an energy source as well as a source of materials with which to make and repair our bodies. Even plants need energy.

Green plants convert and store energy from the sun in the process of **photosynthesis.** Organisms that can make their own food are called autotrophs or **producers.**

Animals and other organisms that do not "make their own food" are called heterotrophs or **consumers.** All heterotrophs (consumers) depend upon the autotrophs (producers) for their energy and for the chemicals of which they are made.

An animal that eats plants is called a primary consumer or an **herbivore.** An animal that eats other animals is called a secondary consumer if it eats herbivores, or a tertiary consumer if it eats other consumers. Since **carnivores** eat other animals, they are consumers. An animal that eats both plants and animals is called an **omnivore.**

As one organism feeds on or eats another, a **"food chain"** is formed. An example of a simplified food chain is shown below:

grass . . . is eaten by . . . grasshoppers, . . . which are eaten by . . . a lizard, . . . which is eaten by . . . a fox, . . . which dies and is consumed by . . . insects and bacteria

Another way of showing this food chain is:

grass → grasshopper → lizard → fox → bacteria and insects

Two other food chain examples are:

marine plankton → sardine → pelican → bacteria

corn → cow → man → bacteria

The ultimate source of energy for essentially all food chains is the sun. When the organism at the end of the food chain dies, the materials from which its body was built are returned to the environment by bacteria, fungi, worms, insects, and other organisms that are called **decomposers.**

It is very important to realize that food chains such as those described here are very simplified versions of what actually occurs. For example, the grass (or grass seeds) in the first example would be eaten by a great variety of insects, birds, and mammals. The grasshopper would be prey for birds, snakes, and other insects as well as lizards. In addition to the fox, birds of prey and other mammals would feed on lizards. The dead fox might be eaten by a coyote, crows, or vultures. We use food chains to make the relationships among parts of an **ecosystem** easier to understand.

A more realistic representation of what actually occurs in nature would include all of the aforementioned organisms and many more. Such a representation would be called a **food web.**

It is also important to realize that at each "step" in a food chain there is a transfer of both energy and materials. The consumer must spend some energy to acquire and use its food and to move about and stay alive. There is energy lost in the animal's waste. Thus, at each step or level in a food chain, energy is lost to the environment and less energy is available to the organism(s) at the next level. Only about 10 percent of the energy is transferred to the next trophic level.

This leads to what is called a food pyramid or a "pyramid of numbers" or, more accurately, a "pyramid of **biomass**." The term "pyramid of biomass" is more accurate because, for example, one oak tree might support many insects because of the large biomass of its leaves. A hypothetical example of a pyramid of numbers follows.

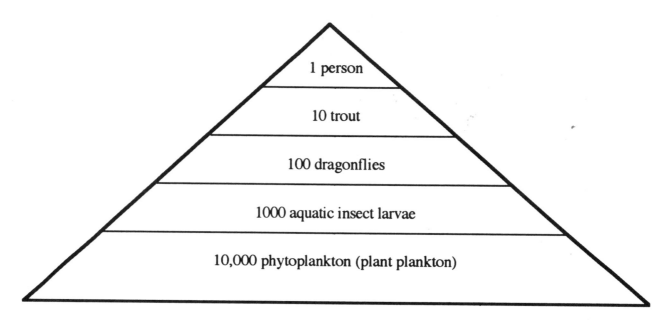

An important ramification of the pyramid of numbers is that the more steps in a food chain there are, the fewer top consumers (such as man) can be supported. A given amount of land will support more people eating lower on the food chain (eating plants) than it will support when people eat higher on the food chain (eating other animals such as pigs or cattle, which eat the plants). Simply put, the Earth can support more vegetarians than it can support carnivores!

It is very important to understand that the lives of all living things depend upon nonliving things, including both energy and materials. The term for the nonliving parts of an environment is "**abiotic** factors." Examples include air, water, and sunlight. These abiotic factors form the basis for all food chains.

Food Chains:

1. What is the difference between a food chain and a food web?

   _____

2. Define, give an example of, and explain the role of each of the following parts of a food chain:

   a. abiotic factors _____

   _____

   _____

   b. producers _____

   _____

   _____

   c. consumers _____

   _____

   _____

   d. decomposers _____

   _____

   _____

   e. scavengers _____

   _____

   _____

3. What would happen to a food chain if the producers were eliminated?

   _____

   _____

4. Where do humans fit in most food chains?

   _____

5. If all humans were vegetarians, what effect would that have on the number of people that the Earth could support?

   _____

   _____

Food Chain Cards

Food Chain Cards

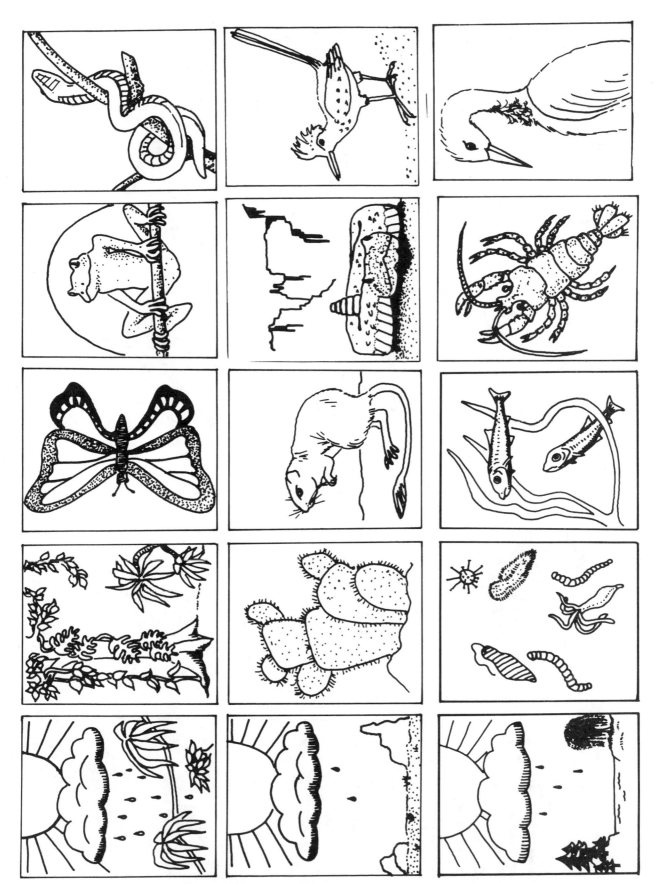

Supplemental Food Chain Cards

(Use these to alter the food chains provided or to adjust them according to the number of students doing the activity.)

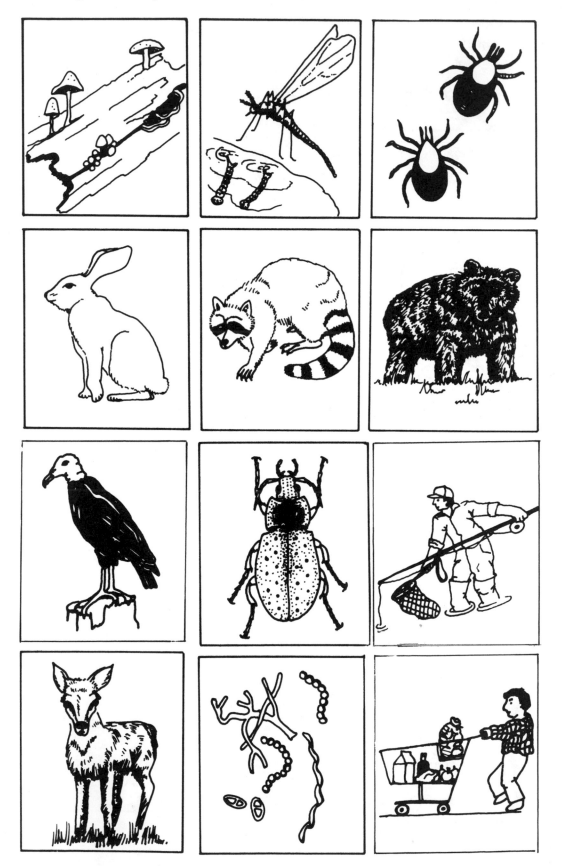

ACTIVITY 17: HIDDEN ENERGY USES _____

Activity Summary

Working in teams, students try to figure out where energy was used in the production, marketing, use, and disposal of a variety of common items. They draw a diagram to represent the materials and energy used for that item. They then share their findings with the rest of the class.

Introduction

When we think of energy use, we usually think of the energy used in our home, our automobile, or at our work. We seldom stop to think of the energy used to make, transport, sell, and dispose of everyday objects such as light bulbs, pencils, food, and soap. In fact, much of the energy used in the United States is used to manufacture and distribute common goods. The table in the student Background Information sheet (17.1) gives an idea of how we use energy.

It is important that students realize that when they purchase an item, they are not only paying for the materials that went into it—they are also paying for the energy used to make, transport, and market it.

An important idea to get across is that manufacturers make only what they can sell. If we don't buy it, they won't make it. If they don't make it, there will be less energy used, less materials used, and less waste to send to the landfill. Realizing that the consumer/purchaser controls the marketplace can give the students a feeling of empowerment, something that is important when dealing with environmental issues that so often seem to be beyond our control.

Of course, manufacturing also means jobs. If we can meet our "needs," as opposed to "wants," with fewer jobs, how should the work force be realigned? These are very interesting ideas to explore with students.

Grouping

Teams of 4–5 students.

Time

45–55 minutes

Anticipated Outcomes

The students will:

- increase their understanding of the amount of energy that is used to make a product.
- increase their understanding of the amount of materials that are used to make a product.
- become more willing to reduce unnecessary use of products.
- become more willing to reuse and recycle.

Materials

—Photocopied student pages:
- 17.1 Hidden Energy Uses: Background Information (one per student)
- 17.2 Hidden Energy Uses: Instructions (one per team)
- 17.3 Hidden Energy Uses: Questions (one per student)

—Materials for the students to analyze, such as:
- aluminum soda can (with plastic neck rings), refillable soda bottle, Styrofoam plate or cup, reusable plastic or ceramic plate or cup, snack with lots of packaging, piece of fruit, trial size (single-use size) deodorant spray can, bar of soap, hair spray in an aerosol can, hair spray in an atomizer, disposable diaper, cloth diaper, disposable lighter (used up), refillable lighter (empty), and so forth.

—Large pieces of paper (1 per team)

—Colored pens or crayons (1 set per team)

Vocabulary

commercial   disposal   raw material

Teacher Preparation

1. Photocopy the Background Information sheet (17.1), Instructions sheet (17.2), and Questions sheet (17.3).
2. Obtain materials. It is valuable to have objects that fulfill the same purpose in different ways, such as an aluminum can and a refillable bottle.
3. Optional: Make a transparency of the diagram on the Instructions page (17.2).

Safety Considerations

None

Procedure

1. Discuss with the students how we all use things without thinking about the energy and materials that go into making them, let alone delivering, using, and disposing of them. Use the example of the pencil on the Instructions sheet as an example.
2. Divide the class into teams of 4–6 students each.
3. Give each team one of the objects.
4. Instruct them to consider and discuss their objects, thinking about:
   - what materials went into making it and where they came from
   - how those materials were obtained and fashioned into the object
   - how the object was marketed
   - how it will be reused or disposed of
   - how energy was used at each step

5. After about 5 minutes, give each team a sheet of paper and have them draw/diagram the materials and energy used to make and utilize their object.

   - Emphasize that these are to be simple sketches with minimal use of words and that artistic ability is not needed.
   - Tell them that they will be asked to explain their diagram to the class.
   - Tell them to underline in red each place where energy is used.
   - Tell them to list any questions or information that they don't know, such as where something comes from, what something is made of, or what it is.

6. After the drawings are done, collect the coloring tools.

7. Have each team share their diagrams, first showing what their object is.

8. Post the diagrams on the bulletin board or wall.

9. It is highly recommended that Activities 18 and 19 be done after doing this activity.

Discussion

1. Were there questions to which you didn't know the answers? How could we find them?

2. In what ways is energy used in marketing or selling?

3. In what ways is energy used in disposing of or reusing an object?

4. For each object, try to think of a way of filling the same need or want using less energy.

5. For each object, try to think of a way of filling the same need or want using more energy.

6. What is the difference between a "need" and a "want"?

7. Some teams had objects that filled the same need in different ways. What are advantages and disadvantages of each?

Answers to 17.3, Hidden Energy Uses: Questions

1. Energy and materials are used in making packaging. The packaging for some products uses more materials and can cost more to produce than the product itself!

2. Manufacturers make and ship goods they can sell. If they can't be sold, they won't make them. We control what we purchase. The manufacturers, of course, try to influence our purchasing, but we decide whether or not to buy an item. Advertisers try to create "wants," and then they try to make us think of those wants as needs. Ultimately, we, the consumers, decide what is produced.

3. All product costs are eventually passed on to the consumer or the taxpayer.

4. A true need is something without which we cannot survive. Many things that we tend to consider needs are actually "wants."

5. Answers will vary, but our true material needs are shelter, food, and water.

6. Answers will vary.

7. Things cannot truly be disposed of in the sense of disappearing. They are put somewhere where we don't have to think of them or deal with them directly. They do,

however, still exist in some form, or at least the atoms from which they were made exist.

8. If we don't buy the products, they won't be produced. If we choose to purchase products with minimal packaging we save on energy and materials. Buying quality, reusable products results in less waste than using disposable products or those that won't last. Recycling is important. Buying in bulk and using reusable packaging helps, as does making or growing one's own goods. Reduce, reuse, recycle, and refuse (to buy destructive products)!

Extensions (See Activity 32 for suggestions for student projects.)

1. Have the students do this activity as individuals, using objects of their choosing.
2. Have the students research answers to questions raised during the activity and report back to the class.
3. Visit places where energy is used, such as farms, mines, manufacturing plants, stores, and disposal facilities.
4. Select one object. Use the library and whatever other sources are available to do this activity in great detail.
5. Graph the data in Table 17-A.
6. Do Activity 18 and then Activity 19.

Modifications

1. Have the students do this activity for objects that fulfill a need or want that can be met in several ways. For example, the need for a drink of a refreshing liquid can be met with a soda in an aluminum can, a refillable bottle, a nonrefillable bottle, a drink from a thermos, a drink of water from a fountain, or an orange. Shaving can be done with an electric razor, a reusable safety razor, or a disposable razor.
2. a. Form groups of 3-5 students.
   b. Give each group an object. (soda bottle, pencil, orange, etc.)
   c. Have each group discuss, among themselves, the "life" of the object, from its origins to its ultimate disposal or use.
   d. Have each member of the group assume a role of the object as they take turns telling the class "their" life story to the class, in the first person. For example, the story of an aluminum can might start out:

   > "I started out as a deposit of aluminum ore in a mountain in South America. One day I felt myself being uncovered and lifted by a huge machine. I was dumped into a large truck and taken to a train. The train carried me to..." etc.

3. The questions (17.3) can be assigned as individual or team work.

References

Miller, G. Tyler, *Living in the Environment*. Belmont, CA: Wadsworth Publishing Company, 1990.

Tourtillot, Leeann, *Conserve & Renew*. Sacramento, CA: California Energy Extension Service; 1990.

17.1 Hidden Energy Uses: Background Information

What do you think of when somebody mentions energy use? Quite likely you think of lights, automobiles, heaters, or other appliances in and around the home. Have you ever considered the amount of energy that goes into manufacturing, transporting, selling, and **disposing** of the thousands of products that surround us?

Consider something as simple as a pencil. Where did the wood, metal, eraser, graphite ("lead"), and paint come from? What were the **raw materials,** how were they obtained and turned into the material used in the pencil? At what steps was energy used? What about energy and materials used in shipping the raw materials and final product? What about energy and materials used in the stores where the pencil is sold? Is energy used to sharpen the pencil? What happens to the stub after the pencil is used?

Table 17-A shows the distribution of commercial energy use in the United States in 1984.

17-A
COMMERCIAL ENERGY USE IN THE UNITED STATES, 1984

Industrial Uses (37%)

heating and steam production 24%
electric drive 8%
raw material, feedstocks, etc................. 5%

Transportation Uses (25%*)

Private cars, etc. 16%
Commercial and public 9%

Residential (22%)

space heating 11%
water heating 3%
air conditioning 2%
lighting 2%
refrigeration 2%
other 2%

Commercial (16%)

space heating...6%
air conditioning.....................................3%
lighting..3%
other..4%

*Actually, transportation amounts to closer to 50% of the energy used if the energy used to make the vehicles, refine fuels, build roads, produce parts, etc., is considered.

Examination of Table 17-A shows that most energy used in the United States is used to make, transport, and sell the thousands of products we buy. If we didn't purchase them, would the manufacturers make them? What if we were to purchase less, waste less, recycle more, and reuse more? Would both energy and material resources be saved?

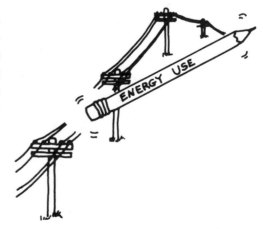

17.2 Hidden Energy Uses: Instructions

1. As a team, think and talk about the energy and materials that have gone into your object. Consider at least the following:

   a. Where did the raw materials come from and how were they obtained?

   b. How was energy used in obtaining the raw materials?

   c. How were the materials processed or refined?

   d. How was the object manufactured?

   e. How was the object transported?

   f. What energy was used in selling or marketing the object?

   g. Was energy used by the consumer in obtaining the object and using it?

   h. Is energy used to dispose of the object?

2. Sketch your object at the center of your paper. Don't worry about making your sketch a work of art. Simple drawings are fine. Draw a diagram or "map" showing the path of the materials used in this object, from **raw materials** in nature to the **manufacturing** to the **marketing** to **use** to **disposal.**

3. In red, underline or circle each point on your map where energy is used.

4. As you do this activity, write down any questions you have. These might be such things as how something is made, where it comes from, or any other things that come up as you consider your object and its energy history.

   An example of a simple energy and materials map (yours will have more detail):

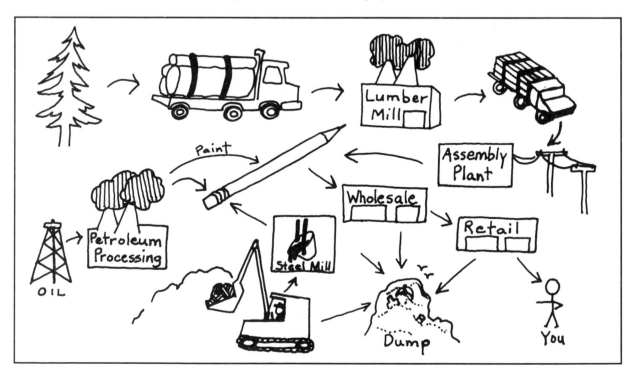

17.3 Hidden Energy Uses: Questions

1. In what ways is packaging an important use of energy and materials?

   _____

   _____

2. Discuss the idea that we, the consumers, control the manufacturing and commercial sectors of the economy.

   _____

   _____

   _____

3. How is the energy used in making a product paid for?

   _____

   _____

4. What is the difference between a "need" and a "want"?

   _____

   _____

5. List several things that you truly NEED.

   _____

6. List several things that most people in our society WANT.

   _____

7. When we throw something "away," has it truly gone away or is it just put somewhere else? Discuss this.

   _____

   _____

8. What happens to the energy stored in something that is "thrown away"?

   _____

   _____

9. What are some ways that you can help reduce the energy used in the manufacture of goods such as those used in this activity?

   _____

   _____

   _____

ACTIVITY 18: "WATTS" THE COST? _____

Activity Summary

Students survey their homes for electrical appliances. They then compute the monthly cost of each appliance, in kilowatt-hours and in dollars.

Introduction

To make decisions about how to conserve energy, we need to understand how we use it. The consumption of electricity by various appliances varies tremendously. Sometimes students think that conserving energy means doing without modern amenities such as compact disc players and television. By learning which appliances use the most energy, students can learn ways to cut electrical use without having to give up all the conveniences of today's culture. Reducing electrical use in space (air) heating by 2 percent can save more energy than is typically used by televisions, stereos, and VCR's combined! They can also learn that the use of electrical appliances adds up, so that every little bit of energy saved helps the environment (and their pocketbook!).

Grouping

Individuals

Time

30–45 minutes to introduce
homework time: variable
45–55 minutes to discuss homework

Anticipated Outcomes

The students will:

- increase their understanding of the energy used by various appliances.
- increase their understanding of how they can save energy at home.

Materials

—Photocopied student pages:

- 18.1 "Watts" the Cost? Background Information, with table of approximate electricity use for various appliances (one per student)
- 18.2 "Watts" the Cost? Instructions and Data (one per student)
- 18.3 "Watts" the Cost? Questions (one per student)
- 18.4 "Watts" the Cost? Letter to Parents (optional) (one per student)

—Samples of various electrical appliances such as hair dryer, toaster oven, radio, shop tools, VCR, television, and the like. In addition to actual appliances, you might obtain the tags or plates showing wattage used by larger appliances. (Contact an appliance repair shop.) Alternatively, you might use photographs of the appliance tags or plates.

—Calculators are highly desirable

—Energy Use Guides from various appliances (recommended)

Vocabulary

kilowatt   kilowatt-hour   watt   wattage

Teacher Preparation

1. Photocopy the Background Information sheet (18.1), Instructions and Data sheets (18.2), Questions sheet (18.3), and optional Parent Letter (18.4).
2. Obtain samples of appliances, labels, and tags to show the students.

SAFETY CONSIDERATION

Tell the students to unplug appliances before examining them for the tags that tell the appliance's wattage.

Procedure

1. It is highly recommended that Activity 17 be done before doing this activity.
2. Decide whether to require the students to check their home appliances for their wattages or to allow students to use the approximate values supplied with the Background Information sheet (18.1).
3. Decide whether to ask the students to bring in old utility bills. (Some parents are reluctant to allow students to bring such documents to school.) If you do, consider using the Letter to Parents provided (18.4).
4. Introduce the lesson by asking students to guess the answers to the following questions:

   a. How much does it cost, in energy, for you to watch TV for an hour?

   b. Which costs more, an hour of listening to the stereo or leaving a light on for an hour?

   c. In your home, what appliance uses the most electricity per month?

   d. How much does your family pay for electricity in an average month?

5. Tell the students that power companies charge us for the watts of energy that we use and that appliances generally have their wattage marked on them.
6. Have the students examine various electrical appliances to find their wattages. This might be done by passing the appliances around or by having them set out at stations and having the students circulate.
7. After the students have had an opportunity to find the wattages, distribute the Instructions and Data Table page (18.2) and teach how to calculate average electrical rate, kilowatt-hours, and cost per month, using the examples on the page. These

calculations look formidable, but are really quite easy. Work through several examples to help the students understand. You might want to have them either round off to the nearest quarter of an hour or the nearest tenth of an hour.

8. Go over the list of appliances, being sure that the students know what the terms mean. What, for example, is a "range" as opposed to an "oven"? What is a "space heater"?

9. Distribute the student Background Information (18.1) and discuss the use of the Approximate Wattages information if you are going to use it. Note that the wattages are given in watts, rather than in kilowatts. This is because most appliances have their wattages in watts.

10. Ask the students to try to bring in an old electrical bill. Distribute the parent letter (18.4).

11. When the students have calculated their data, discuss which appliances use the most and the least energy and the variables that determine energy use. (See discussion questions.) Emphasize that the simplest way to cut back significantly on energy use is to reduce the use of appliances that use a lot of energy, such as space and water heaters, by some percentage. This does not mean, though, that we should thoughtlessly use small-wattage appliances. It all adds up.

Discussion

1. Which appliances generally use the most energy?

2. What fraction of the electrical use is due to the biggest energy user? The top two or three users?

3. For a given kind of appliance (refrigerator, for example), do all makes and models use the same amount of energy?

4. What are some of the factors that influence a family's energy use?

5. How did your calculated energy use compare to the actual amount on the bill? What accounts for any discrepancies?

Answers to 18.3, "Watts" the Cost? Questions

1. For most homes, space heating and air conditioning are by far the main energy users. Refrigerators are next.

2. Answers will vary.

3. Answers will vary.

4. Heating, cooking, food refrigeration, and lighting are generally the most necessary. Some students may claim that television, stereos, etc., are necessities. This provides an opportunity to discuss <u>needs</u> versus <u>wants</u>.

5. Least necessary appliances generally would be:

   • convenience items such as electric can openers, pencil sharpeners, and toothbrushes

   • entertainment items such as stereos and televisions

   • personal appearance items such as hair dryers, curlers, and shavers

This provides another opportunity to discuss both needs versus wants and alternatives to the use of electrical appliances.

6. Most "experts" agree that we could easily reduce our domestic electrical use by at least 15 percent without adversely affecting our lifestyles. Most industrialized or developed countries use significantly less energy per person than we do.

7. Reducing domestic electricity use can help protect the environment in many ways. Reducing energy use means less oil and natural gas will need to be drilled for, less coal mined, and fewer valleys flooded by dams. Burning less oil and coal reduces air pollution. Mining and transporting less coal and oil reduces water pollution. Less energy used results in less demand for nuclear power plants and less production of wastes from them. If you have done activity 17, Hidden Energy Uses, refer to it in the discussion of this question.

Extensions (See Activity 32 for suggestions for student projects.)

1. Calculate the energy use per person in the family.
2. Do a similar activity with gas use (natural gas or propane).
3. Invite a speaker from your local utility company.
4. Contact your local utility company, the U.S. Department of Energy, or your state energy department for information.
5. Contact local appliance sales companies. Ask them to talk to the class about energy-efficient appliances. Consider a field trip to visit an appliance store.
6. Obtain examples of the Energy Guides that are affixed to most major appliances. Teach the students how to read and utilize them.
7. Investigate what wattages are available for comparable appliances. What is the reason for differences in wattage?
8. Do Activity 19.

Modifications

1. Select only certain appliances that all students will have in their homes.
2. Assign different types of appliances to different students.
3. Students can convert all energy users to BTUs to compare how much energy they use in various ways:

1 gallon of gasoline = 115,000 BTUs

1 kW = 3413 BTUs

1 therm of natural gas = 100,000 BTUs

1 gallon of diesel fuel = 123,000 BTUs

References

Anonymous, *Winter Bill Workbook*. San Francisco, CA: Pacific Gas and Electric Company, 1990.

Chiras, Daniel, *Laboratory Activities Masters for Environmental Science*. Menlo Park, CA: Addison-Wesley Publishing Company, 1989.

Miller, G. Tyler, *Living in the Environment*. Belmont, CA: Wadsworth Publishing Company, 1990.

18.1 "Watts" the Cost?: Background Information

How much does it cost to watch television for an hour? How much energy does it take to cook a meal, heat a house, or light a lamp? What does that energy cost? Does it take more energy to toast bread or to boil water? What are the major and minor energy users in your home? How much does it cost to use the various appliances per hour, day, or year? Are they worth that amount? To answer these questions, we need to understand how we are charged for electricity.

When utility companies bill us for the electricity we use, they charge us according to how many **kilowatt hours** we have used.

A **watt** is a unit used to indicate how much electrical power has been used. A **kilowatt** equals 1,000 watts. An appliance's **"wattage"** indicates the amount of watts an appliance uses in an hour.

If 1,000 watts (1 kilowatt) of power is used for 1 hour, that is a kilowatt-hour (kW). Thus, if an electrical appliance that uses 1,000 watts of power is used for 1 hour, 1 kilowatt-hour of power has been used. Ten 100-watt light bulbs left on for 1 hour would also equal 1 kilowatt-hour of power, as would one 100-watt light bulb left on for 10 hours.

A heater that uses 1,500 watts of power per hour uses 1.5 kilowatts of power per hour. If it were used for 2 hours, 3 kilowatt-hours of power would be used. Since 200 watts equals 0.2 kilowatts, a 200-watt television used for 1 hour would use 0.2 kW of power.

Generally, converting electrical energy to heat energy takes a lot of electricity to obtain usable amounts of heat. Thus, appliances that are used to generate heat, such as stoves, water heaters, space (air) heaters, etc., use a lot of electricity. Some other electricity users such as radios and stereos use relatively little electricity in a given period of time. Even they, though, can add a lot to electricity bills when they are used a lot.

By knowing how much electricity costs per kilowatt-hour, we can get an idea of how much it would cost to operate an appliance for a period of time.

In this activity, you will determine how much power various appliances around your home use. Then you will calculate how much each costs you to use per month.

© 1993 by The Center for Applied Research in Education

APPROXIMATE ENERGY USE FOR SOME APPLIANCES

Note: These are approximations. Adjust them as seems appropriate for your family. For example, if you have a large family or use lots of hot water, you might increase the hot water usage. If you have a particularly powerful appliance, or a small model, you might adjust these wattages accordingly. Older appliances tend to use more watts than comparable newer models.

APPLIANCE	APPROXIMATE ENERGY USE (watts/hour or /use)	APPLIANCE	APPROXIMATE ENERGY USE (watts/hour or /use)
air conditioner (room)		iron (hand)	1000
window / wall	1500	microwave oven	1000
central	4500	mixer	125
evaporative cooler	500	oven	1300
portable fan	250	rangetop burner	1200 / burner
blanket, electric	75 / night	self-cleaning feature	6000 / use
blender	350	radio, portable	20
broiler	1500	refrigerator-freezer	
clock	2	manual defrost	3000 / day
clock radio	6	auto. defrost, 16 cu. ft.	3300 / day
clothes dryer	5000 / load	auto. defrost, 22 cu. ft.	5000 / day
clothes washing machine	250 / load (+ water)	stereo components (most need receiver too)	
coffee maker	120 / use	cassette player (+ receiver)	100
computer	75	C.D. player (+ receiver)	14
dehumidifier	275	receiver / radio	75
dishwasher		turntable (+ receiver)	10
normal cycle	1000 / load (+ water)	sewing machine	75
energy saver cycle	500 / load (+ water)	shaver	14
fan		swimming pool	
attic	370	sweep and filter pump	1800
ceiling	100	+ increased water heating	
circulating	200	television	
portable	250	black and white	70
freezer		color	230
auto. defrost, 20 cu. ft.	3800 / day	VCR	25
manual defrost, 22 cu. ft.	2700 / day	toaster	75 / use
frying pan, electric	1000	toaster oven	500
hair dryer	1300	toothbrush	7
heater (space / air)		vacuum cleaner	750
baseboard (6')	3000	water bed (w/thermostat)	280 / day
heat pump	4000	waste disposal	450
portable	1500	word processor/typewriter	50
wall furnace	10,000	other:_____	
central, (w/floor vents)	25,000	other:_____	

Lighting: Check the wattage of the bulbs in the most frequently used lamps and estimate hours of use, or approximate 100,000 watt-hours (100 kW) per month.

Hot Water: This will vary greatly according to length and numbers of showers/baths, clothes and dish washing, whether you have a blanket on the heater, and the setting on the water heater. An average family might use about 350,000 watt-hours (350 kW) per month.

Note: Many homes have gas water heaters, space heaters, ovens, and stoves.

18.2 "Watts" the Cost?: Instructions

In this activity, you will first survey your home, listing the various electrical appliances you have in your home. Then you will estimate how many hours each is used per month. Finally, using an average rate (cost) per kilowatt-hour of electricity, you will compute how much money is spent on each appliance per month.

To calculate your average rate per kilowatt-hour, you will need to obtain one of your family's electrical utility bills. Find the area that indicates kilowatt-hours of electricity used and how much money was charged for that electricity. Then divide the cost by the kW. This will give you your average rate per kW.

For example: If the cost of electricity was $86.88 and 724 kW were used, the average rate was $0.12 per kW.

$$\frac{\$86.88}{724\ \text{kW}} = \$0.12\ \text{per kW}$$

To determine the wattage of an appliance, look for a label, plate, or other marking that gives such information as model number, voltage, and wattage. The abbreviation for watt is "W," so the wattage mark would look like "400 W."

To convert watts to kilowatts, divide watts by 1,000:

$$2{,}500\ \text{watts} = 2.5\ \text{kW} \qquad 350\ \text{watts} = 0.35\ \text{kW} \qquad 25\ \text{watts} = 0.025\ \text{kW}$$

To find the cost of using an appliance per month, multiply the following:

days used × hours used / day × kilowatts × average rate / kW = cost / month

(For some appliances, it makes more sense to calculate the kW per use or per day than per hour.)

SAMPLE CALCULATIONS:

for a 200W color television watched 3 hr / day with a rate of $0.12 / kW:

30 days × 3 hr / day × 0.2 kW × $0.12 / kWh = $2.16 / month

for a 1,500W heater used 5 hr / day with a rate of $0.12 / kW:

30 days × 5 hr / day × 1.5 kW × $0.12 / kWh = $27.00 / month

for a 700W refrigerator that comes on intermittently so that it uses 5 kW / day:

30 days × 5 kW / day × $0.12 / kWh = $18.00 / month

for a clothes dryer that uses 4 kW / load and is used for 9 loads / month:

9 loads × 4 kW / load × $0.12 / kWh = $4.32 / month

Name _____ Class _____ Date _____

18.2 "Watts" the Cost?: Data

type of home: ( ) single family residence ( ) apartment or condominium ( ) other: _____

number of people living in the home: _____ rate based on bill for the month of: _____

other pertinent information: _____

rate calculation: $\dfrac{\text{cost of electricity}}{\text{kWh used}}$: \$ ___ . ___ = \$ ___ . ___ /kWh

HOURLY USE APPLIANCES	days used per month	×	hrs. per day	×	kW per hr.	×	average rate per kW	=	cost per month
air conditioner	_____	×	_____	×	_____	×	\$__.__	=	\$__.__
blanket, electric	_____	×	.075 kW / night			×	\$__.__	=	\$__.__
coffee maker	_____	×	.120 kW / use			×	\$__.__	=	\$__.__
compact disc player (+ receiver)	_____	×	_____	×	_____	×	\$__.__	=	\$__.__
hair dryer	_____	×	_____	×	_____	×	\$__.__	=	\$__.__
heater (space / air)*	_____	×	_____	×	_____	×	\$__.__	=	\$__.__
iron, steam	_____	×	_____	×	_____	×	\$__.__	=	\$__.__
microwave oven	_____	×	_____	×	_____	×	\$__.__	=	\$__.__
oven*	_____	×	_____	×	_____	×	\$__.__	=	\$__.__
personal computer	_____	×	_____	×	_____	×	\$__.__	=	\$__.__
radio, portable	_____	×	_____	×	_____	×	\$__.__	=	\$__.__
rangetop burner (stove) (per burner)*	_____	×	_____	×	_____	×	\$__.__	=	\$__.__
receiver / radio (+CD, turntable, or?)	_____	×	_____	×	_____	×	\$__.__	=	\$__.__
swimming pool filter pump & sweep	_____	×	_____	×	_____	×	\$__.__	=	\$__.__
television (color or b/w?)	_____	×	_____	×	_____	×	\$__.__	=	\$__.__
toaster oven	_____	×	_____	×	_____	×	\$__.__	=	\$__.__
turntable (phonograph)	_____	×	_____	×	_____	×	\$__.__	=	\$__.__
vacuum cleaner	_____	×	_____	×	_____	×	\$__.__	=	\$__.__
video cassette recorder (VCR) (+TV)	_____	×	_____	×	_____	×	\$__.__	=	\$__.__
other: _____	_____	×	_____	×	_____	×	\$__.__	=	\$__.__
other: _____	_____	×	_____	×	_____	×	\$__.__	=	\$__.__

*NOTE: Many homes have GAS heaters, clothes dryers, stoves, and ovens, rather than electric.

TOTAL FROM THIS SIDE: \$_____.____

18.2 continued

lighting: approximately 100 kWh per month (adjust?)   × $ __ . ____ = $ ____ . __

water heater*: approximately 350 kWh per month (adjust?)   × $ __ . ____ = $ ____ . __

refrigerator/freezer: approx. 125 kWh per month (or from other side) × $ __ . ____ = $ ____ . __

freezer: approximately 100 kWh per month (or from other side)   × $ __ . ____ = $ ____ . __

waterbed: approximately 10 kWh per month   × $ __ . ____ = $ ____ . __

clothes washer: _____ loads per month × .25 kWh per load   × $ __ . ____ = $ ____ . __

clothes dryer*: _____ loads per month × 5 kWh per load   × $ __ . ____ = $ ____ . __

dishwasher (normal cycle) _____ loads per month × 1 kWh per load × $ __ . ____ = $ ____ . __

dishwasher (energy saver cycle) _____ loads/mo × .5 kWh per load × $ __ . ____ = $ ____ . __

self-cleaning oven*: _____ cleanings per month × 6 kWh per cleaning × $ __ . ____ = $ ____ . __

other: _____ × $ __ . ____ = $ ____ . __

other: _____ × $ __ . ____ = $ ____ . __

other: _____ × $ __ . ____ = $ ____ . __

*NOTE: Many homes have GAS water heaters, stoves, ovens, and clothes dryers.

TOTAL FROM THIS SIDE: $_____ . _____

TOTAL FROM THE OTHER SIDE: $_____ . _____

TOTAL OF BOTH SIDES: $_____ . _____

<u>electrical</u> portion of your utility bill: $_____ . _____.

    How close did your calculated total come to your actual electrical bill? How do you explain any significant (over 10%) difference?

18.3 "Watts" the Cost?: Questions

1. What are the two main energy users in your home?

    _____

    _____

2. If you cut back your electrical use for the single top energy user in your home by 5 percent, how much money would your family save each month?

    _____

    _____

3. If your family reduced its total electrical bill by 10 percent, how much money would you save each month? What would you do with that money?

    _____

    _____

4. List the three most necessary electrical users in your home. Tell why each is so necessary. What alternatives are there?

    _____

    _____

    _____

5. List the three least necessary electrical users in your home. For each, tell what you would do without it.

    _____

    _____

    _____

6. Discuss the statement: "We can reduce electrical use in our homes by 15 percent and still maintain good lifestyles."

    _____

    _____

    _____

7. How can saving energy in the home help the environment?

    _____

    _____

    _____

18.4 "Watts" the Cost? Parent Letter

Dear Parents:

As part of our study of electricity, electrical use, and energy conservation, we are studying electrical appliances and their energy use and costs. In order to do this study, the students have been asked to:

1. Survey their homes, listing all <u>electrical</u> appliances, their wattage, and how much they are used.

   (The students should find out whether your water heater, clothes dryer, stove/oven, and space (air) heating are electrical or gas.)
2. Obtain a utility bill. This will be used to determine the cost of a kilowatt-hour of electricity and the total electrical cost for the month. An old one will do nicely, so long as it is recent enough to show the current rates.

   Your assistance and cooperation with this assignment will be most appreciated.

   If you have any questions, please contact me at _____.

   Thank you!

Sincerely,

ACTIVITY 19: CONSERVE A WATT _____

Activity Summary

Using the information on electrical appliance use and costs from Activity 18 ("Watts" the Cost?), students consider ways to conserve energy in the home. They also consider ways to conserve energy outside the home. (If this activity can be done in the late fall, students could see real energy savings if they implemented the energy-saving methods during the winter months.)

Introduction

In Activity 18, we saw that some appliances use a lot of electricity and others use very little. While it is important to save energy wherever possible, it is often easy to save lots of electricity by making minor changes in our use of a few major energy-consuming appliances. To do this, we need to understand how much energy various appliances use and how we can reduce that use.

In addition to conserving energy by cutting back on major home appliance use, there are many ways to conserve energy outside the home. To do this, we need both to know how to conserve and to have a willingness to do so. Students need to know what their options are if they are going to make choices to conserve.

Grouping

Teams of 3 or 4 students

Time

Calculation of savings: 45–55 minutes

Generation of lists of ways to conserve and pros and cons, and discussion: 45–55 minutes

Anticipated Outcomes

The students will:

- increase their knowledge of ways to conserve electricity in their homes.
- increase their knowledge of ways to conserve energy outside the home.
- increase their willingness to make choices that reduce energy use.

Materials

—Photocopied student pages:

- 19.1 Conserve a Watt: Background Information (one per student)
- 19.2 Conserve a Watt: Instructions and Data (one per student)
- 19.3 Conserve a Watt: Questions (one per student)
- 19.4 Some Ways to Conserve Energy (optional) (one per student)

—Data from Activity 18, "Watts" the Cost? (18.2)

—Calculators will be useful

—It would be desirable to have a variety of books and pamphlets that tell how to conserve energy. See the listings under "References."

Vocabulary

None

Teacher Preparation

1. Photocopy the Background Information sheet (19.1), Instructions and Data sheets (19.2), Questions sheet (19.3), and, possibly, Some Ways to Conserve Energy (19.4).

2. If Activity 18 ("Watts" the Cost?) has not been done, duplicate the page of Approximate Energy Use for Some Appliances that is part of the Background Information sheet (18.1). Better yet, do the activity and have the students use their data from Activity 18 for this activity.

3. Obtain a variety of books and pamphlets that tell how to reduce energy use in the home.

Safety Considerations

None

Procedure

1. If Activity 18 has not been done, consider doing it. Alternatively, have the students complete the data table (18.2) using the Approximate Energy Use for Some Appliances sheet that is part of the Background Information (18.1) for Activity 18. Another alternative would be for you to provide data on energy use for an imaginary household for all students to use.

2. Issue the Instructions and Data sheets (19.2) and explain what the teams are to do.

3. Have the teams complete Part A in class.

4. Part B can be assigned as homework, or it can be done as a team on a subsequent day.

5. After the teams have calculated potential energy savings and ways to conserve, discuss their results as a whole class. A list of some ways to conserve energy (19.4) has been provided if you desire to use it for your own information or for a handout.

Discussion

1. Do the same appliances use the most energy in most students' homes?

2. How much electricity (and money) would be saved by reducing the energy used by each of the following by 20 percent?

    a. television

    b. clothes dryer

    c. space heater

    d. stereo (or CD or phonograph or radio)

    e. water heater

    f. lighting

3. What keeps people from cutting back energy use?

4. What encourages people to use more energy?

5. What could be done to encourage people to conserve energy?

6. What are some of our alternatives to using energy for:

    a. some necessities?

    b. some nonnecessities?

    c. some luxuries?

7. What are some environmental and political/social problems that result from excessive energy use?

8. What electrical appliance(s) could you do without?

Answers to 19.3, Conserve a Watt Questions

1. Answers will vary, but probably would include space (air) heating, water heating, and refrigeration or laundry uses. Students with gas heating or water heating will, of course, use less electricity for those uses. They should be reminded that the gas used counts as an energy cost, too.

2. Generally, the major energy users fulfill "needs" such as providing warmth, sanitation (hot water), and cooking. That, however, does not mean that energy can't be conserved in those uses.

3. Since most of our energy is used to fill needs, we should carefully consider how we can reduce those few energy uses. Doing something as simple as insulating can cut heating costs by 25 percent. For every degree that the space heater's thermostat is lowered, up to 5 percent is saved on heating costs! Using a water heater blanket and installing low-flow shower heads can save 20 percent of the hot water costs!

4. Answers will vary.

Extensions (See Activity 32 for suggestions for student projects.)

1. It is recommended that Activities 17 and 18 be done before doing this activity.

2. Have students make energy conservation posters and get them posted in local businesses such as grocery stores or hardware stores.

3. Contact your local utility company for suggestions for conserving energy.

4. Students can encourage energy conservation at school by giving presentations to the faculty, making posters to put up in classrooms, and forming an "energy patrol" to check classrooms at lunch or after school to be sure that lights and heaters or air conditioners are turned off.

5. After generating a list of ways to conserve energy in the home, have the students take the list home and discuss it with their parents.

6. Students can do energy conservation presentations in the community, at elemen-

tary schools, churches, business groups, service groups, or for youth groups such as scouts, campfire, or 4-H.

7. Join the National Energy Education Development project (N.E.E.D.). This project provides a wide range of current and varied energy education materials and ideas. Contact:

> N.E.E.D.
> P.O. Box 2518
> Reston, VA 22091
> (703) 860-5029

Modification

Include conservation of other resources besides energy.

References

Anonymous, *Home Energy-Saving Practices Checklist, Winter Bill Workbook,* and *Your Summer PG&E Bill Workbook.* San Francisco, CA: Pacific Gas and Electric Company, 1990.

Javna, John, *30 Simple Energy Things You Can Do to Save the Earth.* San Francisco, CA: The Earthworks Group and Pacific Gas and Electric Company, 1990.

Miller, G. Tyler, *Living in the Environment.* Belmont, CA: Wadsworth Publishing Company, 1990.

19.1 Conserve a Watt: Background Information

Energy conservation makes sense. Not only that, it makes dollars and cents! Nobody wants to waste energy, and nobody wants to waste money. Why, then, do we use so much energy and waste so much of it?

That is a very complex question. It involves personal ethics, choices, priorities, and knowledge. Most of us would be willing to reduce our energy use if we knew how to do it and if it were not too inconvenient. What can we do to save the most energy with the least inconvenience? Just how much are you willing to do to save energy? What choices do you have for saving energy and money? What are the pros and cons of those choices? What are our energy needs and wants?

Space (air) heating uses about 50 percent of the energy that we use in our homes. Water heating uses about 13 percent of the energy used in a typical home; air conditioning, lighting, and refrigeration each use about 9 percent, and all other home uses combined use about another 10 percent. Of course, these figures are averages, and the energy use in your home will probably be different.

How much energy would one save if one were to reduce their space heating energy costs by 10 percent? Since 10 percent of 50 percent is 5 percent, one could save 5 percent of the total home energy bill just by reducing space heating by 10 percent! What if you reduced lighting energy use by 10 percent? Ten percent of 9 percent is less than 1 percent, so reducing lighting by 10 percent would reduce your total home energy bill by less than 1 percent. So, IF you want to save energy by doing only one thing, you should consider reducing your space heating energy use!

Does this mean that we should not conserve on the energy used by appliances that use small amounts of energy? Not at all. Every bit of energy saved helps to preserve both the environment and your bank account! The energy used by "small" energy users such as kitchen appliances, audio systems, and televisions adds up! If you really want to save energy and money, you need to consider all of your opportunities to save.

Transportation is another major energy user. Private automobiles are the largest single energy user over which we have personal control. They use about 14 percent of the total energy used each year in the United States. That is more than home space heating, which uses about 11 percent! If you really want to save both money and energy, you should consider ways to reduce driving!

We should keep in mind, too, that our personal demands determine all the other energy uses. If we reduce our demands for goods, less energy will be spent making and selling them.

19.2 Conserve a Watt: Instructions

Part I: How Much Could I Save?

A. Using the data that you obtained in Activity 18 ("Watts" the Cost?), or using data supplied by your teacher, calculate the percentage of your electrical bill spent on the following types of home energy users. (Use the data table to show your data.)

lighting

television

water heating

space heating or air conditioning

clothes washing and drying

grooming (hair dryer, shaver, curlers, toothbrush, etc.)

refrigerator and freezer

cooking (oven, stove, microwave, toaster, etc.)

audio systems (phonograph, radio, CD, cassette)

B. Discuss your personal data with a team of students. Decide what is an average or typical percentage of energy used for each use by the people in your team. Use that average to calculate:

- how much each type of energy use costs in a typical month
- how much money could be saved by reducing each by 5%
- how much money could be saved by reducing each by 10%
- how much money could be saved by reducing each by 20%

C. How much money would be saved by reducing the entire electricity bill by:

10% per month?   10% per year?

20% per month?   20% per year?

Part II: Ways to Conserve

A. For each energy use, list ways to conserve energy and the advantages and disadvantages of each. Consider not only reducing the use, but substituting alternatives. Consider not only what you can do now, but what you will be able to do when you are living on your own, whether it is in a single-family residence, condominium, apartment, or other arrangement.

B. List other ways of conserving energy in the home.

C. Since the private automobile is a major energy user, list ways to reduce the use of energy by private automobiles.

19.2 Conserve a Watt: Data

Part I: How Much Could I Save?

A. My energy use:

   1. My home electrical use costs about $ _____ per month.

   2. Itemized use:

     lighting . . . . _____ % = $ _____

     refrigerator and freezer . . . . _____ % = $ _____

     television (and VCR) . . . . _____ % = $ _____

     cooking . . . . _____ % = $ _____

     water heating . . . . _____ % = $ _____

     audio systems . . . . _____ % = $ _____

     space heating or air conditioning . . . . _____ % = $ _____

     clothes washing and drying . . . . _____ % = $ _____

     grooming . . . . _____ % = $ _____

B. My team's average cost per month and savings of various percentages:

   1. Our average home electrical use costs about $ _____ per month.

   2. Itemized use:

	average percentage	average cost/mo	$ saved with use reduction of		
			5%	10%	20%
lighting	_____ % =	$ _____	$ _____	$ _____	$ _____
refrigerator and freezer	_____ % =	$ _____	$ _____	$ _____	$ _____
television (and VCR)	_____ % =	$ _____	$ _____	$ _____	$ _____
cooking	_____ % =	$ _____	$ _____	$ _____	$ _____
water heating	_____ % =	$ _____	$ _____	$ _____	$ _____
audio systems	_____ % =	$ _____	$ _____	$ _____	$ _____
space heating or air conditioning. .	_____ % =	$ _____	$ _____	$ _____	$ _____
clothes washing and drying	_____ % =	$ _____	$ _____	$ _____	$ _____
grooming	_____ % =	$ _____	$ _____	$ _____	$ _____

C. Reducing the entire energy bill by 10% would save $_____/month and _____/year. Reducing the entire energy bill by 20% would save $_____/month and _____/year.

Part II: Ways to Conserve

A. use	ways to reduce use or alternative	advantages	disadvantages
lighting			
refrigeration			
television/VCR			
cooking			
water heating			
audio system			
space heating or air conditioning			
clothes washing and drying			
grooming			

B. What are some other ways to conserve energy (electricity or gas) in the home?

_____

_____

C. What are some ways to conserve energy in transportation?

_____

_____

_____

D. What energy uses could you completely eliminate from your home? What would you do instead?

_____

_____

_____

_____

19.3 Conserve a Watt: Questions

1. What were the three major electricity users in the home?

   _____ _____ _____

2. Compare the major energy users with those that use less electricity in regard to their importance—how much electricity is used to fill "needs" as opposed to "wants"?

   _____

   _____

   _____

3. If most of our energy is used to fulfill needs, does that mean we can't reduce the energy used to fill needs? Why or why not?

   _____

   _____

   _____

4. Discuss the following statements:

   a. If we cut back on our space heating, we don't need to conserve on lighting.

      _____

      _____

   b. If we eliminate three of our smaller electricity users, that is enough.

      _____

      _____

   c. Why should I conserve if other people won't?

      _____

      _____

   d. There's nothing that I can do because my parents pay the utility bills.

      _____

      _____

      _____

   e. I want to conserve energy because it is the right thing to do, and it saves money!

      _____

      _____

      _____

19.4 Some Ways to Conserve Energy

The following list is by no means complete. The percentages in parentheses after the suggestions are approximate potential energy (and therefore money!) savings for that use.

All Appliances and Other Energy Users:

- Carefully consider whether you really need the appliance.
- When purchasing appliances, select the most energy-efficient model. (5–25%)
- Keep all appliances in good working order and make them last as long as possible.
- Be concerned about saving energy elsewhere. Recycle, reduce consumption, and look for other ways to save energy.

Lighting:

- Turn off lights whenever they are not in use. Open curtains and blinds if it is not too cold.
- Switch to fluorescent lights wherever possible. (30–38%)
- Use dimmer switches and/or timers. (7–10%)
- When you purchase bulbs, buy one with the needed amount of **lumens,** not watts.

Refrigeration:

- Operate the refrigerator at normal settings.
- Keep the condenser coils clean of dust.
- Check the door gasket for a tight seal.
- Decide what you want before opening the refrigerator door. Open the door as infrequently as possible.

Television/VCR Use:

- Turn them off when they aren't being used.
- Cut back on use. There are thousands of other things to do. (How many can you name?)

Cooking:

- Except when baking, don't preheat ovens. Turn the oven off before the dish is completely cooked.
- Use a microwave or toaster oven when possible.
- Cook complete meals of several dishes at once. Make enough for leftovers.
- When food needs to be thawed prior to cooking, let it thaw on the counter or in the refrigerator, rather than heating it.
- Cook on rangetop burners when possible, rather than in the oven.
- Use the air-dry setting on the dishwasher, rather than using heat to dry dishes.
- Wash dishes by hand, using plastic pans for soap and rinse water.

Audio Systems:

- Turn them off when they are not in use.
- Find some other entertainment.
- Take good care of them so that they last longer.

Water Heating

- Wrap your water heater in a water heater blanket. (6–10%)
- Set the water heater thermostat to 120°F or 140°F if you have a dishwasher. (7–11%)
- Insulate water-heater pipes.
- Install low-flow shower heads and flow restrictors or aerators on faucets. (5–10%)
- Take short showers or baths with less water.
- Don't let the hot water run while shaving or rinsing dishes.
- Operate dishwashers and clothes washers only with full loads.
- Use a solar pool cover or thermal blanket.
- Investigate a solar hot-water system.

Space (Air) Heating and Air Conditioning

- Insulate. (25% of heating costs)
- Rather than turning heaters and air conditioners on, adjust your clothing appropriately.
- Adjust the thermostat. (Lower the heater and raise the air conditioner thermostats.) (5–20%)
- Weatherstrip doors and windows and caulk other air leaks around pipes and other openings.
- Install storm or thermal windows.
- Turn off thermostats or close vents in unused rooms. (up to 10%)
- Install clock thermostats or set-back thermostats.
- Keep the furnace and filter in good repair. (up to 5%)
- Use passive solar energy on sunny days and close curtains on cold days. (8–10%)
- Open windows and doors and use fans for circulating air.
- Turn the gas furnace pilot light off in the warm seasons. (3–9%)
- Avoid using major appliances between noon and 6 P.M.
- Provide shading for air conditioning condenser. (5–11%)
- Install thermal curtains.

Clothes Washing and Drying:

- Operate clothes washers and dryers only with full loads.
- Use a clothesline instead of a dryer.

- Use cold or cool water washes and rinses when possible.
- Be sure the lint filter is clean.

Grooming:

- Don't leave hot or cold water running.
- Wear a hair style that doesn't require blow drying or hair sprays.
- Don't use electric toothbrushes or other unnecessary appliances.

Transportation:

- Walk, ride a bike, carpool, take public transportation. Do whatever you can to reduce the use of the private car with only one person in it!
- Avoid unnecessary trips. Plan your trips so that you do several errands on one trip.
- Keep your car tuned up properly.
- Keep your tires properly inflated.
- Don't carry unnecessary weight in the trunk.
- Make good mileage a high priority when purchasing a car.

ACTIVITY 20: KEEP THE HEAT! _____

Activity Summary

Students test the insulating values of various materials.

Introduction

For most homes, the single largest energy user is heating or air conditioning. Additionally, home energy use accounts for a large portion of the carbon dioxide, sulfur dioxide, and nitrogen oxides that pollute our air.

There are numerous things that can be done to decrease energy use and waste in existing homes. Such retrofitting can include adding insulation to ceilings, adding "blown-in" insulation to walls, caulking, weather stripping, installing insulating blinds or curtains, and replacing inefficient heaters and air conditioners with energy efficient models.

When building a new home or other building, or when adding a room, there are many opportunities for saving energy and money. Proper design, incorporating solar heating and lighting, ample insulation, superinsulating windows and doors, weather stripping and caulking, appliance selection, and many other features add to the initial costs, but pay for themselves in a surprisingly short time.

In this investigation, students test the insulating qualities of a variety of materials. Students can be involved with the experimental design, allowing the instructor to point out the importance of using standardized methods and equipment.

Grouping

Teams of 3–5 students.

Time

Introducing the insulation activity: 5–10 minutes
Building insulation testers: 10–15 minutes
Testing insulators: 30 minutes
Discussing investigation: 30–45 minutes

Anticipated Outcomes

The students will:

- understand how insulation works to prevent heat energy transfer.
- understand the meaning of "R-value."
- appreciate the value of insulation.

Materials

—Photocopied student pages:

- 20.1 Keep the Heat! Background Information (one per student)
- 20.2 Keep the Heat! Instructions and Data (one per team)

- 20.3 Keep the Heat! Questions (1 per student)

—Per team of students:

- 4 two-pound or three-pound coffee cans, with plastic lids (see Modification 2.)
- 4 thermometers (°C)
- 4 cans that will fit inside the coffee cans, such as 10.75-oz. soup cans or 16-oz. vegetable cans
- 1–4 large (250–1000 ml) graduated cylinders or graduated beakers

—Various types of insulating materials to test, including:

- sand
- shredded newspaper
- corrugated cardboard strips
- sawdust
- socks or other thick cloth
- strips of old blankets
- quilting batting
- pieces of Styrofoam
- portions of old coats (check flea markets, garage sales, or second-hand stores)
- construction insulation, including rigid foam, fiberglass, "blown-in"
- feathers
- wool

—Hot water: about 40–60 oz. per team, depending on the size of the interior cans

Vocabulary

insulation   R-value

Teacher Preparation

1. Photocopy the Background Information sheet (20.1), Instructions and Data sheets (20.2), and Questions sheet (20.3).
2. Obtain samples of as many insulation types as possible. (Contact an insulation company for samples, literature, and costs.)
3. Obtain coffee cans and other materials listed above.
4. Contact your local utility company regarding gas and electrical rates and any assistance programs that may be available for adding insulation. Find out how much money would be saved in a typical home by installing various amounts of insulation. Contact a local insulation company to find out how much such insulation would cost when a home is retrofitted and when a home is built. Calculate how long it would take for the insulation to pay for itself through reduced energy costs.
5. Contact your local building inspector regarding insulation recommendations and requirements.

SAFETY CONSIDERATIONS

1. Students should wear gloves and face masks when handling fiberglass insulation.
2. Students should wear safety goggles when heating or handling very hot water.

Procedure

1. Several weeks before doing the activity, ask the students to bring 2-pound or 3-pound coffee cans, with plastic lids, to school. Rinse them out.

2. Several weeks before doing the activity, ask the students to bring several clean 10- to 16-oz. cans. (Each team will need four identical cans that will fit inside the coffee cans.)

3. Prepare a sample insulation tester as described on the student Instructions and Data sheet (20.2).

4. Issue and discuss the Background Information sheet (20.1).

5. Issue and discuss the student Instructions and Data sheet (20.2). Have the students build their insulation testers and predict which will insulate the best.

6. Have the students heat the water to 90–100°C and add it to their testers. Remind them to be careful to keep the insulation dry when adding the water and to add the same amount of water to each can.

7. Have the students record the starting water temperature and record the temperature every five minutes for 30 minutes.

8. Discuss the results.

9. Assign the students to investigate the costs and benefits of adding insulation to homes and water heaters.

10. Discuss the results of their investigations.

Discussion

1. Which materials insulated well? Which didn't?
2. Did the materials that insulated well have any common characteristics?
3. What are the advantages and disadvantages of each material?
4. Why was it important for a team to use the same kind of inner cans and outer container with each test?
5. Why was it important to record the starting temperature of the water in each container?
6. Why was it important to use the same amount of water for each test?
7. What was the purpose of the tester with no insulation, the control?
8. Insulation adds to the cost of building a home. Will that cost be recovered with energy savings?

Answers to 20.3, Keep the Heat! Questions

1. Commercially available foam insulation will probably be the best insulator, but answers will vary.

2. Good insulators generally have lots of spaces in which air is trapped.

3. Good insulators generally will prevent heat loss and heat gain. They slow or reduce heat transfer in either direction.

4. a. Reducing heating and air conditioning will reduce air pollution because less oil, coal, and natural gas will be burned to generate electricity or be burned in furnaces.

   b. Reducing heating and air conditioning will reduce water pollution because less oil will need to be shipped or transferred with pipes, fewer wells will need to be drilled, less coal will need to be mined and shipped. Also, burning fossil fuels contributes to acidic precipitation, which pollutes water as well as the land.

   c. Reducing heating and air conditioning will help protect wildlife habitat by reducing air and water pollution and by reducing the need to drill more wells and mine more coal.

   d. Reducing energy use reduces the need for nuclear power plants and all of their associated environmental, health, and financial problems.

5. Simply turning the heater thermostat down (so that it comes on at, for example, 68°F rather than at 72°F) will reduce heating costs tremendously. For every degree lower in the 60° to 70° range, up to 5 percent is saved on heating costs! Heaters can be turned off or down as low as possible at night or when leaving home for the day. Caulking and weather stripping are inexpensive, easy, and effective. Checking and replacing furnace filters is inexpensive and important. Not heating unused rooms, wearing sweaters, using warmer blankets, closing curtains and blinds at night and opening them on sunny days all help. There are many other ways to save heat and money.

6. Simply turning the air-conditioner thermostat up (so that it comes on at, for example, 78°F rather than at 72°F) will reduce air-conditioning costs tremendously. A setting of 78°, rather than 74°, for example, will save about 12 percent of air-conditioning costs! Air conditioners should be turned off when leaving home for a long period of time. Checking and replacing filters is inexpensive and important. Not cooling unused rooms, using fans, wearing fewer clothes, closing curtains or blinds on the south side, opening windows and doors (without the air conditioner being on), and cooking only when it is cooler will all help to reduce air-conditioning costs. There are many other ways to reduce air-conditioning costs.

Extensions (See Activity 32 for suggestions for student projects.)

1. Record the insulating ability of various insulating materials. Have a contest to see who can find the best insulator.

2. Have the students graph the temperatures as compared to time. Using different colors to plot the data from several insulators on one graph is a good way to compare the insulators.

3. Arrange for guest speakers on the topic of insulation or energy conservation. Possible sources:

   • your local utility company
   • a local insulation supplier / building supply (possible field trip)
   • a local company that installs insulation
   • a building inspector

4. Obtain samples of as many different types of insulation and water-heater blankets as possible.

5. Demonstrate how to install insulation or water-heater blankets.

6. Have an insulation salesperson or installer discuss career opportunities.

Modifications

1. Use cold water in place of hot water. Do the same insulators protect against heat gain?

2. Rather than coffee cans, cardboard boxes can be used. It is important that a team either uses the same box for each test or that they use identical boxes.

3. Beakers, large test tubes, or other containers would work as the water containers. Cans are recommended because metal conducts heat well. Aluminum cans work well.

4. If your thermometers are too long to fit inside the coffee can with its lid, use a cork borer or nail to poke a hole in the center of the lid. Use a rubber no-roll sleeve or masking tape to suspend the thermometer so that it doesn't touch the side of the can.

5. If you have materials, have the students test more than three.

References

Anonymous, *Winter Bill Workbook* and *Your Summer PG&E Bill Workbook*. San Francisco, CA: Pacific Gas and Electric Company, 1990.

Miller, G. Tyler, *Living in the Environment*. Belmont, CA: Wadsworth Publishing Company, 1990.

Tourtillot, Leeann, *Conserve & Renew*. Sacramento, CA: California Energy Extension Service, 1990.

20.1 Keep the Heat!: Background Information

In most homes, heating and air conditioning use more energy than any other item except, possibly, the private automobile. There are many things that can be done to reduce energy used in the home. Appliance use can be reduced. Windows and doors can be weather stripped. Openings can be caulked. Heaters can be turned down or off. Lights can be used less. The list of energy-saving opportunities in the home is a long one!

Many energy-saving methods involve simple behavior changes like turning off unused lights and other appliances. Some involve changing the home itself. There are estimates that current technology could save over 50 percent of the energy used in existing buildings in the United States if it were utilized to the maximum. We have the technology to reduce the energy used in new buildings by over 70 percent! The average home in Sweden used only about one-third as much energy as the average American home of the same size!

One of the best ways to save energy in the home is to be sure that it is properly insulated. **Insulation** prevents the passage of heat energy into the home in the summer and out of the home in the winter. Our clothing keeps us warm by insulting us with a layer of air that is trapped within the fabric. Down, wool, and some synthetic materials are so effective because they trap a lot of air, thereby providing a lot of insulating.

The ability of a material to insulate is indicated by its **"R-value."** The higher the R-value, the better the insulator. A single-pane glass window has an R-value of 1. Double-glazed windows have an R-value of 2, and many triple-glazed windows have R-values of about 5. There are "superinsulating" windows that have R-values of R-10 to R-12! In many areas, the energy saved by such windows would pay for the extra cost in only two to four years! Reducing heat lost through windows is important because about 16 percent of the heat that is lost is lost through windows!

Another place where a lot of energy is lost is through the walls, floors, and ceilings. Installing proper insulation in walls, ceilings, and floors can reduce heating costs by as much as 25 percent or more!

There are a variety of materials available for insulating houses. They range from natural wood and stone to synthetic fiberglass and foam. Some are even made from recycled paper!

In this activity, you will be investigating the insulating properties of various materials. Keep in mind that any energy saved also means that less oil, coal, and natural gas have to be removed from the Earth. That means that there is less chance of oil spills and less habitat destruction. Keep in mind, too, that burning coal, oil, and natural gas pollutes the air and adds to acidic precipitation and many other environmental problems.

20.2 Keep the Heat! Instructions

Your teacher will demonstrate how to build a simple insulation tester. You will use it to test the insulating qualities of various materials.

Your team will make four different insulation testers, or will use one tester to test four different insulators.

If you use only one, be sure to allow time for the inside container to return to room temperature between tests.

1. Obtain three different kinds of insulating materials. Be sure to obtain enough to completely fill the space between the inner container and the outer container.

2. Assemble three insulation testers, using a different type of insulation in each.

3. Assemble one tester with no insulating material other than air. This is a "control" for your experiment. Compare other insulators to it.

4. Measure the volume of your inner container(s). Heat enough water to fill all four of them. Heat the water to 90–100°C.

5. When the water is hot, carefully pour it into the inner container(s). Be sure to keep the insulation dry. Do this for each tester.

6. Record the starting temperature of the water in each container.

7. In each tester, record the water temperature every 5 minutes for 30 minutes.

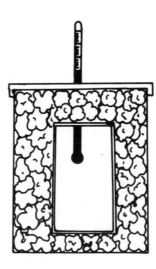

20.2 Keep the Heat!: Data

List the insulation types to be tested.

1. air (no insulation . . . control)

2. _____

3. _____

4. _____

    Predict: Which type of insulation do you predict will keep the water hot longest? (i.e., Which will be the best insulator?) Why?

_____

_____

insulation type	starting temp. (° C)	temperature after this many minutes					
		5	10	15	20	25	30
1. none (air) . . .(control)							
2.							
3.							
4.							
(If you have time and materials, test additional types of insulation.)							
5.							
6.							

20.3 Keep the Heat!: Questions

1. Which of the materials tested was the best insulator?

   your team: _____ the class: _____

2. What properties do the good insulators share that make them good insulators?

   _____

   _____

3. Would a material that is a good insulator against heat loss also be a good insulator against gaining heat? How could you test this?

   _____

   _____

4. How does reducing heating and air-conditioning energy use and costs help:
   a. reduce air pollution

   _____

   _____

   b. reduce water pollution

   _____

   _____

   c. protect wildlife habitat

   _____

   _____

   d. reduce the need for nuclear power plants

   _____

   _____

5. Even though it will pay for itself in a surprisingly short time, insulating a home is expensive. What are some other ways that you could reduce your heating costs in the winter?

   _____

   _____

6. Running an air conditioner takes a lot of energy and is expensive. What are some ways that you could reduce your air conditioning expenses?

   _____

   _____

ACTIVITY 21: CATCH THE SUN! _____

Activity Summary

Students design and build models of homes and investigate various factors that contribute to collecting solar heat in a home.

Introduction

While it is likely that few of your students will actually design their own homes, investigating solar home heating is interesting and enjoyable for most students. They can learn about utilizing solar energy, heat and heat transfer, energy transformations, weather, botany, matter, and even astronomy as they learn about ways to take advantage of the sun's light and heat.

In the basic activity, the students investigate the effect of south-facing windows on air temperature inside of their "houses," which are made from cardboard boxes. In the "Extensions" section, many additional ideas are suggested as possible investigations. It is highly recommended that students be encouraged to investigate some of these factors.

The heat gain of the model home will be greatest when the sky is clear, but it need not be warm or hot. It is interesting and instructive to compare the results gathered on clear, cool days to those gathered on clear, warm days, and those collected on a clear day to data collected on a cloudy day.

Grouping

Teams of 2–3 students.

Time

Introduction and building the "home": 45–55 minutes
Testing the home model and discussing the data: 45–55 minutes

Anticipated Outcomes

The students will:

- increase their understanding of passive solar heating.
- learn about factors that affect the collection of solar energy.

Materials

—Photocopied student pages:

- 21.1 Catch the Sun! Background Information (one per student)
- 21.2 Catch the Sun! Instructions and Data (one per team)
- 21.3 Catch the Sun! Questions (one per student)

—For each team:

- two thermometers
- two identical cardboard boxes with lids
- enough clear plastic wrap to cover two of the larger sides of the boxes (clear acetate sheets such as those used on overhead projectors can be used)
- masking or transparent tape
- knife or single-edged razor blade
- ruler ("T squares" are useful if you can obtain them)

Vocabulary

active solar   fossil fuel   nonrenewable
passive solar   solar

Teacher Preparation

1. Photocopy the Background Information sheet (21.1), Instructions and Data sheets (21.2), and Questions sheet (21.3).
2. Obtain the necessary materials.

SAFETY CONSIDERATION

Caution the students to be careful when using the knife or razor blade.

Procedure

1. Obtain the materials. You might want to standardize the box size and shape so that the students' data are more comparable. You might want to use a variety of box sizes and shapes and let that be a variable to be investigated. Consider having the students obtain the boxes, but remind them that each team will need two identical boxes.
2. Build a sample.
3. Have the students build their "homes" as described on the Instructions sheet (21.2).
4. Have the students place their homes in the sun.
5. Have the students record the temperature inside the boxes every 5 minutes for 30 minutes.
6. Discuss the results.
7. Discuss modifications that could be done to increase or reduce heating. See "Extensions."

Discussion

1. What effect did the window cover have on the heat gain?
2. What would increasing the size of the "window" do to the heat gain?
3. Did the size or shape of the box have any effect on the results?

4. What other factors might we test besides the effect of covering the window? (See "Extensions.")

Answers to 21.3, Catch the Sun! Questions

1. The home with the uncovered window should heat up faster.

2. The home with the uncovered window should get warmer.

3. The home with the uncovered window would probably cool off faster at night.

4. If these were real homes, one might do such things as paint the house a dark color or install more windows to increase the rate and amount of heating.

5. If these were real homes, one might do such things as reduce window area, paint the house white or some other light color, plant shade trees, install a reflective coating on the windows, or insulate to reduce the rate and amount of heating.

6. a. In Anchorage, solar homes would need a lot of south-facing glass. Since it gets so cold there, however, it would be very important to have superinsulated glass.

    b. In Phoenix, it would be important to have shading on the windows designed so that they do not add too much heat to the home in the winter. It is possible to calculate the proper overhang so that light can enter the windows in the winter when the sun is lower in the sky.

    c. Since Sydney is in the southern hemisphere, it would be important to face the windows to the north, rather than to the south.

7. Solar energy can be used to heat water, generate electricity, cook, and even to cool homes.

8. The <u>advantages</u> of solar energy include its lack of pollution, inexhaustability, and the fact that, except for installation and maintenance of the equipment, it is free. Solar energy's main <u>disadvantages</u> are the cost of the original equipment (in some applications) and problems with storage in cloudy weather or at night.

Extensions (See Activity 32 for suggestions for student projects.)

1. Students can make their "houses" as realistic as they wish by adding more windows, doors, peaked roofs, and so forth.

2. Have the students investigate variables such as:

    a. increasing window space

    b. adding windows to other sides

    c. painting the house various colors

    d. covering the house with foil or mylar

    e. insulation in the walls, floor, or ceiling

    f. adding a roof overhang

    g. adding an opening in the top

    h. allowing "leaks" around the window or elsewhere

    i. placing the house in the shade

    j. placing heat-absorbing materials inside the house; examples might be rocks, tiles, or jars of water.

   k. the effect of a peaked roof with or without roof vents

   l. adding open windows

   m. adding blinds or curtains to the window(s)

   n. adding a small fan (solar powered?) and open windows

3. Teams of students can compete to try to design and build the house that will:

   a. gain the most heat in 45 minutes

   b. gain the least heat in 45 minutes

   c. retain the heat gained for the longest period of time when brought inside or into the shade

   d. reach a certain temperature fastest

4. Invite a local architect to discuss solar home designs with the class. Try to find one who can bring slides to show.

5. Visit a local solar home. (Your local building inspector, university, or an architect might be able to help locate one.)

6. Have the students prepare written and oral reports on other uses of the sun such as cooking, cooling, water heating, photovoltaics, solar-powered cars, generating electricity on "solar farms," and so forth.

7. Have the students build solar water heaters, ovens, boilers, solar cell-powered model cars, and other solar devices.

Modification

Students can be provided with a paper template to use to build a small "house." An example can be found in *Hot Water and Warm Homes from Sunlight* by Alan Gould.

References

Anonymous, *Science Activities in Energy: Solar Energy*. Washington DC: U.S. Department of Energy, Education Division, 1980.

Gould, Alan, *Hot Water and Warm Homes from Sunlight*. Berkeley, CA: Lawrence Hall of Science, University of California at Berkeley, 1990.

Miller, G. Tyler, *Living in the Environment*. Belmont, CA: Wadsworth Publishing Company, 1990.

21.1 Catch the Sun!: Background Information

People have always used the sun as a heating source. When we open our window curtains to let the sun in, we are using **solar** energy. When we burn wood in our fireplaces, we are using solar energy that has been stored by trees. Even when we use oil, coal, or natural gas to heat our homes, we are using solar energy that has been stored in these **"fossil fuels"** for millions of years. Since most of our electricity is generated by burning fossil fuels, even most of our electricity is generated by stored solar energy!

As the price of **nonrenewable** fossil fuels increases, and as people become more aware of and concerned about the environmental problems caused by fossil fuels and nuclear power, people are looking more closely at using solar energy for heating their homes. Solar energy can be used to produce electricity, heat water, cook, or even to cool homes!

When we use solar energy without electrical devices to increase circulation, it is called **"passive"** solar technology. A simple window is an example of a passive solar energy collector.

When we use fans or pumps to circulate the heated air or water, that is called **"active"** solar technology. Many rooftop solar water heaters use pumps and so are referred to as active systems.

There are about 500,000 homes in the United States that have passive solar designs. Many of these homes are not in the southern states where one might expect them to be more common. In fact, effective, affordable, and comfortable solar-heated homes can and have been built in most areas of the United States. As energy costs increase and new designs and technology become available, more solar homes will be built.

Solar energy can be focused on materials to be burned or melted in a furnace. It can also be focused on boilers to produce steam to generate electricity. There are several places in the world, including some in the United States, where solar energy is currently being used to generate electricity commercially. A 200-megawatt plant near Los Angeles produces enough electricity for 270,000 people. Such plants cost no more than nuclear power plants, take much less time to build, use a renewable energy source, and do not produce dangerous nuclear by-products.

Solar energy can be converted directly to electricity by solar cells (photovoltaic cells). You have probably seen or used a calculator that is powered by a solar cell. Groups of cells can be coupled together to form panels that can be mounted on houses, cars, and even airplanes! They provide electricity that can be used immediately or stored in batteries. Photovoltaic technology is advancing rapidly, and electricity produced by solar cells may soon be competitive with other sources of electricity. It already is competitive in out-of-the-way places where it is not economical to run electrical lines.

© 1993 by The Center for Applied Research in Education

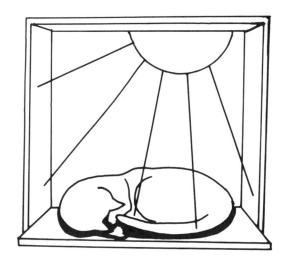

21.2 Catch the Sun!: Instructions

In this activity, you will use cardboard boxes to construct two "homes." Each will have a plastic "window." One home's window will be covered with cardboard. You will then place your homes in the sun and record the air temperature inside of each for 30 minutes.

Your teacher will explain how to construct your "home."

When you cut the cardboard out to form the windows, save one piece to use as a window cover.

The thermometer can either be placed in the home where it is visible through the window, or it can be suspended in the "ceiling" (box top) in such a way that the bulb is inside the home near the ceiling and the temperature can be read from the outside of the box.

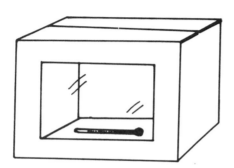 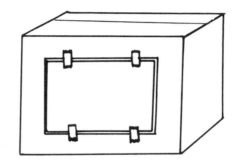

When the thermometer has stabilized, record the starting temperature in each "home." Then place both "homes" in the sun with the windows facing toward the sun. Be sure to place them in a place where they won't become shaded before they have been in the sun for 30 minutes.

Record the temperature of each house every 5 minutes for 30 minutes.

21.2 Catch the Sun!: Data

Record the starting temperatures after the thermometers have stabilized. Then take readings every 5 minutes for 30 minutes.

description of the "home" (materials, dimensions, color, window area, etc.)	temperature readings (°C) after this many minutes:						
	start	5	10	15	20	25	30
(with window covered) dimensions: ____ × ____ × ____ volume: _____ window area: _____ × _____ = _____ material: other notes:							
(with window <u>not</u> covered) dimensions: ____ × ____ × ____ volume: _____ window area: _____ × _____ = _____ material: other notes:							

21.3 Catch the Sun!: Questions

1. Which "home" heated up faster?_____

2. Which "home" got warmer?_____

3. Which home do you think would cool off faster at night?_____

4. If this were a real home, how could you **increase** the amount or rate of heating?

   _____

   _____

5. If this were a real home, what could you do to **decrease** the amount or rate of heating?

   _____

   _____

6. What would be the implications of this activity if you were designing a home to be built in the following places:

   a. Anchorage, Alaska:

   _____

   b. Phoenix, Arizona:

   _____

   c. Sydney, Australia:

   _____

7. Besides space heating, how can solar energy be used?

   _____

   _____

   _____

   _____

8. What are some of the advantages and disadvantages of solar energy?

   advantages: _____

   _____

   _____

   disadvantages: _____

   _____

   _____

ACTIVITY 22: FOSSIL FUEL EXTRACTION _____

Activity Summary

Students "mine" cookies containing raisins, nuts, and chocolate as a simulation of mining for coal, oil, and natural gas.

Introduction

Often, when we discuss saving resources, we think only of saving that particular resource itself. We think of saving oil or electricity or water or trees. It is important to realize the interconnectedness of various resources. For example, when we reduce paper use, we are also reducing water and air pollution, saving habitat for many kinds of plants and animals, saving energy, protecting watersheds, and reducing erosion. When we reduce fossil fuel use, we also reduce air pollution and water pollution and protect habitats. In this activity, students "mine" cookies or brownies to obtain raisins, nuts, and chocolate from within. This serves as a model for removing fossil fuels from the Earth and points out that the removal of fossil fuels has a great impact on the environment.

   While this activity is simple and fun, it is useful as a reminder to students that wasting energy has many effects beyond the wasted energy itself.

Grouping

Individual or teams of 2–3, depending on how many cookies you want to make.

Time

45–55 minutes

Anticipated Outcomes

The students will:

 • increase their understanding of the environmental impacts of mining for fossil fuels or other Earth resources.
 • increase their willingness to reduce energy and other resource waste.

Materials

—Photocopied student pages:

 • 22.1 Fossil Fuel Extraction: Background Information (one per student)
 • 22.2 Fossil Fuel Extraction: Instructions and Data (one per student or team)
 • 22.3 Fossil Fuel Extraction: Questions (one per student)

—Per individual or team of 2–3 students:

 • 1 cookie containing chocolate chips, raisins, and walnut pieces
 • 1 toothpick
 • 1 saucer or small plate

Vocabulary

crude oil   fossil fuel   fractional distillation
nonrenewable resource   strip mining

Teacher Preparation

1. Photocopy the Background Information sheet (22.1), Instructions and Data sheet (22.2), and Questions sheet (22.3).
2. Obtain materials for baking cookies and bake them. Use whatever recipe you like, making at least one cookie per student or team of students. (You might work something out with a home economics teacher to get the cookies baked.)

SAFETY CONSIDERATION

Caution the students not to eat cookies that other people have handled. (You might consider providing some sort of snack to be eaten after the activity. This should reduce the temptation of the students to eat the cookies.)

Procedure

1. Either bake the cookies or arrange to have them baked.
2. Distribute the Background Information sheet and have the students read and discuss it.
3. Distribute the Instructions sheet and discuss the procedures to follow.
4. Distribute the cookies and toothpicks (on saucers, rather than on paper towels or napkins).
5. Have the students "mine" their cookies, recording their data.
6. Discuss the activity.

Discussion

1. What happened to the "land" (represented by the cookie) when you mined for the fossil fuels?
2. Were any crumbs spilled on the floor or table? What is erosion?
3. What would happen to the plants and animals that lived on land that was mined in this way?
4. What could be done to reduce the damage done to the environment by such mining?
5. If we use less energy, we need less fossil fuel. If we need less fossil fuel, we don't need to do so much mining. What can you do to reduce energy use?

Answers to 22.3, Fossil Fuel Extraction Questions

1. Coal is a nonrenewable resource. Surface mining coal severely disturbs the land and the plants and animals that live there. Underground mining and surface min-

ing both produce water pollution. Underground mining is very dangerous. Burning coal produces air pollution, acidic precipitation, and water pollution.

2. Since much coal is used to produce electricity, saving electricity will reduce the need to mine and burn coal. Supporting the passage of strict pollution control laws will help. We need to be willing to pay for the costs of reducing pollution.

3. Oil is a nonrenewable resource. Oil spills can and do occur when oil is mined, transported, and used. Burning oil produces air pollution and contributes to acidic precipitation and water pollution.

4. Anything that we do to save electricity also helps reduce the need for oil. Since so much oil is used for transportation, especially private automobiles, driving less, keeping cars tuned properly, using more fuel-efficient cars and many other transportation-related changes of behavior can help. Supporting the passage of strict pollution control laws will help. We need to be willing to pay for the costs of reducing pollution.

5. Electricity production is the main use for coal in the United States. Saving electricity means less coal will need to be mined and burned.

6. There are many ways to reduce electricity use. Reducing space heating and air conditioning, water heating, and lighting uses are important. See Activities 17, 18, and 19.

7. See question 4.

8. Saving electricity, driving less, supporting public transportation, recycling used motor oil, and many other things can save oil.

9. Natural gas is a nonrenewable resource, and burning it produces some air pollution. It burns much cleaner than other fossil fuels and gives a lot of heat when it burns.

Extensions (See Activity 32 for suggestions for student projects.)

1. This activity is similar to Activity 1, Surface Mining. If you have not yet done it, consider doing it after doing this one.

2. Activity 10, Oil Spill!; Activity 14, Acidic Precipitation; and Activity 15, Global Warming, are also closely related to this activity.

3. Visit a local mine and find out about measures taken to reduce environmental damage.

4. Write to coal and oil companies or organizations to find out about environmental protection measures they take. See Activity 25 for some addresses.

5. To understand fractional distillation, make a mixture of alcohol and water. Have the students distill off the alcohol by heating the mixture to about 80°C.

Modifications

1. Rather than individual cookies, make a pan of brownies. This enables you to bury the nuts, raisins, and chocolate chips deeper.

2. Rather than chocolate chips, use candy-coated chocolate pieces such as M&M's.®

3. Use only chocolate pieces, and have the students keep track of how many chips they successfully remove. (One chip represents a community's energy needs for one

week.) Point out that energy is used in the "mining" process, and it takes time, energy, and money to restore the land. Students can be "charged" chocolate chips based on how much damage they do to the land. For example:

Cookie still in one piece, relatively undamaged:	1 chip charged
Cookie in 2–3 pieces:	2 chips charged
Cookie in more than 3 pieces:	3 chips charged
Cookie in crumbs:	5 chips charged

References

Anonymous, *If the Earth Were a Cookie.* Washington, DC: National Science Foundation, 1991.

Miller, G. Tyler, *Living in the Environment.* Belmont, CA: Wadsworth Publishing Company, 1990.

22.1 Fossil Fuel Extraction: Background Information

Most of the energy we use in the United States comes from **"fossil fuels."** Fossil fuels are those that are derived from plants that died millions of years ago, so they are **nonrenewable** resources. Coal, oil, and natural gas are the main fossil fuels.

Coal is burned to produce electricity and for other heating purposes. About 70 percent of the coal burned in the United States is used for generating electricity, and about 56 percent of the electricity generated in the United States is made by burning coal. Most of the rest is used to produce a substance called coke, which is used in making steel or is burned in various other manufacturing processes.

About two-thirds of the coal mined in the United States is removed by surface mining. Surface **strip mining** involves removing the soil and rocks (and any plants and animals living there!) from the surface, then using machinery to remove the layers of coal underneath. This, of course, wreaks havoc on the strip-mined land. In the United States, mining companies are now expected to restore the newly strip-mined land, but many previously mined areas have not been restored. Restoration is a costly and time-consuming process.

Underground or tunnel mining is used to remove coal that is too deep for surface mining. Acids and other chemicals can be flushed from coal mines and pollute lakes and rivers. When abandoned mines collapse, subsidence of the land above them can occur.

Burning coal produces a lot of air pollution unless effective air pollution control devices are utilized. About 70 percent of the sulfur dioxide emissions in the United States come from burning coal, as do many other air pollutants, including carbon dioxide, which is a major greenhouse gas. Such air pollution is not only harmful in itself, it is also a major cause of acidic precipitation.

Coal is the most abundant fossil fuel. Most authorities agree that there are several hundreds of years' worth of affordable coal available in the world. Unfortunately, much of this is lignite or bituminous coal, which does not produce as much heat as anthracite coal. Anthracite coal also produces much less pollution when burned.

Oil is used for many purposes. About 63 percent of the oil used in the United States is used for transportation. About 3 percent is used for generating electricity, and oil provides about 4.5 percent of the electricity that we generate in the United States. About 25 percent of the oil used in the United States is used for industrial uses, and about 9 percent is used for residential and commercial heating. We obtain many materials from oil, including plastics, fertilizers, pesticides, medicines, waxes, asphalt, natural gas, and gasoline. More than 6,000 different products are made from oil!

Some oil is obtained from wells drilled on land, and some comes from offshore oil wells in the oceans. Drilling for oil involves a lot of machinery and road building.

Wherever drilling for oil occurs, there is the potential for spills. Oil spills can occur during the drilling process, during pumping of the oil from the ground, and during transportation of the oil by pipelines or ships. Spilled oil is hazardous because it contains many toxic chemicals, it can burn, and it is sticky, so it can smother plants and animals.

The oil that comes from the well is called **crude oil,** and it contains many different chemicals. To make useful products from the oil, it needs to be refined. Oil refining of crude oil involves heating it, which causes the various components to vaporize. Since different chemicals vaporize at different temperatures, the vapors are cooled, which causes different fractions to condense at different temperatures, allowing them to be separated. This process is called **fractional distillation.**

Oil is a relatively cheap fuel source and is fairly easy to transport and use. Burning oil, though, produces many air pollutants such as carbon dioxide and oxides of sulfur and nitrogen. Spills and leakage from drilling can contaminate the land, surface waters, and underground water systems.

There are estimates that "affordable" oil supplies may run out in fewer than 100 years, but new finds, new technology, rising prices, new demands, and conservation make estimates very uncertain.

Natural gas is often found along with oil deposits. It is a mixture of methane gas and other gaseous compounds like propane and butane. After being removed from the ground, natural gas is cleaned of impurities such as water and hydrogen sulfide. It is then shipped in pipelines or as liquified natural gas.

About 41 percent of the natural gas used in the United States is used in residential and commercial heating, 41 percent in industrial processes and 3 percent for transportation. About 15 percent is used by utility companies in electricity generation. Natural gas provides about 11 percent of our electricity.

Compared to coal and oil, natural gas is an excellent fuel. It produces much less air pollution and burns hotter. It is easy to transport via pipelines and is a versatile fuel that is easy to use in many ways. Natural gas electrical plants cost significantly less to build than coal plants.

The readily obtainable supplies of natural gas in the United States and the world as a whole are very limited. In the 1960s, there were even predictions that we would run out of natural gas by 1990! There are ways to recover natural gas from coal seams and other sources, but we should not waste this valuable and versatile resource!

22.2 Fossil Fuel Extraction: Instructions and Data

Your teacher will provide you with a cookie. This cookie represents a land area that may contain deposits of coal (represented by raisins), oil (represented by pieces of nuts), and/or natural gas (represented by chocolate pieces). You will also be provided with a toothpick, which represents the mining and drilling equipment used in obtaining the coal, oil, and natural gas.

Your job is to try to remove as much of the coal, oil, and natural gas as possible with as little damage to the environment as possible.

Imagine that the top surface of the original cookie is an area of land on which various kinds of plants and animals live.

In the space below, sketch the cookie surface before and after "mining."

Also, record the amounts of the various resources that you were able to obtain and the amount of "waste" generated. (**Estimate:** about _____% of the original cookie.)

BEFORE MINING

AFTER MINING

resources recovered (as % of the original cookie):

_____% coal (raisins)

_____ % oil (nut pieces)

_____ % natural gas (chocolate)

_____ % waste (crumbs and pieces)

Name _____ Class _____ Date _____

22.3 Fossil Fuel Extraction: Questions

1. What are some problems associated with obtaining and using coal?

   _____

   _____

2. What can be done to reduce or avoid these problems?

   _____

   _____

3. What are some problems associated with obtaining and using oil?

   _____

   _____

4. What can be done to reduce or avoid these problems?

   _____

   _____

5. How can saving electricity help reduce the need for mining and shipping coal?

   _____

   _____

6. List some ways that you could reduce your electricity use.

   _____

   _____

7. How can reducing gasoline consumption reduce the need for mining, shipping, and refining oil?

   _____

   _____

8. List some ways that you could reduce the need for oil?

   _____

   _____

9. What are some advantages and disadvantages of natural gas as an energy source?

   _____

   _____

ACTIVITY 23: THE NUCLEAR POWER PUZZLE _____

Activity Summary

Working in teams, students investigate various aspects of nuclear power. They then present their findings to the other members of the class. As the information is presented, the students in the class record the information on portions of a jigsaw puzzle.

Introduction

In the 1970s and 1980s, nuclear power was a hotly debated issue. A wide variety of factors, including changes in oil costs, effective conservation measures, greater public concern about the safety of nuclear fission, and changing economics resulted in a slowdown of the nuclear power industry in the United States. As we continue to use up fossil fuels and use more electricity, nuclear power is likely to soon become a popular issue again.

For students or adults to make intelligent choices, they need to understand all sides of issues. We make choices about nuclear power when we use electricity, thereby increasing the need for power plants. We also make choices when we elect governmental officials who will have the responsibility of regulating the nuclear power industry. For these and many other reasons, we need to understand how nuclear power works and its advantages and disadvantages.

Grouping

The class should be divided into 7–10 teams.

Time

Introduction: 15–30 minutes
Student research: one to four 45- to 55-minute periods, possibly spread out over several weeks if you are having the students write for information
Presentations: two 45- to 55-minute periods

Anticipated Outcomes

The students will:

- understand nuclear power, including how it works and its advantages and disadvantages.
- increase their ability to evaluate arguments on an issue.
- increase their ability to present information or an argument on an issue.

Materials

—Photocopied student pages:

- 23.1 The Nuclear Power Puzzle: Background Information (one per student)
- 23.2 The Nuclear Power Puzzle: Instructions and Puzzle sheets (one per student)

• 23.3 The Nuclear Power Puzzle: Questions (one per student)

—Transparency of puzzle sheets

—Enlarged puzzle for bulletin board

—Colored felt-tip pens: one set per team or have students share

—Optional: photocopies of Appendix III, How to Write a Letter to Obtain Information

—Printed resources giving information on nuclear power (you might obtain these ahead of time, or you might have the students obtain them)

Vocabulary

breeder reactor	containment vessel	control rod	cooling water
core	enrichment	fission	fuel cycle
fuel rod	fusion	generator	neutron
nuclear	nucleus	radioactivity	reactor
redundant systems	uranium		

Teacher Preparation

1. Decide how many teams to divide the class into. Topics and puzzle sheets have been provided for dividing the class into either 7 or 10 teams.

2. Photocopy the Background Information sheet (23.1), Instructions (mark the time parameters first) and Puzzle sheets (23.2), Questions sheet (23.3), and, possibly, Appendix III: How to Write a Letter to Obtain Information. Note that there are two parts to the puzzle if you use 7 teams and three parts if you use 10 teams. See 23.2.

3. Make a transparency of the appropriate puzzle sheets.

4. Use the transparency to make a large (bulletin-board size) copy of the puzzle.

5. Cut up the enlarged puzzle into puzzle pieces.

6. Optional: Obtain as much printed or other information as you can on nuclear power.

7. Optional. Arrange for the students to use the library's resources.

Safety Considerations

None

Procedure

1. (optional) Write for, or have the students write for, as much information on nuclear power as you want. Appendix III (How to Write a Letter to Obtain Information) might be useful. You might want to provide relatively balanced information only, or obtain biased information and be sure that the students recognize the biases. See the following list. The addresses were obtained from *The Environmental Address Book,* 1991 edition. There are many other organizations listed therein to whom you may wish to write. Some of these are pro-nuclear, some are antinuclear, and some are relatively objective.

Abalone Alliance
2940 16th Street,
   Room 310
San Francisco, CA 94103
(415) 861–0592

**American Council for an
   Energy Efficient Economy**
1001 Connecticut Avenue, NW
Washington, DC 20036
(202) 429–8873

**American Nuclear Energy
   Council**
410 First Street, SE
Washington, DC 20003
(202) 484–2670

American Nuclear Society
555 N. Kensington Avenue
La Grange Park, IL 60525
(312) 352–6611

Americans for Nuclear Energy
2525 Wilson Boulevard
Arlington, VA 22201
(703) 528–4430

Citizens Energy Council
77 Homewood Avenue
Allendale, NJ 07401
(201) 327–3194

**Committee for Nuclear
   Responsibility**
P.O. Box 11207
San Francisco, CA 94101
(415) 776–8299

**Concerned Citizens for a
   Nuclear Breeder**
P.O. Box 3
Ross, OH 45061
(513) 738–6750

**Critical Mass Energy
   Project**
215 Pennsylvania Avenue, SE
Washington, DC
(202) 546–4996

Fusion Power Associates
#2 Professional Drive
Gaithersburg, MD 20879
(301) 258–0545

General Atomics
10955 John Jay Hopkins
   Drive
San Diego, CA 92121
(619) 455–3000

General Electric Co.
3135 Easton Turnpike
Fairfield, CT 06430
(203) 373–2211

**League Against Nuclear
   Dangers**
Rt. 1, 525 River Road
Rudolph, WI 54475
(715) 423–7996

Nuclear Free America
325 East 25th Street
Baltimore, MD 21218
(301) 235–3575

**Nuclear Information and
   Resource Service**
1424 16th Street, NW
Washington, DC 20036
(202) 328–0002

**Task Force Against
   Nuclear Pollution**
P.O. Box 1817
Washington, DC 20013
(301) 474–8311

**U.S. Council for Energy
   Awareness**
1776 I St., NW, Suite 400
Washington, DC 20006
(202) 293–0770

**U.S. Nuclear Regulatory
   Commission (NRC)**
1717 H Street, NW
Washington, DC 20555
(202) 492–7000

Another important pro-nuclear group is the:

Another important antinuclear group is the:

U.S. Council for Energy Awareness
P.O. Box 66080
Washington, DC 20035
(202) 293–0770

Union of Concerned Scientists
26 Church Street
Cambridge, MA 02238
(617) 547–5552

Fact Sheets on a variety of energy sources, including nuclear power, can be obtained from:

**National Energy Education Development
   Project**
1920 Association Drive
Reston, VA 22091
(703) 860–5029

Electric Power Research Institute
P.O. Box 10412
Palo Alto, CA 94303
(415) 855–2000

2. Decide how long you want the presentations to be.

3. Explain the activity to the class and form teams.

4. Allow the students time to complete their research and prepare their presentations.

5. Have the students present their information while the other class members take notes on their puzzle sheets.

Discussion

1. What presentation methods were helpful in teaching/learning about the topic?

2. Do you think that the U.S. government should be supporting and encouraging nuclear fission as an energy source?

3. Can you explain basically how a nuclear power plant works?

4. What are some advantages and disadvantages of nuclear fission as an energy source?

Answers to 23.3, The Nuclear Power Puzzle Questions

1. No, the electricity is the same. The difference is in the source of the heat that produces the steam that turns the turbine that turns the generator.

2. A neutron collides with a large atom such as uranium-235. The uranium atom splits, releasing large amounts of energy and additional neutrons. These neutrons hit other uranium atoms and a chain reaction occurs, producing huge amounts of heat energy. This heat is used to produce steam. The expanding steam turns a turbine. The turbine turns a generator, which produces electricity.

3. Answers will vary. Advantages include lots of energy from a small amount of fuel and relatively little pollution released into the environment if all goes as planned.

4. Answers will vary. Disadvantages include high costs when governmental support is included, great risk if something does go wrong, and a legacy of dangerous waste left to future generations.

5. a. A nuclear power advocate would point out that nuclear power plants are designed to release relatively little pollution into the environment. They have redundant safety systems. Lots of energy can be obtained from relatively little uranium.
   b. A nuclear power opponent would point out that nuclear power plants do release large amounts of heat into the environment and that they produce very dangerous waste products. Even with their redundant safety systems, there have been numerous accidents, some quite serious. High grade, easily obtainable uranium is not abundant.

6. Conserving energy, including electricity, can reduce our need for additional power plants. Many people believe that simple conservation measures could easily save more energy than we now get or are likely to soon get from nuclear power.

Extensions (See Activity 32 for suggestions for student projects.)

1. Obtain as much information as possible on both sides of the nuclear power issue. Have the students either debate the issue or present a panel discussion. This might be before their own class or before other classes.

2. Visit a nonnuclear power plant. Find out how it is similar to and different from a nuclear plant.

3. Arrange for guest speakers who are for and against nuclear power.

4. Obtain copies of propaganda for and against nuclear power. Have the students analyze the arguments presented and how they are presented.

5. Obtain a copy of *Know Nukes* and do the activities described therein. (See "References.")

6. Have students debate the pros and cons of nuclear power.

Modifications

1. Require the teams to use a visual aid in their presentation.

2. Require that each member of the team participate in the oral presentation.

3. Have the team members do "peer evaluations" after the project.

4. Consider having the teams submit written reports. Check with Social Studies or English teachers regarding formats that they teach, including citation procedures.

5. Consider covering up or "whiting out" the vocabulary and topic suggestions on the puzzle pages that are used by the class for note taking. Consider providing each team with its list of topics or vocabulary.

6. You might provide student teams with lists of the main topics that they should cover. These can be added to the puzzle pages to facilitate note taking.

7. Alter the number of teams. If you are using the puzzle sheets, this will require remaking them.

8. Don't provide the students with the information. Have them obtain it themselves. If you do this, consider asking them to leave the information with you for use next year in case you decide to provide the information then.

References

Anonymous, *Energy Fact Sheet: Nuclear Energy*. Reston, VA: National Energy Education Development Project, 1992.

Butterfield, Charlie, and Marjorie McCandless, *Know Nukes*. Keene, NH: Antioch / New England Graduate School, 1982.

Levine, Michael, *The Environmental Address Book*. New York, NY: Putnam Publishing Group, 1991.

Miller, G. Tyler, *Living in the Environment*. Belmont, CA: Wadsworth Publishing Company, 1990.

23.1 The Nuclear Power Puzzle: Background Information

Nuclear power is a way to generate electricity. The electricity made in nuclear power plants is just like the electricity made in a coal, oil, or natural gas powered plant, by a hydroelectric plant, or by a geothermal power plant. The electricity is made by a **generator,** which is turned by a turbine. Whatever can turn the turbine can generate electricity. In a hydroelectric plant, falling water turns the turbine. A turbine can also be turned by steam formed by boiling water with heat from burning coal, oil, or natural gas, or by steam formed with the heat from a nuclear reaction in a nuclear power plant.

In a **nuclear fission** power plant, large atoms such as those of **uranium** are caused to split into smaller products. When they split, the energy that had held the **nucleus** together is released as heat energy. Tremendous amounts of heat energy can be obtained from a relatively small amount of nuclear fuel.

There are many concerns about the safety of nuclear power plants. People are concerned about radiation from the mining process, from waste products, and from the plant itself. There is concern about accidents in the operation of the plants and in the shipping and storage of the fuel and waste products. Indeed, there have been several serious accidents at nuclear power plants, and many minor accidents.

Nuclear fission advocates point out that burning coal and oil to generate electricity produces air pollution and water pollution. They also point out that there are accidents in all kinds of power plants.

The federal governmental agency that is charged with regulating nuclear power is the Nuclear Regulatory Commission. The development of nuclear power is in the jurisdiction of the Energy Research and Development Administration. Both are part of the Department of Energy.

The issue of nuclear power is extremely important. We use a lot of energy, much of it electrical. If we demand electricity, the utility company's job is to supply it. Nuclear power is one way to produce a lot of electricity. Our legislators need to understand nuclear power if they are to make wise laws regulating it. As citizens, we need to understand it if we are going to give direction to our legislators or judge what they do.

We also need to consider our own personal responsibility for the consequences of the generation of the electricity we use. What can we, personally, do to reduce the need for the generation of electricity?

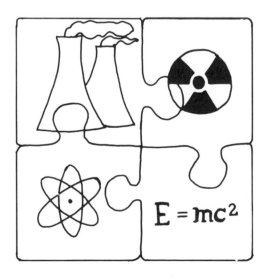

23.2 The Nuclear Power Puzzle: Instructions

Your team is assigned to find out about a part of the Nuclear Power puzzle.

Our topic is: _____

When you have found out about your topic, you are to prepare a presentation to give to the class. When you give your presentation, keep in mind that it should:

- inform the class about the important aspects of your topic
- be presented in an interesting way
- be between _____ and _____ minutes long
- allow time for questions

Each student will be given a page on which to take notes on the Nuclear Power Puzzle. Be sure that you provide the most important information about your topic. To help with this, the puzzle pieces include some vocabulary terms and/or important topics. Be sure to teach about these terms and topics. They are provided as starting points—your presentation should include them and more.

Some hints for giving a good presentation:

- Plan carefully.
- Use note cards, but DO NOT READ THEM TO THE CLASS. Know your material well enough that you need only to refer to your cards occasionally. To avoid the temptation to read your cards, don't write sentences on them; use only key terms and thoughts.
- Have a large, clear, attractive visual aid. This will help make your presentation clear to the class and will support you.
- Practice and practice some more. Have somebody critique your presentation. Practice until you are sure you will do a good job!

Your team will be given an enlarged copy of your portion of the Nuclear Power Puzzle. You should neatly record the most important information on it so that it can become part of a bulletin board to be shared with the class. Drawings or pictures might help.

23.2 The Nuclear Power Puzzle

(7 teams, left half)

1. What is nuclear fission?

terms:

nucleus

neutron

nuclear

radioactivity

uranium

fission

3. How is the fuel for a nuclear power plant made?

terms:

enrichment

fuel cycle

What is nuclear waste?

4. What are some advantages of nuclear power?

cost

abundance

safety

2. How do we get electricity from a nuclear power plant?

terms:

fuel rod

control rod

core

generator

pollution

waste products

diagram:

23.2   The Nuclear Power Puzzle

(7 teams, right half)

5. What are some disadvantages of or problems with nuclear power?

cost

abundance

safety

pollution

waste products

6. What are some safety measures that are taken at nuclear power plants?

redundant systems

cooling water

containment vessel

accidents that have happened

7. What is a "breeder reactor"?

costs

What is nuclear fusion?

theory

heavy water

deuterium

Name _____ Class _____ Date _____

23.2 The Nuclear Power Puzzle

(10 teams, left part)

---

1. What is nuclear fission?

terms:

nucleus

neutron

nuclear

uranium

radioactivity

fission

---

3. How is a nuclear power plant's fuel made?

terms:

enrichment

fuel cycle

U-235, U-238, plutonium

---

2. How do we get electricity from a nuclear power plant?

terms:

reactor

fuel rod

control rod

core

generator

diagram:

23.2 The Nuclear Power Puzzle

(10 teams, middle part)

4. What are some advantages of nuclear power?

cost

abundance

safety

pollution

waste products

5. What are some disadvantages or problems with nuclear power?

cost

abundance

safety

pollution: normal (planned, allowed)

accidental

waste products

6. What are some safety measures that are taken at nuclear power plants?

terms:

containment vessel

cooling water

redundant systems

Have there been accidents at nuclear power plants? Examples:

Name _____ Class _____ Date _____

23.2 The Nuclear Power Puzzle

7. What is nuclear waste?

solid

liquid

thermal

How is nuclear waste disposed of ?

long and short half-life

transportation

storage

8. How are nuclear power plants licensed and regulated?

A. E. C.

N. R. C.

9. Are nuclear power plants economical?

governmental subsidies

Would nuclear power plants be economical without governmental support?

Who pays for subsidies?

10. What is a "breeder reactor"?

theory—how does it work?

costs

What is nuclear fusion?

theory—how does it work?

heavy water

deuterium

23.3 The Nuclear Power Puzzle: Questions

1. Is the electricity generated by a nuclear power plant any different from that generated by

   other means? _____

2. Tell, simply, how a nuclear power plant generates electricity.

   _____

   _____

   _____

3. What are some advantages of nuclear power?

   _____

   _____

   _____

4. What are some disadvantages of nuclear power?

   _____

   _____

   _____

5. It has been claimed that nuclear power is "clean, safe, and abundant."
   a. Discuss this statement from the standpoint of a nuclear power advocate.

   _____

   _____

   _____

   b. Discuss this statement from the standpoint of a nuclear power opponent.

   _____

   _____

   _____

6. What can you do to reduce the need for nuclear (or other) power plants?

   _____

   _____

   _____

ACTIVITY 24: BIOGAS

Activity Summary

Students build small biogas generators, collect the gas produced, and burn it to show that it contains methane.

Introduction

When bacteria decompose organic material such as garbage and sewage, especially in the absence of oxygen, biogas is often produced. Biogas is a mixture of about 60 percent methane gas and 40 percent carbon dioxide.

Biogas has a great potential as a source of energy. The technology is relatively simple and economically attractive. There are estimates that it costs about 80 cents per watt to install a biogas system on a large dairy farm, as compared to about $3 per watt for coal and $5 per watt for nuclear power plants. One power plant in California uses cattle manure to produce enough electricity for 20,000 homes! If all dairy farms in the United States installed biogas collection and utilization systems, they could produce more electricity than we currently get from nuclear power at about 20 percent of the cost. Additionally, biogas is a renewable energy source!

Biogas already is utilized extensively in many areas of the world. There are an estimated 7 million biogas digesters in China. They produce methane for heating and cooking, and the residue is used as fertilizer. There are about 750,000 biogas digesters at work in India. In the United States, about 50 landfills currently recover methane gas, which is used on the site or fed into the community's gas lines. There are more than 2,000 additional sites with potential for large-scale methane recovery.

There are, of course, problems with using methane generated in this way. Some feel that the manure should be utilized as fertilizer. The residue from the burning can be used, but some of the plant nutrients are lost in the process. Burning the methane produces carbon dioxide, but so does burning natural gas (which is methane too!), oil, or coal to generate electricity. Additionally, the methane is going to be produced whether we utilize it or not. Methane is an important "greenhouse gas," and it is suspected of being a major part of the global warming problem.

Since the methane gas produced is flammable (potentially explosive), it is important to treat it carefully. Follow the safety suggestions.

Grouping

Teams of 2 students.

Time

To set up the digester: 30–50 minutes

Varying amounts of time will be needed for the production of the gas, depending on the type of material put into the digester, temperature, etc. 10–20 days at 80°F is a reasonable estimate.

Testing the gas for methane and discussion: 30–45 minutes

Anticipated Outcomes

The students will:

- understand the production of methane gas by anaerobic decomposition.
- appreciate the value of using biogas as an energy source.

Materials

—Photocopied student pages:

- 24.1 Biogas: Background Information (one per student)
- 24.2 Biogas: Instructions (one per team)
- 24.3 Biogas: Questions (one per student)

—Per team of two students:

- 1 one-gallon plastic milk or water jug
- 1 rubber stopper (2-hole, size 6 1/2, to fit in the jug opening)
- 1 manometer tube (glass tube bent as per illustration)
- 1 glass dropper pipette or micropipette or drawn-out piece of glass tubing
- about 4" of rubber tubing into which the glass tubing fits snugly
- 1 hose clamp (also called tubing clamp or pinch clamp)
- about 3 quarts of slurry, prepared as per student Instructions sheet
- 2 lab aprons and safety glasses or goggles

—Matches

—Permanent felt-tip pens and masking tape or labels for identifying generators

—Water and materials with which to make slurries

—Optional: Blender or mixer for making slurry; rubber gloves; funnels with large openings

Vocabulary

activated sludge	anaerobic	biogas
decomposition	landfill	methane
organic	renewable	slurry

Teacher Preparation

1. Photocopy the Background Information sheet (24.1), Instructions sheet (24.2), and Questions sheet (24.3).
2. Obtain materials.
3. Make a sample biogas generator to serve as a model.
4. Locate a place to store the generators. A readily accessible place with adequate space and a temperature of 90°F is desirable.

> **SAFETY CONSIDERATIONS**
>
> 1. DO NOT use a glass bottle or jug for the generator. There is a potential for enough pressure to be built up to cause an explosion. Use a plastic jug.
> 2. Students should always wear aprons and safety glasses or goggles when testing for flammability.
> 3. When testing for flammability, be sure that the burner tip is pointed away from people or flammable materials.
> 4. Students should wear gloves when making the slurry and when disposing of the sludge.
> 5. Students should wash their hands after making slurry and disposing of the sludge.

Procedure

1. Issue the student Background sheet; have the students read it and discuss biogas as an energy source.
2. Show the students a sample biogas generator. Discuss possible materials from which to make slurries.
3. Assign the students to bring slurry material.
4. Have the students build their generators and label them.
5. Have the students make their slurries, recording the types and amounts of components in their notebooks. Alternatively, you could have the class design a data table on which the different slurry types used by different teams are recorded and the dates of methane production are noted.
6. Have the students fill the generators only about 3/4 full, as foam will be generated and it should be kept out of the tubing.
7. Keep the generators in a warm place. Optimum temperatures are 90–100°F, and production slows down quite a bit below 80°F.
8. Check for gas production every day.
9. When the water in the manometer has risen, gas has been produced. Test that gas for flammability by holding a match near the burner tip. (It probably won't burn because it will be mostly carbon dioxide.) Remind the students of safety procedures before they test for gas.
10. As more gas is produced, test it for flammability every day or two. Eventually, methane should be produced.
11. When the methane production has ceased, or when you want to stop producing it, have the students examine the remaining sludge and discuss possible uses for it.
12. Discuss the results with the students.
13. Consider doing extension activities.
14. Consider saving the jugs for use next year.

Discussion

1. What uses are there for methane gas?
2. What could the sludge be used for?
3. What are the advantages of using manure for methane production as opposed to fertilizer?

4. What slurry materials produced the most methane? Produced methane the fastest?

5. What variables might increase or decrease methane production?

Answers to 24.3, Biogas Questions

1. The first gas produced is carbon dioxide (CO_2) which is not flammable.

2. Most bacteria grow more rapidly when they have oxygen to use. When they run out of "free" oxygen in the air, though, some can obtain it from other compounds. They then produce methane gas (CH_4) as a waste product.

3. Answers will vary.

4. Methane can be used for anything that natural gas is used for. This includes cooking, heating, generating electricity, and for various industrial processes.

5. Renewable resources are those that can be regenerated (such as methane, wood, running water, wind, or geothermal steam) or which aren't used up, such as the sun.

6. Advantages of biogas include its renewability, abundance, the fact that methane is a relatively clean burning fuel, and low cost. Also, it helps with the problem of disposal of organic waste.

7. The main disadvantage of biogas is the loss of the organic waste for compost or fertilizer.

Extensions (See Activity 32 for suggestions for student projects)

1. Carefully prepare different slurries and compare their methane production. Which materials work best? What dilution works best? Can salt water be used?

2. Compare methane production at different temperatures.

3. Visit a local landfill or farm where methane gas is being recovered and used.

4. If your local landfill is not recovering methane, write letters to the person in charge and ask why not.

Modifications

1. The gas can be collected in a balloon and used for experiments.

2. See John W. Christensen's book for more details and references.

References

Christensen, John W., *Global Science, Laboratory Manual*. Dubuque, IA: Kendall/Hunt Publishing Co., 1991.

Harley, John P., and Bernard Nebel, *Environmental Science—The Way the World Works, Laboratory Manual*. Englewood Cliffs, NJ: Prentice Hall, 1990.

Miller, G. Tyler, *Living in the Environment*. Belmont, CA: Wadsworth Publishing Company, 1990.

Nebel, Bernard J., *Environmental Science—The Way the World Works*. Englewood Cliffs, NJ: Prentice Hall, 1990.

24.1 Biogas: Background Information

What happens to **organic** garbage when it is buried at the **landfill?** When bacteria grow on the organic material, especially without air **(anaerobically)**, they digest it and give off carbon dioxide gas (CO_2) and **methane** gas (CH_4) as waste products.

Methane is the main component of natural gas, and is relatively clean burning, colorless, and odorless. When organic materials decompose, the methane is normally given off into the atmosphere, where it may contribute to global warming.

What if we could capture this gas and burn it for cooking and heating? Actually, this is already being done in many parts of the world. Even small farms and households can utilize **biogas** generators to provide heat. In China, there are an estimated 7 million biogas generators being used to convert plant and animal wastes into fuel for cooking and heating. India has about 750,000 biogas generators in operation.

In the United States, about 50 large landfills have perforated pipes or other methods of collecting the methane generated by the **decomposition** of garbage. It is estimated that there are 2,000 to 3,000 landfills in the United States that could be tapped for large-scale methane recovery.

Farms that produce a lot of manure, such as hog and dairy farms, can use biogas generators to produce methane. One biogas plant in California uses manure from nearby feedlots. It produces enough power to supply electricity to about 20,000 homes! The residue remaining after the digestion by bacteria is used as fertilizer. Many farms power generators and heaters with the methane they produce. Excess power is sold to local utilities.

Biogas-powered electricity generating plants can be built quickly, simply, and for much less money per kilowatt than coal, oil, or nuclear power plants. Additionally, unlike coal, oil, or uranium, the methane is a **renewable** resource.

When the bacteria have digested most of the organic material, the methane production in a biogas generator slows down and stops. The remaining material is called **activated sludge.** Dried activated sludge can be used as fertilizer.

There are, of course, problems with using organic wastes for biogas production. Some feel that organic plant waste should be used for compost, and that manure should be used for fertilizer. They point out that a lot of natural gas and other energy is used in the production of fertilizers and that using the manure and compost would reduce this use of natural gas.

24.2 Biogas: Instructions

Your teacher will explain how to build a small biogas generator.
   To fuel your generator, you might try:

• manure
• household garbage
• grass clippings or other green plant material
• dried steer manure from a garden supply store

   Whatever fuel you use, mix it with water until it has the consistency of cream. This liquified fuel is called a **"slurry."**

• **Be sure to wear an apron and gloves when making your slurry and to wash your hands afterwards.**

   The bent glass tube is called a manometer. It is used to indicate how much gas is being generated. The water will rise in the tube as gas is produced. It also allows for release of pressure if too much gas is produced.
   When gas is produced, foam will develop. To avoid clogging the openings in the stopper, you will need to leave a 4"–6" air space at the top of the generator.
   The first gas is produced aerobically (using the air from the jug) and will be mostly carbon dioxide (CO_2). After most of the oxygen from the air has been used, the bacteria will begin to produce methane (CH_4).
   When you test the gas for flammability, be sure to:

• **Wear safety glasses or goggles.**
• **Point the burner tip away from people and combustible objects.**

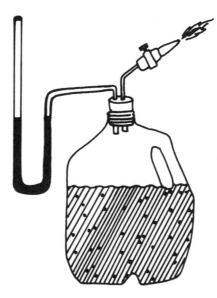

© 1993 by The Center for Applied Research in Education

24.3 Biogas: Questions

1. Was the first gas produced flammable? What was the first gas?

   _____

   _____

2. The chemical formula for carbon dioxide is CO_2. Methane is CH_4. Why is methane produced better in the absence of air (anaerobically)?

   _____

   _____

3. Did different materials produce methane at different rates? Which materials produced the most methane or produced methane first?

   _____

   _____

   _____

4. What could methane biogas be used for?

   _____

   _____

   _____

5. Methane biogas is a renewable resource. What does that mean?

   _____

   _____

   _____

6. What are some advantages of biogas as a fuel source?

   _____

   _____

   _____

7. What are some disadvantages of biogas as a fuel source?

   _____

   _____

   _____

ACTIVITY 25: ENERGY ALTERNATIVES _____

Activity Summary

Student teams investigate various alternatives for meeting our energy needs. Their research includes library research and writing for information from various public and private sources. They then present their information orally and with bulletin boards for the class.

Introduction

Many of us tend to think of energy sources as being coal, oil, natural gas, and nuclear power. In fact, there are many other sources of energy, including several sources of electrical energy. It is important that students expand their thinking to include a wide variety of energy sources and that they learn their advantages and disadvantages.

Grouping

Teams of 1–3 students, depending on how many sources you want the students to investigate.

Time

Introducing the assignment and writing for information: 45–55 minutes
Allow at least 2–4 weeks for the information to arrive
Preparing presentations and bulletin boards: Three to six 45- to 55-minute periods
Presentations: two to four 45- to 55-minute periods.

Anticipated Outcomes

The students will:

- learn about several energy alternatives.
- increase their ability to read and understand printed material.
- increase their ability to organize and present information orally and as a bulletin board.
- increase their ability and willingness to write for information.

Materials

—Photocopied student pages:
- 25.1 Energy Alternatives: Background Information (one per student)
- 25.2 Energy Alternatives: Instructions (one per team)
- 25.3 Energy Alternatives: Questions (one per student)

Vocabulary

alternative energy   energy mix   nonrenewable   renewable

Teacher Preparation

1. Photocopy the Background Information sheet (25.1), Instructions sheet (25.2), and Questions sheet (25.3).
2. Obtain fact sheets and/or other information on as many different energy sources as possible.
3. Optional: Obtain bulletin board materials for the students to use.

Safety Considerations

None

Procedure

1. Obtain fact sheets and/or other information on as many different energy sources as possible. These energy sources are currently most important and should definitely be included:

petroleum (oil)	coal	natural gas	conservation
nuclear fission	geothermal	hydroelectric	solar

Two sources that are often overlooked are conservation and human muscle power. Be sure that the students understand that energy saved by conservation is an energy source and is actually better than obtaining energy from some other source. These are some other alternatives that you might consider:

wind (small and large scale)	biogas (methane)
alcohol	trash as fuel
hydrogen	biofuels (wood, fuel plantations)
oil from shale	oil from tar sands
coal gasification	synthetic natural gas (synfuel)
nuclear breeder reactors	nuclear fusion
small-scale hydroelectric	pumped-storage hydroelectric
ocean waves	ocean currents
ocean tides	ocean thermal gradients
photovoltaic (solar electric cells)	direct solar heating (active and passive)
solar satellites	solar ponds
concentrated solar to produce high temperature heat and electricity	

The following sources provide fact sheets on a variety of energy sources:

Electric Power Research Institute
P.O. Box 10412
Palo Alto, CA 94303
(415) 855–2000

U.S. Department of Energy
Energy Information Administration
1000 Independence Avenue SW
Room 1F-048
Washington, DC 20585
(202) 586–8800

**National Energy Education Development
  Project (NEED)**
1920 Association Drive
Reston, VA 22091
(703) 860–5029

U.S. Department of Energy
Office of Scientific and Technical Information
P.O. Box 62
Oak Ridge, TN 37831
(615) 576–1301

U.S. Department of Energy
Conservation and Renewable Energy Inquiry and Referral Service
P.O. Box 8900
Silver Spring, MD 20907
1–800–(523)–2929

Any Environmental Science textbook will include chapters on energy alternatives, and they generally include references for further information. Some good ones are:

Chiras, Daniel D.; *Environmental Science*
Benjamin/Cummings Publishing Co.
390 Bridge Parkway
Redwood City, CA 94065
(415) 594–4400

Enger, Eldon, and B. Smith;
  Environmental Science
William C. Brown, Publishers
2460 Kerper Blvd.
Dubuque, IA 52004
(319) 588–1451

Nebel, Bernard J; *Environmental Science*
Prentice Hall Publishing Co.
Prentice Hall Building
Englewood Cliffs, NJ 07632
(201) 592–2000

Christensen, John W.; *Global Science*
Kendall/Hunt Publishing Co.
2460 Kerper Blvd.
Dubuque, IA 52004
1–800–338–5578

Miller, G. Tyler; *Living in the Environment*
Wadsworth Publishing Co.
10 Davis Drive
Belmont, CA 94002
(415) 595–2350

You might also write (or have students write) to the following:

**Alternative Energy
Resources Organization**
44 North Last Chance Gulch
Helena, MT 59601
(406) 443–7272

American Nuclear Society
555 N. Kensington Avenue
LaGrange Park, IL 60525
(708) 352–6611

**American Wind Energy
Assoc.**
1730 N. Lynn St., Suite 610
Arlington, VA 22209
(703) 276–8334

**Energy Conservation
Coalition**
1525 New Hampshire
Avenue, NW
Washington, DC 20036
(202) 745–4874

Fusion Power Associates
#2 Professional Drive,
Suite 248
Gaithersburg, MD 20879
(301) 258–0545

**National Energy
Foundation**
5160 Wiley Post Way, #200
Salt Lake City, UT 84116
(801) 539–1406

**National Wood Energy
Assoc.**
P.O. Box 498
Pepperell, MA 01463
(617) 433–5674

**Renewable Energy
Information Center**
3201 Corte Maidas, Unit 4
Camarillo, CA 93010
(805) 388–3097

American Coal Foundation
1130 Seventeenth St., NW
Suite 220
Washington, DC 20036
(202) 466–8360

**American Petroleum
Institute**
1220 L Street, NW
Washington, DC 20005
(202) 682–8000

**Biomass Energy Research
Association**
1825 K St., NW, Suite 503
Washington, DC 20006
(202) 785–2856

Energy Research Institute
6850 Rattlesnake Hammock
Rd.
Naples, FL 33962
(813) 793–1922

**Geothermal Education
Office**
664 Hilary Drive
Tiburon, CA 94920
(415) 435–4544

**National Hydropower
Association**
1133 21st St., NW, Suite 500
Washington, DC 20036
(202) 393–6100

**Passive Solar Industries
Cncl.**
2836 Duke Street
Alexandria, VA 22314
(703) 823–3356

**U.S. Cncl. for Energy
Awareness**
1776 I St., NW, Suite 400
Washington, DC 20036
(202) 293–0770

**American Gas Assoc.
Educational Programs**
1515 Wilson Boulevard
Arlington, VA 22209
(703) 841–8400

**American Solar Energy
Society**
2400 Central Avenue
Boulder, CO 80301
(303) 443–3130

Council on Alternate Fuels
1225 I Street, NW #320
Washington, DC 20005
(202) 898–0711

Enterprise for Education
1320-A 3rd St., #202
Santa Monica, CA 90401
(213) 394–9864

**International Assoc. for
Hydrogen Energy**
P.O. Box 24866
Coral Gables, FL 33124
(305) 284–4666

**National Propane Gas
Association**
1600 Eisenhower Ln. #100
Lisle, IL 60532
(708) 515–0600

Renew America
1400 16th St., NW #710
Washington, DC 20036
(202) 232–2252

U.S. Windpower
6952 Preston Avenue
Livermore, CA 94550
(510) 455–6012

2. Identify and list your resources so that you can check them out to students and keep track of them. Consider placing them on reserve in the library, or allow their use only in your classroom.

3. Plan your schedule, including the following dates:

    a. when to introduce the assignment

    b. when to have the students do their in-class research

    c. when to do the oral presentations

    d. when to have the bulletin board(s) in place and how long they will be up

4. Introduce the assignment to the students. Discuss how to do a good report and what information should be included. Introduce the Background Information and Instructions sheets.

5. Form a team for each energy source that you want the students to investigate and report on. Have the students write for information. Use Appendix III, How to Write a Letter to Obtain Information. Be sure to have the students give a date by which they need to have the information.

6. Allow about 3 to 6 class periods for the students to do their research in class and to prepare their presentations and bulletin boards.

7. Schedule time for the presentations as needed.

8. As the oral presentations are done, discuss what makes a good presentation.

9. Put up, or have the students put up, their bulletin board displays.

Discussion

1. How can conservation be considered an energy source? What are the advantages and disadvantages of conservation as an energy source?

2. Do we currently depend mostly on renewable or nonrenewable energy sources?

3. What are some advantages and disadvantages of each energy source?

4. What are the advantages of renewable energy sources in general?

5. Was the information obtained from organizations representing the various energy sources biased? What about that from governmental organizations? Texts?

6. What can be done to help us move toward more utilization of renewable sources?

7. What can you do in your personal life to help conserve energy?

Answers to 25.3, Energy Alternatives Questions

1. Answers will vary. Good reports present the main information clearly and in an interesting way. Generally, the students should know their information well enough so they don't have to read their reports to the class, although they may use notes.

2. Renewable energy resources are those that are replenished through natural processes. Examples include solar energy, wind, water, and biofuels. Nonrenewable resources are those that are available only in a fixed amount or that are renewed much more slowly than they are used. Examples include coal, oil, natural gas, and uranium.

3. We are currently very dependent on nonrenewable energy resources such as coal, oil, and natural gas. Currently, fossil fuels provide about 95 percent of the energy used in the United States. It is important to develop renewable resources now be-

cause if we wait until the nonrenewable resources are depleted, there will be a period of energy shortages as renewable resources are developed. Another reason is that coal, oil, and natural gas can be used to make products such as medicines, chemicals, and plastics that cannot be made from other materials. Burning such valuable and versatile resources is not the best use for them.

4. The government has supported the development of nonrenewable resources and continues to do so in a variety of ways. If such governmental supports were eliminated, renewable resources such as solar and wind would be much more financially competitive. If the government is to continue to support nonrenewable resource development, many feel that the government should also support renewable resource development. Such support would spur the development of renewable resources.

5. Energy saved through conservation is at least as useful as energy obtained from other sources. For example, if a barrel of oil is saved through conservation, that oil is available for use, now or in the future. Generally, the conservation doesn't cost as much money, use as many resources, or pollute as much as does obtaining energy from other sources.

6. *Advantages:* Generally, conservation doesn't have the financial, resource, and pollution costs of other energy sources. It is something to which we can all directly contribute. It is renewable.
Disadvantages: Some forms of conservation require changes of behavior, and all require education. Some are inconvenient. Some cost money.

Extensions (See Activity 32 for suggestions for student projects)

Consider having the students do written reports. If these are to be graded, they should all be due on the same date. Check with English or Social Studies teachers for the formats that they teach for citations.

Modifications

1. If you are grading the presentations or bulletin boards, be sure the students know your criteria at the start of the project.
2. Students might be given the option of a written or oral report.
3. You might decide not to have the students prepare bulletin boards.
4. Have the students develop their own planning calendars.
5. The student presentations could be done as promotional advertisements for their source, or as skits or songs.

References

Altman, Paula, *Energy Education Resources—Kindergarten through 12th Grade.* Washington, DC: U.S. Department of Energy, 1991.

Chiras, Daniel D., *Environmental Science.* Redwood City, CA: Benjamin/Cummings Publishing Co., 1991.

Levine, Michael, *The Environmental Address Book.* New York, NY: Putnam Publishing Group, 1991.

Miller, G. Tyler, *Living in the Environment.* Belmont, CA: Wadsworth Publishing Co., 1990.

Nebel, Bernard J., *Environmental Science.* Englewood Cliffs, NJ: Prentice Hall, 1990.

25.1 Energy Alternatives: Background Information

What are our sources of energy? In the United States, most of our energy comes from **"non-renewable"** resources such as coal, oil, natural gas, and uranium. Nonrenewable resources are those that are not readily replenished and can be "used up."

Some of our energy is obtained from such **renewable** resources as the sun, wind, and water. Renewable resources are naturally replenished and can't be "used up," although they may not be where we want them when we want them.

Every energy source has advantages and disadvantages. Advantages might include convenience, cost, small environmental impacts, renewability, and other factors. Disadvantages of some energy sources include high cost, inconvenience, pollution, limited supplies, nonrenewability, and lack of technology. When we consider resources, it is important to consider both advantages and disadvantages.

As our population increases, it is increasingly important to find ways to use our resources, including energy, more wisely. As we consume our nonrenewable resources, it is increasingly important to begin to switch to more renewable resources. Many of the energy sources we use the most now also pollute our air, water, and land. Some are dangerous, even deadly for us and for other living things, now and for many generations to come. We need to find ways to reduce that pollution and find alternatives to those sources.

Our tendency has been to rely on one, two, or only a few sources of energy. It is becoming increasingly apparent that we now need to look at a **mix** of a variety of energy sources. In some places, wind may be a good energy source, while in others it is not very useful. Hydroelectric plants can provide electricity in some areas, but not in others. Ocean tides or currents may be useful along the coast, while coal or solar energy may be more useful elsewhere.

As we switch more and more to **alternative** sources of energy, new career opportunities are developing. The coming years will see a need for scientists and engineers to develop new energy sources. Once energy sources have been developed, people will be needed to manufacture, market, install, and service them.

One energy source that must not be forgotten is conservation. Finding a barrel of oil, extracting it from the ground, transporting it, refining it, and using it all involve energy expenditures and cost money. Each step represents some wasted energy and pollution. Conservation, on the other hand, can cost nothing except a change in behavior! Some conservation measures, such as the installation of solar water heaters, insulation, or insulated curtains, involve expenditures of money and energy, but they eventually save more than they cost. Money and energy used to obtain energy from nonrenewable sources, on the other hand, are never recovered.

It is important that we learn about the advantages and disadvantages of the energy alternatives that we now have and that we are likely to have in the future.

© 1993 by The Center for Applied Research in Education

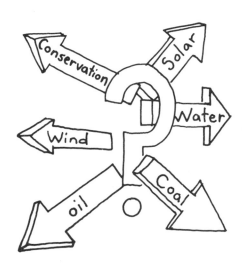

Name _____ Class _____ Date _____

25.2 Energy Alternatives: Instructions

Your team has been given the assignment of finding out about an energy source.

Your energy source is: _____

After completing your research, you will be teaching the rest of the class about it by giving an oral presentation and putting up a bulletin board.

As you do your research and prepare your report and display, keep in mind that your task is to teach the class the most important things about your source.

Here are some hints to help you prepare a good lesson:

- Share the responsibilities among all team members. Divide up the work.

- Meet as a team frequently and discuss progress and problems.

- Plan carefully. Make a calendar. Set and meet deadlines. Don't procrastinate.

- Keep your audience in mind. What type of lesson is interesting to the people in your class? What sort of bulletin board display is interesting?

- Make and use good, clear, easily understood visual aids and displays.

- Know your topic well. Be sure to present the most important information, rather than some unimportant details or statistics that nobody will remember. Include the following:

  √ Is your resource renewable or nonrenewable?

  √ How do we use it? (A diagram might help here.)

  √ How much energy does it currently provide? How important is it likely to be in the near future? In the more distant future?

  √ What are the advantages and disadvantages?

- Practice your presentation thoroughly. Have someone critique it. Practice some more. Then practice still more until you are completely confident that you will do an excellent job.

- Use this calendar:

Meet with team, begin planning, divide up tasks: _____

Send for, telephone for, or start to obtain information by: _____

Work on project: _____, _____, _____ , _____

Meet as a team, report on progress: _____, _____, _____

Plan visual aid(s) and bulletin board: _____ Visual aid(s) to be done by: _____

Put together presentation: _____

Practice presentation: _____, _____, _____, _____

Final presentation due: _____

25.3 Energy Alternatives: Questions

1. What are some characteristics of reports that were successful in teaching about the energy topic?

_____

_____

_____

2. Distinguish between "renewable" and "nonrenewable" energy resources. Give some examples of each.

_____

_____

_____

3. Why is it important to develop our renewable resources now, before the nonrenewable resources have been used up?

_____

_____

_____

4. Should the government (i.e., the taxpayers) help pay for the development of renewable energy resources? Why or why not?

_____

_____

_____

5. How can conservation be considered an energy resource?

_____

_____

_____

6. What are some advantages and disadvantages of conservation as an energy source?

_____

_____

_____

unit

Six

Human Issues

- **Population—More Is Less**
- **Food? What Food?**
- **We "Auto" Drive Less**
- **Toxic in the Home**
- **Wants and Needs**
- **What's Happening?**
- **Do It!**

ACTIVITY 26: POPULATION—MORE IS LESS _____

Activity Summary

Students calculate what happens to a population that increases (or decreases) exponentially at varying rates. They see what effect population changes have on per capita availability of finite resources. They then consider whether increased population would have a positive or a negative effect on various environmental factors. Finally, they imagine themselves living 40 years from now and write a letter to their imaginary grandchild.

Introduction

The issue of overpopulation is THE overriding environmental issue of our time. As population increases, more stress is put on the Earth's finite resources. As people endeavor to raise their standards of living, even more stress is put on the Earth. An understanding of population dynamics is crucial to understanding our environmental problems and possible solutions.

One aspect of the population issue is the simple magnitude of the numbers involved. As death rates have decreased, the human population has increased exponentially. In some areas, mainly the more developed countries, this growth has slowed as resources have been depleted, people have learned the importance of slowing or stopping population growth, and birth control methods have become available. In Europe, the population was growing by only 0.3 percent annually in 1990, while the growth in the United States was 0.7 percent. In other areas, though, the population has been growing much more rapidly as medical and agricultural advances have combined to reduce death rates and increase fertility. Africa's annual growth rate in 1990 was 2.9 percent, while Latin America's was 2.1 percent. While those percentages may not seem large, exponential growth results in very large increases in just a few years. Today there are about three births for each death worldwide. Part I of this activity is intended to demonstrate graphically the results of exponential growth in population and the potential results of exponential population reduction.

In Part II of this activity, the students consider the consequences of rapid population growth. Open space, clean water, adequate food supplies and other characteristics of a desirable and healthy environment become much more difficult to obtain and maintain as the population increases. Generally, increased population results in more pollution, depletion of natural resources, crowding, stress, and other undesirable developments. We need to consider not only the quantity of life, but the quality of life.

Finally, in Part III, the students consider what the future might be like if population continues to grow at its present rate. At the current rate of growth, the Earth's population will double in less than 40 years. Few demographers expect, though, that the Earth will be able to sustain such rapid population growth. The results of such growth are impossible to predict with accuracy, but there certainly will be major changes in all aspects of the human experience.

Grouping

Parts I and II: 12 approximately equal teams
Part III: individuals

249

Time

Part I: 30–50 minutes
Part II: 20–40 minutes
Part III: 20–40 minutes, or as homework

Anticipated Outcomes

The students will:

• understand the effect of exponential growth on populations.
• increase their understanding of the relationship between population and resources.
• know the meanings of the terms on the vocabulary list.
• consider the effect of increased human population on the environment.

Materials

—Photocopied student pages:

• 26.1 Population—More Is Less: Background Information (one per student)
• 26.2 Population—More Is Less: Instructions, Parts I and II (one per team)
• 26.2 Population—More Is Less: Instructions, Part III (one per student)
• 26.3 Population—More Is Less: Questions (one per student)

—For each team:

• 1 red, 1 green, and 1 black pen, pencil, or crayon
• 12 calculators
• graph paper

—13 apples, candy bars, large soft cookies, or other easily cut food
—Knife
—Overhead transparency of 26.2 and graph paper
—Colored pens for writing on transparencies
—Optional: overhead transparency of Table 26.4, Instructor's Data Sheet

Vocabulary

birth rate	carrying capacity	death rate
demography	doubling time	emigration
exponential growth	immigration	population

Teacher Preparation

1. Photocopy the Background Information sheet (26.1), Instructions sheets for Parts I, II, and III (26.2), and Questions sheet (26.3).

2. Obtain the materials.

3. Make overhead transparencies of the Instructions sheet (26.2, Parts I and II), and graph paper.

4. Optional: Make a transparency showing the data from the Instructor's Data Sheet (26.4).

SAFETY CONSIDERATION

Be careful when cutting the apple at the end of Part I.

Procedure

PART I: EXPONENTIAL GROWTH

1. Ask the students whether they think that, 40 years from now, when they have their own families, they will have better, worse, or the same lifestyle as they and their parents do now. Discuss the meaning of "better lifestyle."

2. Ask the students whether they think the world's population is increasing, decreasing, or is stable. Tell them that it is increasing.

3. Ask the students what relationship there might be between population and lifestyle. Discuss finite resources and introduce the term "per capita."

4. Ask the students how fast they think the world's population is increasing, both as a percentage and as a number per year.

5. Distribute the Background Information sheet, 26.1. Have the students read it.

6. Discuss the Background Information sheet with the class.

7. Distribute the Exponential Growth Instructions sheet, 26.2, Part I. Discuss the assignment with the students.

   • Be sure they know how to use the calculators and round off numbers to the nearest whole number.

   • If necessary, help them determine how to make their graphs.

8. Assign each of the teams one of the following growth rates:

0.5%	1.0%	1.5%	2.0%	2.5%	3.0%
−0.5%	−1.0%	−1.5%	−2.0%	−2.5%	−3.0%

9. Allow about 20–30 minutes for the students to do their calculations and graphs.

10. Make an overhead transparency of the data, project it, and discuss it.

11. Give each team an apple (or soft cookie or candy bar). Cut out (or add) part of it proportional to the population change over the 20-year time period, depending on the growth rate they calculated. (See the following calculations.) Discuss how the apple represents any finite resource such as food, water, land, or minerals. Discuss the effect that various population growth rates have on the amount of the resource per capita.

A population starting at 100 and growing at a rate of 0.5 percent for 20 years will have 110 people. One hundred percent of the resource (apple, candy, pie, or ?) divided among 110 people means that each one will only receive 91 percent of what they would have received if the population had remained at 100. (100/110 = .91 = 91%). The figures are:

growth rate	new allocation (% of original allocation)	growth rate	new allocation (% of original allocation)
0.5%	91%	−0.5%	111%
1.0%	82%	−1.0%	122%
1.5%	74%	−1.5%	135%
2.0%	67%	−2.0%	149%
2.5%	61%	−2.5%	167%
3.0%	55%	−3.0%	185%

PART II: QUALITY OR QUANTITY?

1. Distribute the sheet entitled "More Is Less; Part II: Quality or Quantity?"
2. Explain the assignment to the students.
3. Have the students do the assignment in teams of 2–4, possibly the same teams that worked together for Part I.
4. Discuss the results of the activity.

PART III: DEAR GRANDCHILD

1. Distribute and explain the writing assignment of "Dear Grandchild," 26.2.
2. After the students have completed the assignment, discuss their realizations and feelings.

Discussion

PART I

1. Were you surprised at how rapidly the population changed with only a small rate of growth?
2. How can a country's birth rate decline yet its population increase?
3. Distinguish between a reduced rate of population growth and a reduced population.
4. How might population increases in the more developed countries affect your life 10, 20, 30, or 40 years from now?
5. How might population increases in the less developed countries affect your life 10, 20, 30, or 40 years from now?

6. How might population increases in your local area affect the lifestyle there in 10, 20, 30, or 40 years from now?

PART II

1. Did the "good" things (green) tend to increase or decrease with increased population?

2. Did the "bad" things (red) tend to increase or decrease with increased population?

PART III

What were some of your thoughts as you wrote your letter?

Answers to 26.3, Population—More Is Less Questions

1. As a population increases exponentially, there is an ever-increasing rate of growth, resulting in a steeper and steeper population growth curve.

2. Generally, increased population results in a decrease of things that we consider desirable and an increase of most undesirable things. Refer to students' activity sheets for examples.

3. It is not possible for the entire world to live as we in the United States do. If 4.3 percent of the population of the world use 30 percent of the resources, each 1 percent use 30/4.3 or about 7 percent of the resources. Thus, for 100 percent of the world to use an equivalent amount, they would use 700 percent of the resources! (Another way to look at this is to point out that we in the United States use about 7 times as much as the average person on Earth. To be fair, we should cut our resource consumption to about 1/6th or 1/7th of what it currently is. How do the students feel about that?)

4. Answers will vary, but it is very important for population growth to be halted in all areas.

5. Answers will vary.

6. Answers will vary.

7. Generally, an increase in human population will result in:

   a. more extinctions

   b. lower quality of air and water, at least until technology catches up with growth (IF it does!)

   c. less space available

   d. less food available per capita

   e. more stress and conflict as competition for resources increases

   f. less energy per person

   g. more competition for jobs and housing

   h. more chance of spread of contagious disease due to crowding

   i. Answers will vary, but there will probably be less freedom and fewer resources available.

   j. Answers will vary.

8. Answers will vary. Some nations already do.

9. Answers will vary. Some nations already do.

10. Answers will vary. Students should address both their own family size and their use of resources. (If it is not comfortable for you, you don't have to get into a discussion of HOW to control family size. You might discuss why many people feel that they should do so.)

Extensions (See Activity 32 for suggestions for student projects.)

PART I

1. Obtain copies of the latest U.S. and/or World Population data sheets from the Population Reference Bureau. They also publish activity guides to go with their data sheets:

> Population Reference Bureau
> 1875 Connecticut Avenue, NW, #520
> Washington, DC 20009
> (202) 483–1100

2. Have students study the writings of Thomas Malthus, Paul Ehrlich, and other writers on population issues.

3. Have the students graph their prediction of what would happen to resources per person on the same graph as their exponential population change graph.

4. Invite guest speakers on population issues including:

   a. ways of preventing pregnancy, including abstention

   b. abortion

   c. women's rights

   d. resource distribution

   (Some of these topics are controversial. Be sure to check your district's policies regarding controversial issues. Also, be sure to screen speakers carefully. They can sometimes do more harm than good!)

5. Have students make a bulletin board of a graph of the human population through time, including projected population for the next 100 years. It can be illustrated with magazine pictures.

PART II

1. Discuss the role of technology in the population resources question.

2. Have the students make a bulletin board of the arrows from this activity, illustrated with magazine pictures.

PART III

1. Have the students write a letter to a friend or grandchild 40 years from now if the world's population is reduced—through peaceful humane means—by 50 percent from today's population. Compare this scenario to that of the letter with doubled population.

2. Have students make a bulletin board depicting the idea that the United States has about 4.3 percent of the world's population but uses about 30 percent of the world's energy and mineral resources and produces about a third of the world's pollution and trash. (That's a pretty big slice of the pie!)

Modifications

PART I

1. Students can reduce or extend their computations and graphing as far as you wish. To correlate with Part III, you might have them carry them out to 40 years.
2. Have one team calculate a very high growth rate such as 7 percent or more.

PART II

Add other factors, both good and harmful.

PART III

Have the students write a letter to a classmate who is currently their friend, imagining that they haven't seen each other for 40 years.

References

Anonymous, *EdVentures in Population Education*. Washington, DC: Zero Population Growth, 1984.

Brouse, Deborah, and Pamela Wasserman, *For Earth's Sake*. Washington, DC: Zero Population Growth, 1989.

Miller, G. Tyler, *Living in the Environment*. Belmont, CA: Wadsworth Publishing Company, 1990.

Wasserman, Pamela, and Andrea Doyle, *Earth Matters*. Washington, DC: Zero Population Growth, 1991.

26.1 Population—More Is Less: Background Information

What is the most pressing environmental issue of our time? Is it acid rain? Air pollution? Deforestation? While some authorities might answer differently, most would agree that the problem of human **population** growth is of major importance.

To see why this is so, we need to consider two aspects of human population growth: the **quantity** of human life and the **quality** of human life. First, let us consider the quantity of human life.

Population growth occurs when the number of organisms entering a population exceeds the number of organisms leaving it. The population of a city, for example, grows if the people moving into it **(immigration)** plus the number of people born in it is greater than the sum of the number of people moving out **(emigration)** and the number of deaths. When considering the Earth, we need to consider the **birth rate** (number of live births per 1,000 people in a year) as compared to the **death rate** (number of deaths per 1,000 people per year).

For most of human existence, the death rate nearly equalled the birth rate, and the population grew very slowly. It took perhaps 2 billion years for the human population to reach 1 billion, about the year 1810. It took only 117 more years to add the second billion (1927), only 33 years to add the third billion (1960), 14 years to add the fourth billion (1974), and only 13 more years to reach 5 billion in 1987. It is predicted that the Earth's population will reach 6 billion people by 1998. This type of growth is called **"exponential growth."** Part I of this activity will allow you to investigate exponential growth.

As you do Part I, keep the following growth rates in mind:

The World:	1.8% per year	Africa:	2.9% per year
Latin America:	2.1% per year	Asia:	1.9% per year
United States:	0.7% per year	Europe:	0.3% per year

Those who study populations, **demographers,** often consider the **doubling time** for a population. We can see that the population of Earth is expected to double between 1960 and 1998, a doubling time of less than 40 years! Compare this to the 117 years that it took to double from 1 billion in 1810 to 2 billion in 1927, and the 47 years that it took to double again to 4 billion!

Any place on earth can support only a certain number of any type of organism. That is its **carrying capacity**. We do not know what the Earth's carrying capacity for people is. Some demographers feel that we have already exceeded it. Others think that our ability to manipulate our environment will enable us to support even more people. Regardless of how many people can possibly subsist on Earth, how many of us <u>should</u> there be? Is our goal to have as many people as possible existing on Earth, or is our goal for people to have happy, healthy, fulfilling lives? The United States has about 4.3 percent of the world's population but uses about 30 percent of the resources that are consumed each year. Is it possible for *all* people to achieve the standard of living that we in the United States now enjoy?

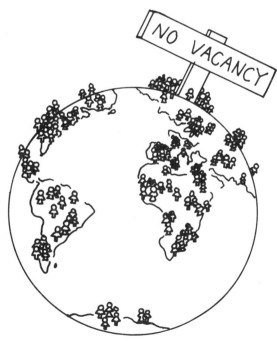

© 1993 by The Center for Applied Research in Education

26.2 Population—More Is Less: Instructions
Part I: Exponential Growth

Your team will be assigned a population growth rate, stated as a percentage. Note that a negative population growth rate means simply that the population is getting smaller.

Use a calculator to determine the population each year for a population that starts at 100. Round off decimals to the nearest whole number. As you do your calculations, record your data on the table below.

For example, if you were assigned a growth rate of 7 percent, the first part of the table would look like this: [calculations: $100 \times 1.07 = 107$ $107 \times 1.07 = 114.49$]

year #	population	year #	population
0	100	11	_____
1	107	12	_____
2	114	13	_____

As you do your calculations, one team member should graph the population change. Before beginning your graph, your team should:

• decide which axis should represent the year and which should represent the population
• decide what the units should be on the population axis
• graph a population growth of 0 percent

population growth rate assigned: _____

year #	population	year #	population
0	100	11	_____
1	_____	12	_____
2	_____	13	_____
3	_____	14	_____
4	_____	15	_____
5	_____	16	_____
6	_____	17	_____
7	_____	18	_____
8	_____	19	_____
9	_____	20	_____
10	_____		

26.2 Population—More Is Less: Instructions
Part II: Quality or Quantity?

1. As a team, discuss the items listed below. Decide whether each item is generally "good" for people and the environment or is generally "harmful."

   • If it is "good," place a green "+" in the space beside the item.
   • If it is "harmful," place a red "−" in the space.
   • If your team really can't decide, place a black check in the space.

__ clean water	__ polluted air	__ food	__ opportunities for solitude
__ energy	__ minerals	__ wildlife	__ endangered species
__ noise	__ space to live	__ acid rain	__ contagious disease
__ buildings	__ cars and roads	__ garbage	__ traffic congestion
__ overgrazing	__ unemployment	__ poverty	__ available housing
__ hunger	__ soil erosion	__ oil spills	__ international conflicts
__ material luxuries	__ forests	__ crowded cities	__ recreational space

2. Now consider the effect of a significantly increased human population on each item. If increasing the human population would tend to increase the item, write the item inside the arrow pointing upward. If increasing the human population would tend to decrease it, write the item inside the arrow pointing downward.

   • Use a red writing tool for the "harmful" things.
   • Use a green writing tool for the "good" things.

Increased human population tends to

Increased human population tends to:

DECREASE:

INCREASE:

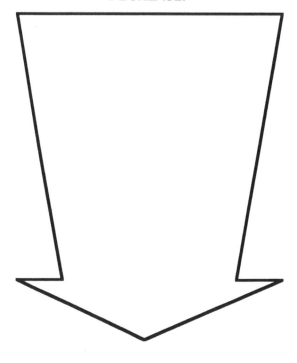

26.2 Population—More Is Less: Instructions
Part III: Dear Grandchild

If the current trends continue, the population of the world will be about twice as large 40 years from now. What do you think your life will be like in 40 years? Will you have children? Grandchildren? What will their lives be like? What will the environment be like in the area where you now live?

Write a letter to your grandchild, who is 10 years old. In your letter, discuss:

- what you do for a living
- what you do for recreation
- how the world has changed
- what you eat
- your energy source
- what you would have done differently
- your hopes and dreams for your grandchild
- offer one simple piece of advice to your grandchild

date: _____

Dear _____

_____

_____

_____

_____

_____

_____

_____

_____

_____

_____

(Continue on the back of this paper or on a separate paper.)

26.3 Population—More Is Less: Questions

1. Summarize the effect of exponential growth on a population.

   _____

   _____

2. In Part II of this activity, you saw some relationships between population and some parts of the environment. What sorts of things tend to increase with population increases? What sorts of things tend to decrease?

   _____

   _____

   _____

3. The United States has about 4.3 percent of the Earth's human population and is responsible for about 30 percent of the annual resource use and pollution. What does this tell us about the lifestyle that is possible for the world's population?

   _____

   _____

   _____

4. Which is more important, to halt population growth in the rapidly growing less-developed areas such as Africa or in the more slowly growing developed areas such as the United States? Discuss your answer.

   _____

   _____

   _____

5. List some advantages of a reduced human population.

   _____

   _____

   _____

6. Discuss the relative importance of quantity of life vs. quality of life.

   _____

   _____

   _____

© 1993 by The Center for Applied Research in Education

7. How does human population growth affect the following?

   a. extinction of other species

   _____

   b. quality of air and water

   _____

   c. space available for recreation

   _____

   d. food available for people

   _____

   e. stress and conflict

   _____

   f. energy resources available per person

   _____

   g. competition for jobs and housing

   _____

   h. the spread of contagious diseases

   _____

   i. your lifestyle in the next 40 years

   _____

   j. your descendants' lifestyles

   _____

8. Should governments enact and enforce laws to limit population? Explain your answer.

   _____

   _____

9. Should governments encourage population control through such measures as education, tax incentives for smaller families, and making birth control more available? Explain your answer.

   _____

   _____

10. What can you do, personally, to help with the overpopulation problem?

    _____

    _____

26.4 Population—More Is Less
Instructor's Data Sheet

CHANGES IN A POPULATION STARTING AT 100, WITH VARIOUS GROWTH RATES

	YEAR NUMBER										
	0 (start)	1	2	3	4	5	6	7	8	9	
GROWTH RATE					POPULATION						
-3.0%	100	97	94	91	89	86	83	81	78	76	C
-2.5%	100	98	95	93	90	88	86	84	82	80	O
-2.0%	100	98	96	94	92	90	89	87	85	83	N
-1.5%	100	99	97	96	94	93	91	90	89	87	T
-1.0%	100	99	98	97	96	95	94	93	92	91	I
-0.5%	100	100	99	99	98	98	97	97	96	96	N
0.0%	100	(A growth rate of 0% results in an unchanged population.)								100	U
+0.5%	100	101	101	102	102	103	103	104	104	105	E
+1.0%	100	101	102	103	104	105	106	107	108	109	
+1.5%	100	102	103	105	106	108	109	111	113	114	B
+2.0%	100	102	104	106	108	110	113	115	117	120	E
+2.5%	100	103	105	108	110	113	116	119	122	125	L
+3.0%	100	103	106	109	113	116	119	123	127	130	O

← W

	YEAR NUMBER										
	10	11	12	13	14	15	16	17	18	19	20
GROWTH RATE					POPULATION						
-3.0%	74	72	69	67	65	63	61	60	58	56	54
-2.5%	78	76	74	72	70	68	67	65	63	62	60
-2.0%	82	80	78	77	75	74	72	71	70	68	67
-1.5%	86	85	83	82	81	80	79	77	76	75	74
-1.0%	90	90	89	88	87	86	85	84	83	83	82
-0.5%	95	95	94	94	93	93	92	92	91	91	90
+0.5%	105	106	106	107	107	108	108	109	109	110	110
+1.0%	110	112	113	114	115	116	117	118	120	121	122
+1.5%	116	118	120	121	123	125	127	129	131	133	135
+2.0%	122	124	127	129	132	135	137	140	143	146	149
+2.5%	128	131	134	138	141	145	148	152	156	160	164
+3.0%	134	138	143	147	151	156	160	165	170	175	181

© 1993 by The Center for Applied Research in Education

ACTIVITY 27: FOOD? WHAT FOOD? _____

Activity Summary

By participating in a simple relay game, students see that the transfer of materials and energy between organisms in a food chain is not 100 percent efficient. Discussion leads to a better understanding of problems of food and population.

Introduction

It is generally agreed that the typical American diet has too much meat and too little fiber. Nutritionists would encourage most Americans to eat less meat for health reasons.

There are reasons, other than health, to reduce meat consumption. As the world's population increases, ways to feed more people need to be found. The food that goes to beef cattle, hogs, chickens, and other animals on American farms and ranches could be used to feed people directly. Ecologists estimate that only about 10 percent of the energy contained in a food organism becomes available to the organism that consumes it. Thus, the land that grows corn to support beef cattle that would support "X" people could, theoretically, support about "10 X" people eating corn. Modern agricultural methods often used in the United States also use a lot of energy, most of it coming from fossil fuels. It is estimated that the American agricultural industry uses about 10 to 15 units of fossil fuel energy to put one unit of food energy on the table. Subsistence farmers elsewhere, on the other hand, produce about 10 units of food for each one they expend.

Other people promote vegetarianism for humanitarian reasons. They feel that it is immoral to take an animal's life for human food.

It is worthwhile for students to consider their eating habits. Many students have poor diets. They may not be undernourished, but many are malnourished and/or overnourished. One advantage of meats is that they provide a variety of the amino acids that we need for protein synthesis. With an understanding of nutrition, these amino acids can also be obtained from a properly balanced vegetarian diet.

This activity teaches about food chains and food pyramids, also known as pyramids of numbers or pyramids of biomass.

Strictly speaking, a food chain does not include the physical environment. It is important, though, that students understand that the physical environment provides the basis for all food chains.

Grouping

Teams of 5–7 students.

Time

One 45- to 55-minute period

Anticipated Outcomes

The students will:

- increase their understanding of food chains and food pyramids
- increase their understanding of the environmental value of eating lower on the food chain
- learn more about nutrition
- increase their willingness to reduce their meat consumption

Materials

—Photocopied student pages:
- 27.1 Food? What Food? Background Information (one per student)
- 27.2 Food? What Food? Questions (one per student)

—Popcorn (about 1 quart per team for the activity, plus some to eat afterward)

—An area, suitable for a relay, about 40 yards by 30 yards (or more) in size

—"Cones" or other objects to mark the start and end points for the relay (see a P.E. teacher)

Vocabulary

food chain	malnourished	per capita
undernourished	vegetarian	

Teacher Preparation

1. Photocopy the Background Information sheet (27.1) and Questions sheet (27.2).
2. Obtain materials.

SAFETY CONSIDERATIONS

1. To reduce the eating of the popcorn by the students during the activity, tell them that popcorn will be provided for eating after the activity.
2. Be sure that the area where the relay will be done is reasonably smooth and free of holes, sprinkler heads, or other hazards.

Procedure

1. If the class has not yet done Activity 16 (Food Chains), do it. If they have, review the concept of food chains and energy and materials being passed from one trophic level to another.
2. Form teams of 5 to 7 students each. If the teams are not equal, have some students run twice.
3. Within each team, assign each student a trophic level role, such as plant, herbivore, first carnivore, second carnivore, scavenger, decomposer, and so forth. In each team, the student with the largest hands should represent the sun. Have the students line up in order behind the "sun."

4. Discuss (or have students tell about) each trophic level. Explain that the popcorn represents energy and materials that are to be passed from one level to another.

5. Explain the rules.

   a. The "suns" will be given as much popcorn as they can hold in their two hands. They may not make a pouch out of shirts, skirts, and so forth.

   b. They are to run to the marker, circle it, and return to the next person in the food chain.

   c. The popcorn is passed to the next person in the food chain, who then runs to the marker, circles it, returns, and passes it to the next person.

   d. This is continued until the entire food chain has run the relay, including any who need to run a second time because of uneven numbers in the teams.

   e. When the entire team has completed the relay, the last person is to hold the popcorn above his or her head as a signal that the team has completed the relay.

   f. Remind them to run quickly but carefully and not to eat popcorn that has fallen on the ground or that others have handled. Tell them that clean popcorn will be provided for eating later.

   g. Discuss the activity. See Discussion topics below.

Discussion

1. What was the limiting factor affecting how much popcorn could be carried? (At the start, students will often think that the student with the largest hands will give his or her team an advantage. In reality, the limiting factor is the student with the smallest hands.)

2. Look at the ground. What does the popcorn on the ground represent? (heat energy and materials lost to the environment)

3. When did most of the popcorn spill? (at the transfer point, unless there was an accident) What would happen if there were fewer transfers?

4. An example of a food (energy) chain might be: sun → corn → beef cow → man. Could more people be supported if the cow step were eliminated and people ate the corn? (Point out that the sun, while not "food," is the basis of all food chains.)

5. What are some advantages and disadvantages of vegetarianism?

Answers to 27.2, Food? What Food?: Questions

1. Most of the energy contained in a food is not available to the consuming organism because it is given off as heat, is expended in the food-getting process, or is not extracted from the food and is passed out of the body as waste.

2. Answers may vary. Water, available sunlight, and soil fertility are natural limiting factors. The availability of labor, machinery, and chemicals are limiting factors in human food-growing systems.

3. Starvation increases the death rate and so limits populations. Undernourishment and malnourishment affect the reproductive capacities of men and women, infant mortality rate, and death rate.

4. Malnutrition occurs when the diet does not supply enough of the proper proteins, vitamins, minerals, and other nutrients needed for good health. It also occurs when

there is too much of some nutrients such as fats and sugars. <u>Undernourishment</u> is a condition of not having enough food.

5. Cutting back on meat consumption certainly helps reduce the demand for land, water, and other materials used in growing meat. It can also help reduce fat intake.

6. Answers will vary.

7. Advantages of raising one's own food include such things as being able to control (or eliminate) chemicals such as pesticides, saving money, and the enjoyment that many derive from gardening. Disadvantages include the time and effort required, space requirements, environmental limitations such as soil fertility, climate, and weather.

Extensions

1. Have the students record the types and amounts of food that they eat for a week or more. Have them record (privately) their weight at the start and the end of the week. Have them design a data-recording table. Discuss parameters and controls for this experiment. Discuss what happened to the food. If they ate 20 pounds of food, why didn't they gain 20 pounds?

2. If you keep animals such as guinea pigs, rats, mice, and so forth in the classroom, have the students keep accurate records of the food and water given to them for a month. Collect and record the weight of wastes cleaned from the cage. Compare food and water consumed to waste collected. How can the differences be explained? (gases such as CO_2 and water vapor given off, evaporation, wastes absorbed by shavings or papers in the cage, etc.)

3. Investigate the diets of people in areas where there are chronic food shortages. Compare the percentage of meat and vegetables in their diets to typical diets in the United States, as represented by the students in the class. How can the differences be explained?

4. Have the students explore and report on the pros and cons of vegetarianism.

5. Have a vegetarian meal for the class. Either have the students each prepare part, work out something with a home economics teacher, or invite vegetarian restaurants to donate samples of their wares.

6. Have the students prepare vegetarian cookbooks, including only dishes that they have tried.

7. Have the students try out vegetarian recipes.

8. Are vegetarian entrees offered in the school cafeteria? Have students investigate the nutritional requirements of the food services program in your school.

9. Have the students find out about and illustrate food pyramids, pyramids of numbers and/or pyramids of (bio)mass. Have them illustrate this concept either with a bulletin board or a three-dimensional model.

10. Research report topics: the green revolution, pest control, organic/sustainable yield agricultural systems, fish farming, food irradiation, seed banks (genetic storage banks), biological magnification of chemicals in foods.

Modifications

1. The activity can be done indoors. Be sure to have a broom or large dust mop for clean-up.
2. Play another round with uneven teams. This will help bring home the idea that more energy and material is lost at each level. (Having the students explain why shorter teams are desirable can be an assessment method.)

References

Miller, G. Tyler, *Living in the Environment.* Belmont, CA: Wadsworth Publishing Company, 1990.

Tourtillot, Leeann, *Conserve and Renew.* Sacramento, CA: California Energy Extension Service, 1990.

27.1 Food? What Food?: Background Information

As the world's population increases, so does the need for food. About one fourth of the people living today are not adequately fed. Each year, 20 to 40 million people die because of under-nutrition or malnutrition. People need not only enough food, but they need the right kinds of food to be healthy.

Food provides us with the energy and chemicals that we need for life. Growing, harvesting, processing, shipping, and preparing food are extremely important processes and industries. Our food industry, from growing and processing to selling food, employs about 20 percent of the work force, uses about 17 percent of the commercial energy consumed, and generates about 18 percent of our gross national product, including food that feeds many people in other countries. Few things are as important as food. Yet, even in the United States, many people are **malnourished** or **undernourished.**

World food production more than doubled between 1950 and 1984, and food prices dropped. Even so, in many areas, the average food production **per capita** has actually dropped by over 20 percent! This drop has been caused by a variety of factors, including population increases, changes in dietary habits to include more meat, decrease in soil fertility, droughts, and other factors.

Generally, at each step in a **food chain** most of the energy stored in an organism is not transferred to the organism that consumes it. If 100 calories are stored in corn and the corn is eaten by a human, the human retains about 10 calories. The rest is used or lost as heat or in waste products. If that same 100 calories in corn is fed to cattle (or hogs or chickens), the cattle gain about 10 calories. If a human then eats the beef, he or she gains only about 1 calorie!

Energy provides us with more than food. We also get various nutrients, including minerals, vitamins, and proteins. Meat is an important source of protein-building amino acids for many Americans. Those amino acids can also be obtained from vegetables, too, and many people have chosen to be **vegetarians.**

There are many reasons that some people decide not to eat meat. Too much meat is not healthy, principally because of its fat content. Meat is expensive. Some people object to killing animals for food. Some are concerned about the land, fuels, expertise, money, water, and other resources that are used to grow meat. They point out that those resources could be used to grow plants that would feed many more people than the meat will.

We also need to be aware of the chemicals used in growing and processing many of our foods. Fertilizers, pesticides, and fungicides are used extensively in growing many foods in the United States and in other countries. Preservatives, coloring agents and other chemicals may be added before we purchase food. Many people are concerned about the safety of these food additives.

For these and other reasons, the study of nutrition is not only interesting, it is vital!

27.2 Food? What Food?: Questions

1. What happens to the approximately 90 percent of the energy that is "lost" at each transfer of energy in a food chain?

    _____

    _____

2. What are some factors that limit how much food can be grown in an area?

    _____

    _____

3. In what ways is food a limiting factor for human populations?

    _____

    _____

4. Distinguish between malnourishment and undernourishment.

    _____

    _____

5. Could reducing one's meat consumption provide some of the benefits of vegetarianism? Discuss the idea of cutting back on meat consumption.

    _____

    _____

    _____

6. Some people have suggested that, in the long run, sending food to famine victims may cause more harm than it helps. Some suggest attaching conditions to aid sent to famine victims. What do you think of this?

    _____

    _____

    _____

7. What are some advantages and disadvantages of growing at least some of one's own food?

    _____

    _____

    _____

    _____

ACTIVITY 28: WE "AUTO" DRIVE LESS _____

Activity Summary

Student teams complete various surveys of transportation habits and choices. They then graph and analyze the data.

Introduction

Most Americans are dependent on the private automobile. We use it for about 98 percent of all urban transportation, 85 percent of all travel between cities, and 84 percent of all travel to and from work—69 percent of us drive to and from work alone in a private automobile. The average number of people in a typical passenger vehicle is only 1.2! Only 15 percent of us carpool, and a mere 7 percent of us ride public transportation to and from work!

As individuals and as a society, we pay a huge price for our addiction to the private automobile. The Background Information sheet, 28.1, gives some statistics about our use of the automobile and its effects.

As the streets become more crowded, as oil prices go up and air pollution increases, mass transit is going to become a more attractive option to many Americans. There are, however, many attitudinal blocks to the acceptance of public transportation in America. By examining their own attitudes and surveying to determine the attitudes of others, students can gain some understanding of what it will take to move Americans out of their private automobiles.

Grouping

Teams of 2 students.

Time

Introducing the activity: 20–30 minutes
Students complete surveys outside class
Graphing and discussing the data: 45–55 minutes

Anticipated Outcomes

The students will:

- increase their understanding of some of the factors that influence transportation choices in the United States.
- increase their willingness to conserve fuel.
- increase their understanding of the effects of private automobile use in the United States.
- increase their ability to graph and analyze data.

Materials

—Photocopied student pages:

- 28.1 We "Auto" Drive Less: Background Information (one per student)
- 28.2 We "Auto" Drive Less: Instructions and Survey Forms (varies)
- 28.3 We "Auto" Drive Less: Questions (one per student)

—Graph paper

—Transparencies of the surveys and graph paper with axes drawn

Vocabulary

carpool   public transit   subsidy

Teacher Preparation

1. Decide which surveys you want to use, how many students should be in a team, and how many teams you want to do each survey.

2. Photocopy the Background Information sheet (28.1), Instructions and Survey forms (28.2), and Questions sheet (28.3). Note that each team does Survey I and one of the others. Some survey form pages need to be cut in half.

SAFETY CONSIDERATION

Caution the students to be careful of traffic and people while doing their surveys.

Procedure

1. Introduce the activity by discussing the advantages and disadvantages of the use of the private automobile as the main means of transportation for most Americans today. Be sure to include social costs such as isolation, time wasted, financial costs (both direct costs such as purchase, gasoline, maintenance, and insurance, and indirect costs such as taxes, land costs, medical insurance costs, and the like), accidents, land dedicated to roads, parking, car lots, and so forth. Ask the students about their families' automobile ownership.

2. Discuss the advantages and disadvantages of various alternatives to reliance on the private automobile, including:

- walking
- cycling
- motorcycle
- carpooling
- bus
- train

3. Point out that automobiles are usually fueled by gasoline, a nonrenewable re-

source. Point out, too, that we currently import between 40 and 50 percent of our oil. Ask what would happen if the supply of petroleum were to be severely disrupted, either because of world economic and political events or simply because the supplies got used up. What would it take to get most people to reduce their gasoline consumption by 25 percent or more?

4. Issue the Background Information sheet (28.1) and the Instructions sheet (28.2). Have the students form survey teams of 2 or 3 students and assign them their survey forms (28.2).
5. Discuss the taking of the surveys, as per the Instructions sheet.
6. Assign a due date for the surveys. Assign the number of people to be surveyed.
7. When the students return their survey forms to class, have the teams with the same survey forms compare and combine their data.
8. Discuss how to graph the data, including the selection of axes (which data should go on the vertical axis and which on the horizontal), selection of units, and labeling of axes. Each team should then graph their data. Teams with narrative responses to their questions should make up groups for similar answers.
9. Either have the students show their data and graphs to the class or make overhead transparencies of the data and/or graphs to use while discussing the data.
10. Discuss the data. (See Discussion questions below.)

Discussion

1. How much of a price increase would it take to get most drivers to reduce their driving significantly? What other ways are there to encourage the use of public transportation?
2. Did age seem to have an effect on the amount of the price increase needed? Why or why not?
3. Which of the actions considered for reducing gas consumption were preferred by the most people?
4. Did age seem to influence which actions were preferred? Why or why not?
5. What are some of the advantages of riding public transportation? Disadvantages?
6. Did age have an influence on the opinions about public transportation?
7. If the price of gasoline is raised, who will be hurt more, the rich or the poor?
8. If public transportation is made more convenient and affordable, who will be helped more, the rich or the poor?
9. If public transportation were used more, what benefits would result?
10. What could be done to encourage people to use public mass transportation in your area?

Answers to 28.3, We "Auto" Drive Less Questions

1. Answers will vary. For most people, a small increase such as 20 cents is not much of a deterrent to driving. Price increases do not affect all groups equally. Those with low incomes are affected disproportionately.
2. Answers will vary. From an environmental perspective, such a plan would be a good

idea because the higher price would discourage unnecessary driving and promote fuel efficiency as well as support public transportation.

3. Answers will vary. Some disadvantages are the loss of privacy, inconvenience, and in some cases, increased time for a given trip.

4. Answers will vary. Some advantages include the opportunity to socialize, the convenience of being able to do something other than drive a car, money saved, time saved when one considers the time it takes to maintain and earn the money to pay for a car, and a multitude of environmental advantages ranging from air pollution to land use.

5. Answers will vary.

6. Answers will vary. (There is an interesting activity dealing with this in the *California Class Project* by Olga Clymire.)

Extensions (See Activity 32 for suggestions for student projects.)

1. Combine the data from several classes and compare each class's data to the larger sample.

2. Find out whether sex, occupation, or financial status have an impact on the answers to the survey questions.

3. Visit a workplace that encourages carpooling, vanpooling, or other use of mass transportation. Talk to the person who runs the program.

4. Many students in suburban areas have never ridden public transportation, especially trains. Take a field trip utilizing public transportation.

5. Obtain a detailed map of your community. With the students, devise a plan for determining how much land is dedicated to the private automobile. Be sure to include parking lots, sales, parts and tire stores, repair facilities, roads, and manufacturing plants. Check with city planners to find out how much land mass transit would take.

6. Students can make up other surveys, including students, faculty, and so forth.

7. Have the students calculate how much money actually is spent on the private automobile when the following are included:

purchase price	taxes to pay for roads, signals and signs, courts, police
operation (fuel, oil)	purchase price of land for driveways and garages
maintenance (repairs)	part of the cost of medical insurance
automobile insurance	damages not covered by insurance

8. Have student teams devise plans for increasing carpooling in your community. Have the students present their plans to the city council or other appropriate agency.

9. Have student teams make a plan for a city the size of your community that uses a transportation mix that includes walking, cycling, trains, buses, electric trains, and private automobiles.

10. Students can investigate the demise of the public streetcar system in cities in the United States in the 1930s and 1940s, which was orchestrated by General Motors, Firestone Tire, and Standard Oil to increase their sales of motor vehicles and buses.

Modification

Modify the survey forms or make your own as you see fit.

References

Christensen, John W., *Global Science: Laboratory Manual* and *Teacher's Guide*. Dubuque, IA: Kendall/Hunt Publishing Company, 1991.

Clymire, Olga (principal writer), *California Class Project*. Costa Mesa, CA: Orange County Superintendent of Schools, 1988.

Miller, G. Tyler, *Living in the Environment*. Belmont, CA: Wadsworth Publishing Company, 1990.

28.1 We "Auto" Drive Less: Background Information

In the United States, we are addicted to the private automobile. Like many drugs, it gives us the feeling of power and freedom. Also like many drugs, it is habit forming and harmful.

Just how addicted to the automobile are we?

- About 98 percent of our urban travel is done in private automobiles.
- About 85 percent of all travel to and from cities is done in private automobiles.
- About 84 percent of all travel to and from work is done in private automobiles.
- The United States, with less than 5 percent of the world's population, has about one third of the world's automobiles.
- About one of every six dollars spent in the United States is spent on automobile-related purchases.

Just how harmful are private automobiles?

- In the United States, about 48,000 people are killed in motor vehicle accidents each year, and an additional 300,000 are seriously injured.
- At the current rate, about 1 out of every 60 babies born in the United States will be killed in an automobile accident before he or she reaches the age of 21.
- Automobile accidents and governmental **subsidies** to support the automobile cost about $400 billion per year, which averages $2,350 for every car and truck in the United States.
- At least one third of the average city's land is devoted to roads and parking. In some cities such as Los Angeles, they take up two thirds of the total land area!
- Automobiles account for about half of our air pollution.
- Many high school students want their own car so badly that they take jobs so that they can earn the money a car requires. For many of them, the long hours of work and using the car result in low achievement at school. Unfortunately, many even drop out of school.
- The use of private automobiles accounts for about 14 percent of all the energy used in the United States. Making, selling, and providing parts, materials, and roads for cars constitutes another large portion of our country's energy consumption.

There are many alternatives to the private automobile, but most of us don't use them. Sixty-nine percent of us drive alone to and from work, 15 percent of us carpool, and only 7 percent take public transportation.

Given the many problems caused by cars, why do we use them so much? Consider your own attitudes toward the use of the private car. What advantages and disadvantages does it have for you? Is our addiction to the private automobile worth all the death, air pollution, energy waste, and money that it costs?

28.2 We "Auto" Drive Less: Instructions

Teams of students from your class will be conducting surveys to determine people's opinions about a number of transportation-related questions. After you collect your data, your team will share its data with that collected by one or more other teams investigating the same question.

After you have shared your data with the other team(s), your combined team will graph the data collected by both (all) teams.

When you ask somebody your survey question, you should first be sure that:

a. You understand the question and how to record answers.

b. The person has not already answered the survey question for another team.

c. The person tells you his or her age.

When you record the responses, be careful to record them in the correct column.

After someone answers your question, be sure to thank the person.

Some survey questions may require you to summarize the response in a few words. If so, be sure that they accurately reflect the response of the person interviewed.

SURVEY I: PEOPLE PER CAR
(TO BE DONE BY UNDERLINE TEAMS)

Select a safe place along a busy street, preferably at "rush hour." Observe the automobiles that pass, noting the number of people in each car, including the driver. Tally your information below. Count the people in the first 100 cars that pass. Do not count commercial vehicles such as delivery trucks, buses, taxis, and so forth. (If there is very little traffic, count the people in the first 25 or 50 cars that pass.)

Location surveyed: _____ date: _____ time: _____ A.M. P.M.

© 1993 by The Center for Applied Research in Education

NUMBER OF PEOPLE IN THE CAR, INCLUDING THE DRIVER					
1	2	3	4	5	more than 5

SURVEY II: HOW MUCH TO CHANGE?

Be sure to record the response of the person in the appropriate age column. Ask at least 12 people, including 3 from each age group.

    Question: How much of a reduction in the amount you drive would the following increases in the price of a gallon of gasoline cause you?

	Age Group											
	16–20			21–30			31–40			41+		
Price Increase	no	some	major	no	some	major	no	some	major	no	some	major
		reduction			reduction			reduction			reduction	
$ .20/gal.												
$ .50/gal.												
$1.00/gal.												
$1.50/gal.												
$2.00/gal.												

-- ✂ --

SURVEY III: THE LONE DRIVER!

Be sure to record the response of the person in the appropriate age column. Ask at least 12 people, including 3 from each age group.

    Question: When you drive to work or school, do you usually drive alone?

Ages	yes	no
16–20		
21–30		
31–40		
41+		

SURVEY IV: DIFFICULT CHOICES

Be sure to record the response of the person in the appropriate age column. Ask at least 12 people, including 3 from each age group.

Question: If gasoline consumption in the United States absolutely **had** to be reduced by 25 percent, which of the following measures would you support?

ACTION	Age Group							
	16–20		21–30		31–40		41 +	
	agree	disagree	agree	disagree	agree	disagree	agree	disagree
1. Triple the price of gas and use the money to develop alternative energy sources.								
2. Ration gasoline. Issue coupons. Unused coupons could be sold, traded, or given away.								
3. Increase the minimum age for a driver's license to 21 years.								
4. Lower air pollution standards so more coal and less oil would be burned by industry.								
5. Ban students from driving to school if a bus is available.								
6. Ban the driving of cars with even-numbered licenses 2 days a week and ban odd-numbered cars 2 other days.								
7. Use military action to obtain oil from other countries.								
8. Require that all new cars get 30% more miles per gallon.								
9. Other:								

SURVEY V: PUBLIC TRANSIT USERS

Be sure to record the age of the person in the age column. Ask at least 12 people, including 3 from each of the following age groups: 16–20   21–30   31–40   41+

Ask this question of people who frequently use public transportation such as a bus, rapid transit system, or train.

Question: What is the main advantage of using public transportation?

age	Response—main advantage	age	Response—main advantage

---✂---

SURVEY VI: PUBLIC TRANSIT—IF ONLY. . .

Be sure to record the age of the person in the age column. Ask at least 12 people, including 3 from each of these age groups: 16–20   21–30   31–40   41+

Ask this question of people who seldom or never utilize public transportation.

Question: What would make public transportation attractive enough for you to utilize it?

age	Response	age	Response

28.3 We "Auto" Drive Less: Questions

1. In your survey, was raising the price of gas a small amount a very effective way to discourage private automobile use? Was the effect equal in all groups? Discuss.

   _____

   _____

   _____

2. In Europe, gasoline costs about 3 to 4 times as much as it does here. Would it be a good idea to triple the price of gas and use the extra money to build or promote an effective public transit system? Discuss.

   _____

   _____

   _____

3. What are the disadvantages of public transit systems?

   _____

   _____

   _____

4. What are the advantages of public transit systems?

   _____

   _____

   _____

5. What are your personal attitudes about public transit?

   _____

   _____

   _____

6. How could cities be built to facilitate, rather than discourage, public transit?

   _____

   _____

   _____

   _____

ACTIVITY 29: TOXICS IN THE HOME _____

Activity Summary

Students practice reading product warning labels and then survey their homes for common (and uncommon!) toxic materials. After identifying the toxic materials, students identify less toxic alternatives and learn how to dispose of hazardous household materials.

Introduction

When most of us hear the term "toxic waste," we think of nuclear waste, the Love Canal incident, medical waste washing up on beaches, or severe air or water pollution. Most of us, though, have a number of hazardous substances in our homes. These include paints, stains, solvents, many cleaning agents, pesticides and fertilizers, various automotive chemicals ranging from oil to battery acid, shoe polish, medicines and drugs, mothballs, disinfectants, deodorants, insect repellents, alcohol, tobacco, and a great variety of other substances.

Many of these substances are relatively safe if used properly. Unfortunately, many of them are frequently used or stored improperly. People ignore or fail to read the warnings on the labels. Toxic chemicals are often stored within reach of small children or too close to heat sources or where they can get knocked off a shelf or where they can mix with other substances. Substances are often mixed improperly, either with chemicals with which they are incompatible or in concentrations that are too strong. These and many other situations result in hundreds of deaths and thousands of injuries every year.

Additionally, when the containers are discarded, they usually contain unused chemicals or some residual chemicals. These can spill and/or mix while in transit to the landfill. Once at the landfill, they often are carried away by water that seeps into the site. This leachate pollutes the surrounding land and can enter ground water and streams and be carried far downstream.

For these, and many other reasons, it is important that students (and their parents) become educated about hazardous wastes found in the home. They need to know what is there, how to store and use it properly, how to dispose of it, and what alternatives are available. It is also important that they know what to do in case of a spill or accidental poisoning. This activity is primarily a survey of chemicals in the home. It is highly recommended that you invite guest speakers from agencies that dispose of hazardous household products and from hospital emergency rooms to visit your class.

Grouping

Whole class, teams of 3–5, individuals

Time

Two 45- to 55-minute periods plus time at home.

Anticipated Outcomes

The students will:

- survey their homes for hazardous substances.
- examine labels of household products for warnings.
- list alternatives for hazardous substances.
- identify proper means of disposing of hazardous substances.
- increase their awareness of toxics in the home.

Materials

—Photocopied student pages:

- 29.1 Toxics in the Home: Background Information (one per student)
- 29.2 Toxics in the Home: Instructions and Data Table (one per student)
- 29.3 Toxics in the Home: Questions (one per student)

—Overhead transparencies of product warning labels

—Optional, recommended: literature, brochures, stickers from local poison control or hazardous waste agencies

Vocabulary

caustic	corrosive	flammable	ingest
leachate	toxic	volatile	

Teacher Preparation

1. Photocopy the Background Information sheet (29.1), Instructions and Data Table (29.2), and Questions sheet (29.3).
2. Obtain samples of common household products that have warning labels on them.
3. Photocopy labels with different warnings on them. Use the photocopies to make overhead transparencies.
4. Make transparencies of the Data Table (29.2).

SAFETY CONSIDERATIONS

1. Do not allow students to bring containers of hazardous materials to school.
2. Be sure to follow the warning labels when you use any of the products in the classroom. Set a good example. Seek to use safer alternatives.
3. Do not store hazardous chemicals in your classroom.
4. Tape the lids of any containers that you bring to the classroom for samples.

Procedure

NOTE: SEVERAL OF THE SUGGESTED EXTENSIONS CAN BE VERY VALUABLE.

1. Show examples of several common household products that have warnings on their labels. Allow teams of 3 to 5 students to examine the containers and read the labels aloud to the class.

2. Discuss product-labeling requirements and the meanings of the terms on the labels. Use transparencies that show one or more warning labels. Point out the liability disclaimer.

3. Give the students the Instructions and Data Table sheet (29.2).

4. Have the students survey their homes for toxic materials and bring their data to class.

5. Use a transparency of the Data Table (29.2) to compile data from the whole class. Have the students raise their hands while you or a student use tally marks on the transparency to record which types of hazardous substances are most common. If a student did not record a material type on his or her own data table but knows that he or she has the material at home, include the student in the tally.

6. Distribute and discuss the Background Information sheet, including the Household Hazardous Materials Chart. Discuss the alternatives suggested. BE SURE TO POINT OUT THAT THIS CHART SHOWS ONLY A VERY SMALL PORTION OF THE HAZARDOUS MATERIALS FOUND IN THE AVERAGE HOME!

7. Optional but strongly recommended: Invite a guest speaker from whatever agency is responsible for disposal of hazardous household materials in your community. That might be the fire department, public works department, county solid waste commission, a private waste disposal company, or other agency. As part of the speaker's presentation, find out how he or she recommends disposing of hazardous household materials and containers.

8. Optional but strongly recommended: Invite a guest speaker from a local poison control center or emergency room to discuss treatment of injuries and poisonings resulting from improper use of household materials including medicines. See Extension 2.

Discussion

1. Were you aware that you had toxic materials in your home?

2. Do the warning labels provide enough information?

3. What would you do if you thought that your little brother had swallowed some harmful substance?

4. Why is it important to dispose of containers properly? What is leachate?

5. Are you willing to reduce your use of toxic materials? Why or why not? If so, how?

Answers to Questions 29.3, Toxics in the Home Questions

1. Answers will vary. You might remind the students that alcoholic beverages and tobacco are toxic.

2. All the materials listed are hazardous except baking soda.

3. a. check breathing, use CPR if needed, call 911, ambulance, poison control, emergency room

   b. ambulance, 911, drug line, poison control center, emergency room

   c. county health department, fire department, waste disposal company

   d. fire department, 911, county sheriff, state highway patrol

   e. poison control, physician, health department

   f. read labels carefully, discuss safe use and storage with all family members, store in locked cabinet, encourage switching to alternates, dispose of containers properly

4. Know about safe use, storage, and alternates. Educate family and friends. Read labels carefully; store and use properly.

Extensions (See Activity 32 for suggestions for student projects.)

1. See Procedure steps 7 and 8. (Arrange for guest speakers from waste disposal agency and hospital or poison control center.)

2. Have students design an emergency phone number list. Duplicate and distribute the list. The list should include:

Emergency response number (911?)	nearest hospital emergency room
police, fire department, ambulance	nearest relative
poison control center	two neighbors or other responsible adults
family doctor	parents' work phone numbers

3. Use a computer to make labels with emergency telephone numbers. Duplicate these for attachment to telephones. Such labels might be available from fire departments or other agencies.

4. Have students prepare a home hazardous substances presentation to give to younger students.

5. Invite the Red Cross or other agency to train the students on first aid for poisoning (and other first aid procedures).

6. Have the students make posters telling about home hazards and disposal of wastes. Have them arrange to have the posters displayed in local hardware, grocery, garden supply, and other stores.

7. Visit a local landfill to see how household trash and other materials are disposed of. Find out about monitoring of the site for leaks and illegal dumping of toxics.

8. Collect newspaper and other articles about toxic spills.

9. Have the students work with local agencies on a poison prevention educational program for younger students. Have your students get local businesses or service agencies to sponsor the program by purchasing commercially available educational materials.

10. Have the students test the alternatives suggested on the Hazardous Household Materials Chart and compare them to the usual toxic alternatives.

11. Have the students bring in warning labels from containers, newspaper articles, and pictures to make a hazardous materials bulletin board.

12. The students can investigate "toxic home syndrome."

13. The students can investigate radon in homes. Some science supply companies sell test kits.

Modification

You might want to send a letter home to explain the home survey to the parents.

References

Anonymous, *Hazardous Household Products.* Sacramento, CA: California Department of Health Services, 1990.

Clymire, Olga (principal writer), *California Class Project.* Costa Mesa, CA: Orange County Superintendent of Schools, 1988.

Comnes, Leslie, *Toxics: Taking Charge.* Hayward, CA: Alameda County Office of Education, 1989.

Daniel, Joseph E. (editor-in-chief), *1992 Earth Journal.* Boulder, CO: Buzzworm Books, 1992.

Miller, G. Tyler, *Living in the Environment.* Belmont, CA: Wadsworth Publishing Company, 1990.

29.1 Toxics in the Home: Background Information

Toxic materials are those that are dangerous or that can be dangerous if not used correctly. Many common household materials can be dangerous, even fatal, if not used properly. Hundreds of people, mostly children, die every year from misuse of ordinary household substances such as paints, cleaners, and pesticides. Do you know what hazards your home contains? What do terms like **caustic, volatile, corrosive,** and **flammable** mean? What happens to the container of a hazardous substance once the contents have been used?

In the United States, if a product contains certain toxic materials in certain amounts, it is supposed to bear a warning label. If the amount of the toxic chemical is low enough, though, the label isn't generally required. Labels may be absent, incomplete, or misleading. Some estimates indicate that as much as 85 percent of the warning labels are incorrect or misleading! So, even if a product doesn't have a warning label, it is wise to treat it carefully and use good judgment.

What kinds of household substances are likely to be hazardous? The most common hazardous household substances include:

- garden supplies, including pesticides, poisons, fertilizers, plant foods
- cleaners (drain, oven, spot removers, polishers, bleach, liquid cleaners)
- automotive chemicals (motor oil, battery acid, antifreeze, gas treatments)
- paints, lacquers, varnishes, thinner, stains
- glues, adhesives, solvents
- medicines, disinfectants, alcohol

For many toxic substances, there are less-hazardous alternatives. Some of these are listed on the "Household Hazardous Materials Chart."

An important thing to remember about toxic household products is that the container they came in usually contains some residue. If the used or partly used container is put into the trash, a number of problems may occur. When the trash is in the trash can, some relatively nontoxic materials may mix with others and form more dangerous chemicals. The trash collectors are exposed to these toxic chemicals. When the trash is taken to the landfill, water will eventually reach the trash and may dissolve and carry the toxics away from the landfill into the aquifer, nearby streams, or other areas. This water, which has dissolved chemicals, is called **leachate.** Modern landfills are designed to contain the leachate, but not all landfills are built and operated in such a way that the containment efforts always work. Even if they work well today, can we guarantee that the leachate will be contained for dozens or even hundreds of years?

What, then, should one do with hazardous household waste? Your teacher may arrange for a speaker on the topic. What should you do if somebody **ingests** some poisonous substance?

HOUSEHOLD HAZARDOUS MATERIALS CHART

SUBSTANCE	PROBLEM	PROPER DISPOSAL	ALTERNATIVES
abrasive cleaners scouring powder	CORROSIVE TOXIC	Use it all up. Rinse container.	baking soda or borax, lemon juice, toothpaste for small stains
ammonia-based cleaners	CORROSIVE TOXIC	Use it all up. Contact waste disposal company.	white vinegar diluted with water, elbow grease. NOTE: DON'T MIX AMMONIA-BASED CLEANERS WITH BLEACH!
chlorine or bleach-based cleaners	CORROSIVE TOXIC	Use it all up. Contact waste disposal company.	dry bleach, white vinegar, baking soda, or borax. NOTE: NEVER MIX BLEACH OR CHLORINE WITH AMMONIA!
drain openers and cleaners	CORROSIVE TOXIC	Use it all up. Contact waste disposal company.	pour boiling water down drains, use plunger or "snake"
oven cleaners	CORROSIVE TOXIC	Use it all up. Contact waste disposal company.	Clean oven as you use it. Use oven liner to catch drips. Use baking soda for scouring.
spot cleaners	TOXIC FLAMMABLE	Use it all up. Contact waste disposal company.	club soda, lemon juice, cornmeal and water paste, dry clean
antifreeze	TOXIC	Recycle.	none
engine degreasers cleaners, solvents	FLAMMABLE TOXIC	Recycle. Contact waste disposal company.	scrub with a brush, catch spills on a rag, fix leaky gaskets
motor oil	FLAMMABLE TOXIC	Recycle.	none. Fix leaky gaskets
enamel or oil-based paints	FLAMMABLE TOXIC	Use it up or donate it. Contact waste disposal company.	latex or water-based paints
latex or water-based paints	TOXIC	See above. Allow "empty" can and painted item to dry outdoors.	Use limestone-based whitewash or cassein-based paints.
thinners, solvents	FLAMMABLE TOXIC	Use it all up. Recycle. Contact waste disposal company.	Keep used solvent in closed jar until sludge settles, pour off and save the reusable solvent.
aerosol spray cans	FLAMMABLE	Use it all up. Contact waste disposal company.	Use equivalent products without aerosols...use atomizers.
drugs and medicines	TOXIC	Use per directions. Contact waste disposal company.	unknown
pesticides, poisons insecticides	TOXIC	Contact waste disposal company.	See any of the numerous books on "organic" pest control.

29.2 Toxics in the Home: Instructions and Data Table

After obtaining your parents' permission to do so, survey your home for products that may contain hazardous substances. Record your findings on the data table below. As you do so, note any containers that are leaking, labels that are falling off or difficult to read, or chemicals that have passed their expiration date. **(Don't touch any leaking containers!)** Report these to your parents and recommend that the problem be fixed or the expired chemical properly disposed of. There are many types of toxic chemicals in most homes, but be sure to look for these:

paints, solvents, cleaners, medicines, pesticides, glues, automotive chemicals

Also note what chemicals the products contain, any warnings on the label, the condition of the container and label, and whether it is stored safely.

area of house	product(s) found	contents or chemicals	warnings on label	condition of container and label; stored safely? notes
kitchen				
bathroom				
garage				
other				

Name _____ Class _____ Date _____

29.3 Toxics in the Home: Questions

1. What were the most common hazardous chemicals in your home and class?

   _____

2. Circle the hazardous or toxic chemicals in the list below:

drain cleaner	laundry detergent	furniture polish
paint	baking soda	alcoholic beverages
air fresheners	ant spray or stakes	hair spray
aspirin	cold capsules	tobacco products
bleach	floor polish	snail bait

3. Tell what you would do in the following situations:
   a. A small child has swallowed several aspirin.

   _____

   b. A friend is sick from a drug overdose.

   _____

   _____

   c. You have a container of a hazardous chemical that you want to dispose of.

   _____

   _____

   d. Some unknown powder has spilled from a truck driving down your street.

   _____

   _____

   e. You have been using a chemical and you feel ill.

   _____

   _____

   f. Your parents have some toxic chemicals that they want to keep at home.

   _____

   _____

4. What can you do to reduce the hazards of toxics in your home and to the environment?

   _____

   _____

ACTIVITY 30: WANTS AND NEEDS _____

Activity Summary

Students brainstorm to develop a list of things they have (or might have) in their homes. They then interview a senior citizen to find out how they lived when they were the students' age. From this, the students develop the distinction between things they want and things they need. This enables them to realize that they have alternatives and choices and that their values help to determine the choices they make.

Introduction

Most of us, child and adult alike, tend to get caught up in the materialism of our society. We equate happiness with "things." We come to think of things as necessities rather than as conveniences or luxuries. What did people do before the invention of television, plastic bags, and disposable beverage containers?

It is important to realize that most of our "things" fulfill <u>wants</u> rather than <u>needs</u>. When we realize that we can live without televisions, hair dryers, and gasoline-powered lawn mowers, we then can exercise our power to choose. It is important to make informed choices. Too often we make choices without considering the real price paid for our material goods. For example, consider the following questions:

- How does watching hours of television impact our social interaction skills?
- Have our children learned how to interact with one another at a party without alcohol or other drugs?
- How many hours do we work to pay for our "labor-saving" devices?
- What are the environmental costs of our labor-saving devices and the things we buy for convenience or because they are currently popular?

It is an interesting paradox that several studies have shown that people in "primitive" cultures tend to have more time for relaxation and socializing than do many of us in our industrialized society. Other studies have shown that homemakers in the 1930s and 1940s actually spent less time doing housework than many homemakers do now. Many of us consider a great vacation one in which we get away from our things and go camping or backpacking!

Many people don't realize that we do have alternatives. People met their needs in different ways in different times. Our students need to realize that many things they perceive as necessities are actually <u>wants</u> rather than <u>needs</u>. Once they understand that, they can begin to take the power and responsibility for making informed choices.

Grouping

Whole class and groups of 2–4.

Time

Brainstorming list: 30–45 minutes
Preparing for interview: 30–45 minutes

Doing interview: 15–30 minutes or more

Discussing interview and implications: 30–55 minutes

Anticipated Outcomes

The students will:

- increase their understanding of the difference between "wants" and "needs."
- better understand the lifestyles, both past and present, of older people.
- better understand the options we have and their advantages and disadvantages.
- become more willing to simplify their lifestyles and reduce their material desires.

Materials

—Photocopied student pages:

- 30.1 Wants and Needs: Background Information (one per student)
- 30.2 Wants and Needs: Instructions and Data (one per team)
- 30.3 Wants and Needs: Questions (one per student)

—Optional: tape recorder or video tape recorder

Vocabulary

None

Teacher Preparation

1. Photocopy the Background Information sheet (30.1) and Questions sheet (30.3).
2. Arrange for senior citizens to visit the class:
   a. Contact retired teachers, friends, relatives.
   b. You might try local senior citizen centers or retirement communities.
   c. Meet with the senior(s) and discuss the activity.
   d. Arrange for transportation or any other assistance that may be needed.
3. Photocopy the Instructions and Data sheets (30.2) after discussing the interview with the students and adding to the Data table.
4. Optional: Arrange for a tape recorder or video tape recorder.

SAFETY CONSIDERATION

Arrange for safe transportation for the senior citizen guest(s).

Procedure

1. Introduce the concept of "wants vs. needs" as follows:
   a. On the board or overhead, list the following:

- television
- refrigerator
- portable compact disc player
- electric lights
- aluminum cans
- paper towels
- plastic wrap
- automobile

(Add others if you wish.)

b. For each of the above, have the students rate them as an absolute necessity, an unnecessary luxury that some people want, or somewhere in between. Do this by having the students line up in a continuum as you name the item. For example, have those that think that television is an absolute need line up on the left, those that think it is an unnecessary luxury line up on the right, and the others distribute themselves in between according to the value they give to the item. (This is called a "values continuum.")

c. Discuss the students' choices.

2. Have the students brainstorm a list of common activities and appliances and other items that are commonly found or done in and around the home. Use this list to add to the Data table (30.2).

3. Have the students discuss what alternatives people might have utilized 50, 60, or 100 years ago. How did people get along without it? What did they do or use instead?

4. Introduce the idea of interviewing a senior citizen (at least two generations older than the students) about life when he or she was a teenager.

5. Discuss how to interview an older person. (See the Instructions sheet, 30.2)

6. Ask the students if they know of somebody who might be willing to come to class and be interviewed. Decide whether to have a small team of students interview the senior(s) in front of the class or for several teams to interview several seniors.

7. Arrange for the interview(s). Consider video taping it or making an audio tape.

8. Conduct the interview(s).

9. Have the students write letters of appreciation.

10. Discuss the results of the interview. Relate their discussion to the values continuum done at the start of the lesson.

Discussion

1. What are the basic human needs? Do these differ for different people? In different places?

2. What is the difference between a want and a need?

3. What influences our wants?

4. Do most of the things you have fulfill wants or real needs?

5. How do our wants often conflict with our needs?

6. Discuss the statement that "Conservation isn't doing without. It is doing better with less."

Answers to 30.3, Wants and Needs Questions

1. True needs are universal—everybody in every culture shares the same needs. Different people, however, have different wants.

2. Our basic physical needs are food, water, air, and shelter. Beyond the physical needs, we need feelings of friendship, affection, security, a feeling of being valued, and some others to be emotionally healthy.

3. a. materials to build it; air and water pollution; electricity; social costs such as isolation; negative influences; reduced development of personal interaction skills; lack of exercise (physical and mental)

   b. materials to build it; air and water pollution; fuel costs; large quantities of space devoted to parking and roads; isolation; loss of time (mass transit allows for other uses of the time while one rides the bus or train); injuries and loss of life

   c. materials; air and water pollution; noise; lack of exercise

   d. materials, including oil; air and water pollution; litter; hazards to wildlife

   e. materials; energy; air and water pollution; litter; broken glass

   f. materials; electricity

   g. materials; air and water pollution; time; possible ozone depletion; energy

   h. materials; air and water pollution; effects on wildlife; possibility of accidents; poisons farm workers; possible health risks to consumers

4. Answers will vary. Students will often claim that they need hair spray, hair dryers, televisions, and the like.

5. Answers will vary. Point out how nice it would be to have a three-day work week and be able to have time to relax, do hobbies, enjoy one's family, and so forth.

6. Answers will vary.

Extensions (See Activity 32 for suggestions for student projects.)

1. Interview other seniors, especially those who may have moved from different regions.

2. Obtain magazines and newspapers from 40 or 50 years ago. Compare them to today's publications, especially with regard to the types of events reported and the articles advertised.

3. Have the students do an oral history project. The video or audio tape made as part of the interview can be the basis for this project. See the "Foxfire" book series by Eliot Wigginton.

4. Have the students commit to doing without (television, automobiles, plastic bags, aluminum cans, hair spray, or ???) for some period of time. Emphasize that what they are really doing is doing something else instead of watching television. Discuss their alternatives before doing the project and their realizations afterwards.

5. Work with Social Studies and English teachers to make this an interdisciplinary project. Industrial Arts, Art, Home Economics and other departments might also be interested.

6. Compare life in the United States 50 to 100 years ago to life today in less-developed regions of the world.

7. Show the film *The Lorax,* which is based on a Dr. Seuss book with the same title. Discuss the meaning of the film. It is available for purchase or rent in 16-mm film or video-tape formats from Phoenix Films, 468 Park Avenue South, New York, NY 10016 (phone 800–221–1274).

8. Discuss what the world will be like 50 or 100 years from now if we keep using up our resources.

Modification

The students can visit the seniors where they live and conduct the interviews there. This should be done in small teams so as to reduce the intrusiveness.

References

Geisel, Theodor Seuss, *The Lorax.* New York, NY: Random House, Inc., 1971.

Tourtillot, Leeann, *Conserve and Renew.* Sacramento, CA: California Energy Extension Service, 1990.

Wigginton, Eliot, *The Foxfire Book* (et al.). New York, NY: Anchor/Doubleday, 1972.

30.1 Wants and Needs: Background Information

Have you ever wondered what it was like "in the good old days"? What about the not-so-good old days? How have times changed, and how have they stayed the same? How did people survive without our modern conveniences?

For most of human history, people have lived quite differently than we do today in the industrialized or "developed" nations. As people developed different sources of energy and invented various machines, their lives changed. Today, in our country, most of us don't have to find firewood or carry water from a stream to cook a simple meal. Most of us have electricity and electrical appliances. We have cars, telephones, televisions, hair dryers, and microwave ovens. We use and discard paper napkins, aluminum cans, and plastic bags without thinking about it.

But are these appliances and other objects really needed, or are they conveniences that most of us seem to want? What are our real needs?

Our physical needs include food, water, space, and shelter. We also have needs such as love, friendship, and a feeling of value and importance.

Many of the things that we take for granted or consider necessities have become common only in recent years. Many were invented only in the last 25 years or so. If these things are such recent inventions, they must not really be necessities. Rather, they are things to which we have become accustomed. Eventually, such things may come to seem as if we need them. It is important to keep such things in perspective. What are our alternatives? What would we do without them? What prices do we pay for them, including the price that our environment pays for their production and use? What did people do before television? Before hair dryers? Were they all bored, unattractive social misfits?

Does it make sense to work 20 hours to pay for an appliance that will save us some work, and then pay more money and spend more time to exercise at a gym? Making and using electrical appliances takes energy and materials and generates air and water pollution. Our labor-saving devices cost us money, for which we labor. We work for money with which to buy them, operate them, and repair them. Are they worth it?

Do we buy things because they are really important, needed or useful? Or do we buy things because the advertising agencies and manufacturers sell them to us? Are we healthier or happier because of our "things"?

It is interesting to think about the fact that many people leave their home and their "things" when they have a chance for a vacation. Many even go camping or backpacking and really leave the "modern conveniences" behind.

Maybe we should all think carefully about what we really want out of our lives and what we really need. Which is more valuable to you, some time to relax with friends or the latest gadget or fashions? Which do you need more, clean air and water, or more manufacturing plants, trucks, and oil wells? Are roads and shopping malls more important than open spaces and wilderness?

30.2 Wants and Needs: Instructions

When you interview a senior citizen, here are some things to keep in mind:

1. Have your interview planned thoroughly. Don't waste the person's time (and yours). Know who is going to do and say what, but don't get so tied to a plan that you don't allow the person being interviewed to talk freely.
2. Talk directly to the person whom you are interviewing.
3. Speak clearly. Be aware of any hearing difficulty.
4. If you can have a tape recorder or a VCR available, it will make it easier to remember what was said and relieve you of the task of taking notes.
5. Allow the person to tell stories and just talk about his or her experiences.
6. As the person talks, look for questions that build on what he or she says.
7. Except for when completing the Data table, try to avoid short-answer questions. Try to ask "open ended" questions that allow and encourage the person to tell his or her story. For example:

   rather than: "Did you like living here when you were a child?"
         ask: "What was it like to be a child living here?"

   rather than: "Did you have a television when you were a teenager?"
         ask: "What did you do for entertainment when you were a teenager?"

As part of your interview, but not the whole thing, you should find out whether the person had the objects on the Data table. If not, what was used instead?

Also find out if the person did the things listed. If not, what did he or she do that was similar or filled the same want or need?

Be sure to assure the person that you aren't trying to pry into his or her personal life. You are just trying to find out what it was like when the person was your age. If he or she seems at all touchy about a question, move on to another one.

Name _____ Class _____ Date _____

30.2 Wants and Needs: Data

Person interviewed:_____ age: _____ year born: _____

Where did the person live as a teenager? _____

Was it a city or country area? (describe) _____

DID HE OR SHE HAVE THE FOLLOWING APPLIANCES OR OBJECTS?

	Did he or she have it?	If not, what was used instead?
automobile		
television		
VCR		
radio		
space heater		
air conditioning		
refrigerator		
freezer		
electric lights		
food processor		
microwave oven		
clothes dryer		
hair dryer		
dishwasher		
paper towels		
paper napkins		
paper plates		
disposable razors		
aluminum cans		
hair spray		

DID HE OR SHE DO THE FOLLOWING THINGS?
HAVE THE PERSON DESCRIBE HIS OR HER ACTIVITIES.

go to church
_____

go to parties
_____

drive around in cars
_____

play video games
_____

play board games or card games
_____

read for pleasure
_____

play sports
_____

go to school
_____

do chores
_____

have a job outside the home
_____

date
_____

use public transportation
_____

_____

_____

_____

© 1993 by The Center for Applied Research in Education

Name _____ Class _____ Date _____

30.3 Wants and Needs: Questions

1. What is the difference between a need and a want?

   _____

   _____

2. List the true needs that each of us has.

   _____

3. Besides money, what costs do we incur with the use of each of the following:

   a. television _____

   b. automobiles _____

   c. power lawn mowers _____

   d. plastic bags _____

   e. disposable beverage containers _____

   f. electric hair dryers _____

   g. aerosol spray cans _____

   h. pesticides _____

4. What "things" are there at your house without which you could live just as well?

   _____

   _____

   _____

5. Job "A" provides enough money to pay for a large home, many electrical appliances, and expensive clothes. It also takes 48 hours per week. Job "B" pays enough money to pay for a modest home, a few basic appliances, and inexpensive clothes. It takes 24 hours per week. Which job would you choose and why?

   _____

   _____

   _____

6. Discuss the idea that conservation means doing more with less.

   _____

   _____

   _____

ACTIVITY 31: WHAT'S HAPPENING? _____

Activity Summary

Students study current events by collecting and summarizing articles on environmental issues. They give reports to the class, including actions that they as individuals might take to improve the situation.

Introduction

Environmental issues seldom grab the headlines as they did in the 1970s, but there are still numerous articles on them to be found in popular publications. Occasionally, there is a major problem or other event that does make the headlines. It is important that students learn to read articles on environmental issues and that they learn to think about and analyze them. Most important, they need to consider how current environmental events might affect them and how they might improve the situation.

Grouping

Individuals or teams

Time

Introduce the assignment: 10–15 minutes

Students collect articles for 3–6 (or more) weeks

Student oral reports on current events: varies, approximately 20 minutes per week

Anticipated Outcomes

The students will:

- increase their willingness to read articles on environmental issues.
- read articles from environmental journals.
- improve their ability to analyze written articles.
- improve their ability to present information orally.
- learn more about current environmental issues.
- better understand how they can have an impact on environmental issues.

Materials

—Photocopied student pages:

- 31.1 What's Happening? Background Information (one per student)
- 31.2 What's Happening? Instructions and Article Cover Sheets (the number varies)
- 31.3 What's Happening? Questions (one per student)

Vocabulary

None

Teacher Preparation

1. Photocopy the Background Information sheet (31.1), Instructions and Cover sheets (31.2), and Questions sheet (31.3).
2. Check your school and public libraries for environmental publications. Talk with the librarian about the possibility of starting subscriptions if they don't have many.
3. If you are using the Cover sheets (31.2), cut them in half along the dashed line.

Safety Considerations

None

Procedure

1. Check your school and local libraries for environmental publications. Students might do this. If they don't subscribe to enough, talk with the librarian about subscribing to more.
2. Check with local environmental organizations about the possibility of their donating subscriptions to their publications to the school library. Alternatively, they might have members who would donate their publications as they finish with them each month. (Students might make these contacts.)
3. Decide for how long you want the students to keep their current events files, how many articles they are to do each week, and what kinds of articles are to be required. Also decide how you want the oral reports to be done. Duplicate an appropriate number of the Cover Sheets (31.2). Here are some alternative ways to give this assignment:

   a. Each member of the class is to do:
      - written current event summaries on 3 newspaper and 1 magazine article each week for 4 weeks
      - one short oral report on an article or a topic each week
      - Current events portfolios which are to be submitted for evaluation every two weeks.

   b. Divide the class into quarters.
      - One fourth of the class will be responsible for keeping the class abreast of current environmental events for each quarter of the school year. They are to meet as a team and decide how to do this. Make and post a schedule. Remind the students each week.
      - Each student, whether it is his or her quarter to be the environmental reporter or not, is to keep a current event summary file that the teacher will collect periodically. The student is to do summaries of three articles each week.

   c. Divide the class into teams of three students. Each team is to collect and report on the current environmental events for a week and will do an environmental news report to the class on Monday of the following week. With 30 students in a class, a 30-week school year allows for each team to do this 3 times, thus allowing for development of their presentation skills.

d. Different students or teams of students could be responsible for different topics, such as air, water, population, toxics (hazardous substances), energy, wildlife, food, open space, solid waste, oceans, land use, or laws. They would develop files of articles and report to the class periodically. Teams could change topics after 2 or 3 weeks.

e. Different teams of students could be responsible for different media types. Once a week, each team could report on the main environmental issues dealt with by their media. After 3 or 4 weeks, each team rotates to a different media type. A possible division of responsibilities could be:

- local newspapers and local television news broadcasts
- regional newspapers or newspapers with large distributions
- national television news broadcasts
- television specials and documentary programs
- popular news-oriented magazines such as *Time* and *Newsweek*
- environmental, nature, and science magazines such as *National Audubon, Sierra, National Wildlife,* and *National Geographic*
- publications of local environmental groups and/or agencies

4. Be sure to make your expectations clear to the students, including any grading criteria. Students might be involved in developing presentation formats and evaluation criteria. Consider filling in the Instructions sheet (31.2) before duplicating it.

Discussion

1. Were the articles from different sources equally informative? Were some sources biased?

2. Did the media present solutions or just tell about problems? Was the issue presented as an isolated event or was it shown in relation to issues?

3. How does the media affect our views about environmental issues?

4. Why is it important to keep informed about local issues as well as about national or world issues?

5. Is it easier for you to have an influence on local issues or national issues? Does this mean that you should not keep informed about national or worldwide issues?

6. What are some ways that you can have an influence on national and/or world issues?

Answers to 31.3, What's Happening? Questions

1. Answers will vary. Any article (or speech or broadcast) will have a bias. General news publications often tend to emphasize the sensational or whatever sentiment is currently "in."

2. Answers will vary. Environmental publications, rightfully, present arguments from an environmental viewpoint. They don't always agree, though, about what is best for the environment.

3. Answers will vary. Solutions that are suggested often are not ones that we as individuals can put into effect in our daily lives.

4. Answers will vary. One approach is to ask, "What is the worst that could happen if this side is wrong? Now, what is the worst that could happen if that side is wrong?" It is also important to learn as much about the subject as possible and think about what seems most logical and simplest. It is also valuable to ask what ulterior motives the "experts" on each side might have.

5. Answers will vary. Publications, including both books and magazines, that specialize are useful.

6. Answers will vary. It is important that understanding be a starting point and foundation for the concern and action.

7. Ostriches employing this defensive technique are called dinner! What you don't know can hurt you! It is vital to know as much as possible about the things in your environment that affect you. It is also useful to simplify your life so that you have more control over the outside influences.

8. If a person attempts to attack global problems without addressing local issues, he or she often feels frustrated and powerless. By dealing with local issues, you can see success. Furthermore, the global (or national) issues are actually made up of lots of local and personal issues. For example, the accumulation of CO_2 in the atmosphere is caused largely by the burning of fossil fuels. Those fossil fuels are burned to produce electricity and products that we as individuals purchase. If we reduce our purchases and save energy, less fossil fuels will be burned.

Extensions (See Activity 32 for suggestions for student projects.)

1. Oral presentations can be videotaped and critiqued, looking for ways to improve them.

2. Students can do bulletin boards as part of their reports.

3. If there is a bulletin board or display case available on the campus, students could use it to publicize environmental information or local environmental issues or events.

4. Students can write letters to the editor of local newspapers.

5. Students can write an environmental column for the school newspaper.

6. Students can produce environmental pieces for local radio or television news programs. Find out about local public access television programming or public service announcements.

7. Students can maintain an environmental library in a portion of the school library. Contact local environmental groups for donations of subscriptions, reference materials, back issues of publications, and other materials.

Modifications

1. Modify the Instructions and Cover sheet (31.2) to suit your needs.

2. Rather than duplicate the Cover sheets for each article, give one to each student and have him or her use it as a model.

Reference

Clymire, Olga (principal writer), *California Class Project*. Costa Mesa, CA: Orange County Superintendent of Schools and the National Wildlife Federation, 1988.

31.1 What's Happening?: Background Information

The 1970s were called the "Environmental Decade." Many people were very concerned about environmental issues ranging from air pollution to overpopulation. The concern of the people resulted in legislation intended to address the multitude of environmental problems facing us. Some of the legislation included:

- The National Environmental Policy Act
- The Clean Air Act
- The Endangered Species Act
- The Safe Drinking and Water Act
- The Toxic Substances Control Act

States established various environmental agencies and offices. The federal government established the Environmental Protection Agency and the Department of Energy. The Atomic Energy Commission was reorganized into the Nuclear Regulation Commission and the Energy Research and Development Administration within the Department of Energy.

In the 1980s, many people, both in and out of government, turned their attention away from environmental issues. Some thought that the measures taken in the 1970s had taken care of the problems. Some became involved in other issues. Others became frustrated because the solutions were not simple or the results didn't come about fast enough. Still others became disenchanted when they found that some measures taken to protect the environment resulted in problems of their own, such as increased costs, less convenience, and even the loss of some jobs.

Now we find that the environmental problems of the 1970s are still unsolved. In fact, many problems, such as overpopulation, are even greater than before. As we have learned about environmental issues, we have found that there are few easy solutions to the problems. Every issue has more than one side. We cannot, however, ignore the problems or leave them to the "experts." It is imperative that every one of us learns about what is happening in our environment now. Why? Because we are directly affected by our environment. The air we breathe, the water we drink, the food we eat, and the energy we use are all affected by environmental influences. We, in turn, affect our environment, sometimes in harmful ways and sometimes in helpful ways. Only by becoming informed of environmental issues can we make wise choices in our daily lives.

By becoming more informed, most of us also become more concerned about environmental issues. When we become more concerned, many of us want to become involved in working toward improving our environment. As we work toward a better environment, we become even more informed. Thus, learning about environmental issues gives us the exciting opportunity and ability to work toward solutions.

31.2 What's Happening?: Instructions

Your teacher will tell you how many articles you are to do current events reports about, how frequently they are to be done, and what is expected in the report.

Record the details of your assignment below. Be sure to ask questions if anything is not clear.

1. Due date(s): _____

2. What I am to do: _____

   type(s) of articles: _____

   _____

   _____

   _____

   number: _____

   how to do the reports:

   _____

   _____

   _____

   _____

   _____

   _____

   _____

   _____

   _____

   _____

   _____

31.2 What's Happening?: Article Cover Sheets

Name _____ **Class** _____ **Date** _____

article title: _____ topic: _____

Attach this cover sheet to a copy of the article or to the article itself **if** the publication belongs to you and you want to cut it out. (Don't damage library publications!) If it is about a television or radio program, give the title, channel, network, time, and date of broadcast.

publication _____ _____ _____
                                name   date   page

source: ☐ home ☐ school library ☐ _____ library ☐ other _____

summary of the article (who, what, when, where, why, etc.): _____

_____

my opinions and reaction to the article: _____

_____

how this affects me; what I can do: _____

· ✂ ·

Name _____ **Class** _____ **Date** _____

article title: _____ topic: _____

Attach this cover sheet to a copy of the article or to the article itself **if** the publication belongs to you and you want to cut it out. (Don't damage library publications!) If it is about a television or radio program, give the title, channel, network, time, and date of broadcast.

publication _____ _____ _____
                                name   date   page

source: ☐ home ☐ school library ☐ _____ library ☐ other _____

summary of the article (who, what, when, where, why, etc.): _____

_____

my opinions and reaction to the article: _____

_____

how this affects me; what I can do: _____

_____

31.3 What's Happening?: Questions

1. Are general news publications unbiased in their reporting? Should they be? Discuss.

   _____

   _____

2. Are environmental organizations' publications unbiased? Should they be? Discuss.

   _____

   _____

3. Do most of the articles about environmental problems suggest solutions? Should they? Discuss. _____

   _____

4. Even "experts" frequently disagree. If opposite sides of an environmental issue both seem to have good arguments and believable "experts" supporting them, how would you decide on which side to base your actions?

   _____

   _____

5. Do the general news publications and broadcast media seem to go into depth, or do they just do superficial coverage of environmental issues? If they do superficial coverage, what can one do to find out more?

   _____

   _____

6. Discuss the idea that understanding leads to concern, which leads to involvement, which leads to more understanding, which leads to more concern, etc.

   _____

   _____

7. There is a story that when ostriches see predators approaching, they hide their heads in the sand because they think that if they don't see the predator it won't hurt them. Some people seem to take the attitude that "What I don't know won't hurt me" with regard to environmental issues. What do you think of this?

   _____

   _____

8. Discuss the idea of "Think globally, act locally."

   _____

   _____

ACTIVITY 32: DO IT! _____

Activity Summary

A format is provided for student projects. Suggestions for student projects are also given. NOTE: EVEN THOUGH THIS ACTIVITY IS PRESENTED AS THE LAST ONE IN THIS BOOK, THERE IS NO REASON WHY STUDENTS SHOULD NOT BE DOING PROJECTS THROUGHOUT THE COURSE OF THE SCHOOL YEAR. THIS ACTIVITY CAN BE USED AS A GUIDE TO PROJECTS UNDERTAKEN WHENEVER APPROPRIATE.

Introduction

Learning about environmental issues can be very frustrating and discouraging for students. As they learn about environmental problems, many will want to become involved in finding solutions, but they often have trouble seeing how they can have an impact. Actually becoming involved in working on environmental projects can help students feel that they can have a positive impact and can help them develop the skills needed to work on any issue. It might even open the door to career possibilities.

It can be very rewarding for junior high and high school students to become physically involved in projects to help the environment. If they can work with others from their community, especially adults, they can benefit from others' knowledge, experience, and skills. Working with others also helps the students feel more optimistic and powerful.

It is easy to feel as if what we do as individuals doesn't count. Students, and most of us, often use this as a rationalization for doing nothing or for doing something that we know we shouldn't do. It is worthwhile to keep the following in mind and to point them out to students:

- We as individuals and consumers determine what our government and industries do. If enough of us don't buy certain harmful products, especially if we let the manufacturer know why we aren't buying them, they will stop making them. Conversely, if we support environmentally sound industries, they will flourish. As voters, or future voters who can influence those who can vote now, we can influence our government. Legislators do pay attention to their popularity polls, and, especially if we join together with others, we can influence them.

- When it seems as if one person's vote doesn't count, consider the following. People often think that it takes 51 percent of the population to win an election. This is not so, as the following shows: (The percentages are for the 1988 Presidential election.)

  1. Only about 71 percent of the population is of voting age.
  2. Of that 71 percent, only about 70 percent are registered to vote. Seventy percent of 71 percent is 50 percent.
  3. Of that 50 percent, only about 50 percent actually vote. Fifty percent of 50 percent is 25 percent.
  4. Therefore, to have a 51 percent majority of the voters in a two-party election, it would take only about 13 percent of the population! But . . .
  5. There are more than two parties, so it actually takes <u>less</u> than 13 percent of the population to win an election! In 1988, George Bush was elected President with less than 20 percent of the total population voting for him.

- Students know very well that some people are more influential than others. They know who sets the styles on campus, who decides what is "in" and what is "out." They also know that a governor, mayor, or city council person has more influence than somebody who doesn't participate in the governmental system. Point out that the influence of a few people can affect the population as a whole. They can learn how to be influential. If they go to a city council meeting and speak intelligently on an issue, they will have more influence than does the 99 percent of the population who never go to a city council meeting. If they write a letter to a legislator, they will have more influence than 1,000 people who don't!

- Suggest that they "think globally and act locally." Their actions in their local communities will have impacts far beyond the local community.

- If we try to help improve the environment, we won't win every battle, but we will win some. If we don't take actions to help the environment, it will certainly get worse.

- Our environmental problems have been accumulating and getting worse for over a hundred years. We aren't going to solve them in a week, a month, or a year. The longer we wait, though, the more difficult the solutions and choices will become. We are going to spend the next 24 hours (days, weeks, or years!) doing something. Why not spend at least some of the time doing something good. Be not simply good. Be good for something!

Grouping

Individual or small groups

Time

Introducing the activity: 20–30 minutes

Doing the projects: varies

Anticipated Outcomes

The students will:

- become involved in actually working toward a better environment.
- increase their ability to plan and complete a project outside the school setting.

Materials

—Photocopied student pages:

- 32.1 Do It! Background Information (one per student)
- 32.2 Do It! Instructions and Project Description sheets (one per student or group)
- 32.3 Do It! Questions (one per student)
- 32.4 Do It! Project Ideas (one per student, or have students share them)

Vocabulary

None

Teacher Preparation

Photocopy the Background Information sheet (32.1), Instructions and Project Description sheets (32.2), Questions sheet (32.3), and Project Ideas (32.4).

SAFETY CONSIDERATION

As you review the students' project proposals, be aware of any hazardous projects. Consider exposure to hazardous chemicals, water, traffic, and equipment or materials. Discuss safety measures with the students. If necessary, have the students change their projects or find other ones.

Procedure

1. Decide if you want to specify whether you want these to be individual or group projects, or whether students can choose. If groups are assigned or allowed, what will be the size?

2. Decide on a schedule, including the following dates:

   a. begin assignment—make assignment

   b. students commit to their projects and submit their Project Description sheet (32.2)

   c. optional: dates for progress reports

   d. project to be completed; Questions sheet (32.3) due

   e. written (or oral) report due

3. If these projects are to be graded or evaluated, decide on the criteria and explain them to the students.

4. Introduce the project assignment by using the Background Information sheet (32.1), Instructions and Project Description sheets (32.2), and Project Ideas (32.4).

5. Have the students select a project and submit a Project Description sheet.

6. Read the Description sheets, making any appropriate comments and suggestions.

7. Have the students begin their projects after receiving your approval.

8. Periodically, have the students meet with you to give progress reports. Ask if there are any problems, what has been accomplished so far, what is next, and what the long-term plan is. Consider obtaining this information in writing. Give the students lots of encouragement and support. Sometimes the most valuable learning comes from problems that the students encounter.

9. At the conclusion of the projects, have the students give short (1- to 5-minute) reports to the class.

10. The Questions sheet (32.3) can serve as a project summary report.

Discussion

1. Do you feel that doing this project actually helped to improve the environment?

2. What did you learn about how to do such a project effectively?

3. What did you learn about environmental problems and their solutions?

4. What problems did you encounter? How did you solve them? What did you learn from them?

5. In what ways, if any, has this project had an effect on your daily life and/or your future?

Answers to 32.3, Do It! Questions

1. Answers will vary.

2. Answers will vary.

3. Answers will vary. Encourage the students to be specific.

4. Answers will vary. Emphasize that problems and "failures" can be valuable learning experiences. Accomplishing something is better than doing nothing!

5. Answers will vary. Point out that what they learned from doing this project will help them in the future.

6. Answers will vary.

7. Answers will vary.

a. Students need to realize that their actions do count. They have lots of energy, ability, money, and influence. Also, the habits they develop now will carry over into adulthood.

b. We are all part of the problem. We all need to be part of the solution, or at least most of us do!

c. The global problems are actually the result of lots of actions by individuals. Also, we can change our local environment much more easily than we can change the state, nation, or world. If enough individuals and groups work for local improvements, however, the state, nation, and the world will be changed!

d. One who leads a simple self-sufficient life may have little negative impact on the environment, but will also have little positive impact. If the environment is to improve, we need to become involved. Point out, though, that none of us is perfect. If students feel that they must be perfect to help, they will not become involved. Taking a few little actions today may lead to bigger and better actions in the future. One step at a time will get the job done, but we need to keep taking those steps, striving to be "better." Remind them that "The longest journey begins with but a single step."

Extensions

1. As you discuss the projects, ask the students what might be done to increase the good done by the project, how it could be extended and expanded, and whether they plan to continue.

2. Most of the sources used as references in this book provide suggestions for projects.

3. Some schools have Independent Study, Student Assistant, other courses, or other ways in which students could continue and expand their projects.

4. There are several awards programs that recognize student environmental projects. Consider participating in these. They provide recognition and positive reinforcement for the students and your class. Two programs that have simple procedures for participating are:

National Energy Education
Development Program (NEED)
1920 Association Drive
Reston, VA 22091
(703) 860–5029

President's Environmental Youth Awards
Office of Environmental Education
U.S. Environmental Protection Agency
401 M Street, SW
Washington, DC 20460
(202) 260–4962

5. Many student environmental projects could be suitable for science fair projects.

6. If the students receive any certificates of appreciation, arrange to have them presented at a school board or other public meeting.

7. Contact your school newspaper, local newspapers, radio, or television stations about the projects. Arrange for an awards presentation ceremony. Also invite the school and district administration, PTA and so forth. Arrange for some positive publicity for your students (and your program!).

Modifications

1. Before duplicating the Assignment and Description sheets (32.2), alter them as you see fit.

2. The list of ideas provided (32.4) suggests 44 possible projects. There is room to add your own. Do so, especially if there are local projects with which the students can become involved.

3. Assign a relatively simple project early in the year and another more advanced one later in the year. Spend time discussing project plans with the students.

4. Rather than written reports, have the students prepare videotaped reports or slide shows.

5. If you are going to assign more than one project per student, require that one be an individual project and one be done with a group of at least two other students.

References

Miller, G. Tyler, *Living in the Environment.* Belmont, CA: Wadsworth Publishing Company, 1990.

U.S. Bureau of the Census, *Statistical Abstract of the United States, 1991.* Washington, DC: U.S. Government Printing Office, 1991.

32.1 Do It!: Background Information

Learning about environmental issues can be very frustrating. There are many problems—air pollution, water pollution, overpopulation, wildlife problems, energy shortages, and a myriad of other concerns. It is easy to feel overwhelmed and helpless. If we all felt helpless, we'd all give up and the situation would, indeed, be hopeless. Fortunately, we are not helpless and the situation is not hopeless!

If we analyze our environmental problems, we realize that even the biggest problems are actually the combination of lots of "little" choices by individuals. Other choices by those individuals (us) would reduce the problems.

Air pollution is an example. Most air pollution comes from private automobiles, generation of electricity, and factories that make various products that we purchase. If we drove our cars less, walked, bicycled, and used mass transit more, there would be much less air pollution. Living nearer to our jobs, carpooling, and keeping our cars well tuned also would help. If we as individuals save electricity, less coal and oil will be burned to generate electricity. If we demand fewer unnecessary products, purchase well-made things and take care of them, recycle, and reuse materials, industry will make less air pollution. All of these are choices that we as individuals can make.

The role of our government is to protect us and enable us to live healthy, happy lives. We sometimes feel that our vote doesn't count. You may feel that you can't influence the government if you aren't old enough to vote. That isn't so. Most people don't become involved in the governmental process. That means that those who do become involved have a disproportionate influence. If you investigate issues and then talk to voters, you will have an influence. Working on local issues may produce faster results than working on national or statewide issues, and both are very important. You can be very influential. One well-written letter from you will have more influence than a hundred people who are old enough to vote but don't, and most don't!

There are dozens of projects you can do to help improve the environment right now. Simply picking up litter, recycling, fixing a dripping faucet, donating time or money to an environmental organization, teaching other people about environmental issues, and saving electricity at home are all ways that really will help. Joining environmental organizations can help you stay informed and add to their power.

Sometimes we feel frustrated because we don't immediately see the results of our efforts to help the environment. We need to be patient and know that what we do does help, even if we don't always see it. It has taken us a long time to get ourselves into our current predicament, and we should not expect to solve our problems in a short time. The longer we wait to start working on them, however, the harder they will be to solve. We will make some mistakes as we try to help the environment, but we will also do a lot of good. Why not start now?

CONSERVATION

32.2 Do It!: Instructions

The best way to learn how to work toward a better environment is to actually become involved in a project designed to help the environment. In other words, **Do It!**

The keys to doing a successful project are:

- Find a project that is interesting to you and that you truly want to do.
- Plan your project carefully and realistically.
- Be willing to make commitments and keep them.
- Turn problems into learning experiences, solve them, and continue.
- Keep your mind on your real goal. Be flexible, but keep moving toward your objective. Don't let egos, personalities, and so forth get in the way.

Keep the above ideas in mind as you plan your project. Your teacher will give you the details of this assignment. The planning guide below may help you plan and complete an excellent project. You may want to add other steps, or you might eliminate some.

DATE	**STEPS TO A SUCCESSFUL PROJECT**
_____	Think of ideas. Talk them over. Envision what will be done and what the project will accomplish. What problems will be encountered and how will they be addressed? Find a project that you really want to do.
_____	Fill out and submit the Project Description sheet, 32.2.
_____	Begin working on the project.

- Find and contact local people who can help or whom you can help.
- Consult libraries or people for information.
- Gather materials.
- If necessary, send or telephone for information.
- Get to work!
- Seek help if you need it.

_____	First Progress Report due.
_____	Second Progress Report due.
_____	Third Progress Report due.
_____	Actual project to be done.
_____	Write report and/or plan oral report.
_____	Answer questions on Questions sheet, 32.3.
_____	Submit written report, questions, do oral report, or other assignment.

Name _____ Class _____ Date _____

32.2 Do It!: Project Description

Project Title: _____

1. **Goal:** What, as exactly as possible, do you hope or expect to accomplish by doing this project? In what way will the environment be helped?

   _____

   _____

2. In addition to the good done for the environment, what do you expect to learn?

   _____

   _____

3. Steps to reach the goals: (Be as specific as possible. Include target dates.)

   (1) _____

   (2) _____

   (3) _____

   (4) _____

   (5) _____

   (6) _____

   (7) _____

4. What problems do you anticipate?

   _____

5. What help will you need?

   _____

6. Where might you get that help? (People, agencies, organizations, etc.)

   _____

7. Are there any safety issues about which to be concerned?

   _____

8. When do you plan to actually start the project? _____ Finish?_____

9. How will you evaluate your project? How will you know whether you achieved your goal?

   _____

   _____

32.3 Do It!: Questions

1. Briefly describe your project.

   _____

2. What was your main goal in doing this project?

   _____

3. Did you accomplish your main goal? If you did, what were the keys to that success? If not, what prevented you from attaining your goal?

   _____

4. What problems did you encounter? What did you learn from them?

   _____

   _____

5. Do you think that your project actually helped to improve the environment? Discuss your answer.

   _____

   _____

6. Discuss how this project will affect you in the future, if at all.

   _____

   _____

7. Discuss the following ideas:
   a. I'm only a kid. What I do doesn't matter.

   _____

   _____

   b. It's not my job. Let somebody else do it.

   _____

   _____

   c. Think globally, act locally.

   _____

   _____

   d. Be not simply good. Be good for something.

   _____

   _____

32.4 Do It! Project Ideas

The ideas below can serve as starting points for projects. They should be modified to suit your particular circumstances. Some are most suitable for individual students and others are most suitable for group projects. When you select a project, whether it is from this list or not, be sure that you really want to do it. Then, plan carefully and DO IT!

1. Contact a local environmental organization and participate in one of its projects.
2. Learn how to fix dripping faucets. Check several homes and fix any leaks found.
3. Learn how to weatherstrip doors and windows. Check several homes and weatherstrip them.
4. Work with the appropriate agencies and plant trees in parks, schools, or other public areas.
5. Study an environmental issue, prepare and teach lessons to classes of younger students.
6. Make some attractive posters promoting conservation. Be specific. Get them put up in stores.
7. Organize an environmental essay or poster contest for younger students.
8. Arrange to do some public-service announcements on local radio or television.
9. Do a creek clean-up. Recycle the recyclable materials.
10. Work with your local waste management company to do a household toxic waste clean-up.
11. Plan and do a recycling campaign in your town or neighborhood.
12. If your town has curbside recycling pick-up, organize a campaign to promote participation.
13. If your town doesn't have curbside recycling pick-up, work to start a curbside program.
14. Plan several vegetarian meals. Prepare them and serve them to friends.
15. Prepare and distribute a handbook of locally available environmentally good products.
16. Organize a litter pick-up program for local roads or parks.
17. Contact environmental groups and bookstores. Establish an environmental library at school.
18. Attend city council meetings. Learn about local environmental issues. Speak out.
19. Write letters to the editor of your local newspaper.
20. Start an environmental column in your school newspaper.
21. Start an environmental club on your campus.
22. Make up a skit, song, or rap about conservation. Perform it in public or at school.
23. Volunteer to help a wildlife rescue organization.
24. Learn to do a simple automotive tune-up. Tune several cars so that they run more efficiently.
25. Find out where to recycle oil. Set up a used oil collection and recycling program.
26. Volunteer to work with recreation, Y.M.C.A., or other groups to lead nature hikes for kids.
27. Organize an "Earth Day" program for your school or other schools.
28. Get local service organizations to subscribe to environmental magazines for school libraries.
29. Work with your local water department to promote water conservation.

30. Arrange for political candidates to discuss environmental issues with social studies classes.

31. Find out about threats to local open spaces and work to protect them.

32. Arrange for environmental action bulletin boards at local bookstores, libraries, etc.

33. Set up a table at a hardware store. Demonstrate energy- and water-saving devices.

34. Start a neighborhood composting project.

35. Set up a school recycling program for cans, glass, white paper, computer paper, oil, and so forth.

36. Help to recycle toys by helping with a Christmas toy drive.

37. Get permission and post signs at local markets indicating environmentally "good" products.

38. Post signs at markets promoting the use of boxes or cloth bags rather than paper or plastic.

39. Talk to local store owners or managers. Arrange for clerks not to automatically use bags.

40. Write letters to governmental officials about environmental issues.

41. Translate a brochure on household hazardous chemicals into another language.

42. Organize a "No TV Week" (or two or three or more!) among the students at your school.

43. Set up a display about environmentally "good" careers. Arrange for speakers.

44. Make a certificate, to be signed by graduating students, pledging to consider the environmental and social consequences of any job or career they might consider.

45. Create a board game that teaches about environmental issues and values. Arrange to play it with groups of elementary school children.

46. Meet with the purchasing agent for your school district or a local company to discuss the purchase of recycled products and recycling waste from the district or company.

47. Work with your district's business manager and your local utility company to arrange for an "energy audit" of one or more schools in your district. The audit should include examination of both hardware and behaviors, and should provide cost saving estimates to various changes that might be made. Try to arrange for some of the money saved as a result to be returned to the school directly.

48. Set up a recycling program at a local retirement community or apartment complex.

49. Arrange for local service stations or auto repair shops to give discounts on tune-ups during Earth Week. Publicize this program.

50. Work with an Auto Shop teacher to develop an environmental unit, including recycling of oil, fuel economy, and tuning up a car for minimizing air pollution and fuel waste.

51. Work with a Home Economics teacher to develop a unit on conservation in the home, including avoiding wasteful packaging, reducing waste, recycling, alternatives to toxics, etc.

52. Work with a Wood Shop teacher to develop a unit on environmentally sound building, including insulation, use of solar energy for space and water heating and lighting, alternative building materials, etc.

53. Work with the city or county to organize a tree planting campaign. Be sure to include young children and senior citizens.

54. Volunteer at a local Humane Society or animal shelter.

55. Learn to repair leaky faucets, contact local service agencies, and work with them to fix leaky faucets in the homes of needy people. Be sure to also contact your local water agency.

Appendices

Appendix I: Governmental Agencies

Appendix II: Selected Private Organizations

Appendix III: How to Write for Information

Appendix IV: How to Write a Letter to a Governmental Official

APPENDIX I: GOVERNMENTAL AGENCIES _____

City council meets: _____ Mayor: _____ _____
                       time and place   name   phone #

City council members: _____ , _____ , _____

County Supervisor: _____ _____ meets: _____
                       name   phone #   time and place

State Assembly: _____ _____ Senate: _____ _____
                name   phone #   name   phone #

Governor: _____ _____ _____
             name   phone #   address

U.S. GOVERNMENTAL AGENCIES

(Consult your local telephone book for local offices of federal legislators and agencies.)

President _____
1600 Pennsylvania Avenue, NW
Washington, DC 20500

Representative _____
U.S. House of Representatives
Washington, DC 20515

Senator _____
U.S. Senate
Washington, DC 20510

ENVIRONMENTAL PROTECTION AGENCY
401 M Street SW
Washington, DC 20460

Executive Branch

**U.S. Council on
Environmental Quality**
722 Jackson Place, NW
Washington, DC 20503

Soil Conservation Service
P.O. Box 2890
Washington, DC 20013

**U.S. Department of the
Interior, Bureau of Land
Management**
1849 C Street, NW, Room 5600
Washington, DC 20240

**U.S. Department of
Agriculture, Forest Service**
P.O. Box 2417
Washington, DC 20013

U.S. Department of Energy
1000 Independence Avenue, SW
Washington, DC 20585

**U.S. Department of the
Interior, Fish and Wildlife
Service**
1849 C Street, NW
Washington, DC 20240

**U.S. Dept. of Agriculture
Natural Resources & Envt.
Division**
14th Street & Independence
Avenue, SW
Washington, DC 20250

U.S. Department of the Interior
1849 C Street, NW
Washington, DC 20240

**U.S. Department of the
Interior National Park
Service**
Interior Building
P.O. Box 37127
Washington, DC 20013

Senate Committees On:

- **Agriculture, Nutrition and Forestry:** Rm 328-A, Russell Bldg., Washington, DC 20510
- **Commerce, Science, and Transportation:** U.S. Senate, SD-508, Washington, DC 20510
- **Energy and Natural Resources:** Rm. SD-364, Dirksen Bldg., Washington, DC 20510
- **Environment and Public Works:** Rm. SD-458, Dirksen Bldg., Washington, DC 20510

House of Representatives Committees On:

- **Agriculture:** Rm. 1301, Longworth House Office Bldg., Washington, DC 20515
- **Energy and Commerce:** 2125 Rayburn House Office Bldg., Washington, DC 20515
- **Interior and Insular Affairs:** Rm. 1324, Longworth House Office Bldg., Washington, DC 20515
- **Environmental and Energy Conference:** H2-515 Ford House Office Bldg., Washington, DC 20515

(These addresses are from *The Environmental Address Book,* 1991, by Michael Levine, Putnam Publishing Group, New York, NY, and the *1992 Conservation Directory* of the National Wildlife Federation, Washington, DC. Their currency or accuracy is not guaranteed.)

APPENDIX II: SELECTED PRIVATE ORGANIZATIONS

There are literally hundreds of private environmental organizations. This list is not intended to be comprehensive. For a very complete list, see the National Wildlife Federation's *Conservation Directory*. This book is revised annually. The addresses below were taken from the 1992 edition of the *Conservation Directory*. Another excellent resource is *The Environmental Address Book*, by Michael Levine (1991, The Putnam Publishing Co., 200 Madison Avenue, New York, NY)

Alliance for Environmental Education
10751 Ambassador Drive, #201
Manassas, VA 22110
(703) 335–1025

Defenders of Wildlife
1244 19th Street, NW
Washington, DC 20036
(202) 659–9510

Friends of the Earth
218 D Street, SE
Washington, DC 20003
(202) 544–2600

League of Conservation Voters
1707 L Street, NW, Suite 550
Washington, DC 20036
(202) 785–8683

National Wildlife Federation
1400 Sixteenth Street, NW
Washington, DC 20036
(202) 797–6800

Planned Parenthood Federation
810 Seventh Avenue
New York, NY 10019
(212) 541–7800

Sierra Club
730 Polk Street
San Francisco, CA 94109
(415) 776–2211

World Wildlife Fund
1250 24th Street, NW
Washington, DC 20037
(202) 293–4800

Center for Science in the Public Interest
1875 Connecticut Avenue, NW
Washington, DC 20009
(202) 332–9110

Environmental Action, Inc.
1525 New Hampshire Avenue, NW
Washington, DC 20036
(202) 745–4870

Greenpeace, U.S.A., Inc.
1436 U Street, NW
Washington, DC 20009
(202) 462–1177

National Audubon Society
950 Third Avenue
New York, NY 10022
(212) 832–3200

Natural Resources Defense Council
40 West 20th Street
New York, NY 10011
(212) 727–2700

Rain Forest Action Coalition
301 Broadway, Suite A
San Francisco, CA 94133
(415) 398–4404

U.S. Public Interest Research Group
215 Pennsylvania Avenue, SE
Washington, DC 20003
(202) 546–9707

Worldwatch Institute
1776 Massachusetts Avenue, NW
Washington, DC 20036
(202) 452–1999

Conservation Foundation
1250 24th Street, NW
Washington, DC 20037
(202) 293–4800

Environmental Defense Fund
257 Park Avenue South
New York, NY 10010
(212) 505–2100

Izaak Walton League
Box 824
Iowa City, IA 52244
(319) 351–7037

National Parks and Conservation Association
1015 31st Street, NW
Washington, DC 20007
(202) 944–8530

Nature Conservancy
1815 North Lynn Street
Arlington, VA 22209
(703) 841–5300

Scientists Institute for Public Information
355 Lexington Avenue
New York, NY 10017
(212) 661–9110

Wilderness Society
900 17th Street, NW
Washington, DC 20006
(202) 833–2300

Zero Population Growth
1400 16th Street, NW
Washington, DC 20036
(202) 332–2200

APPENDIX III: HOW TO WRITE FOR INFORMATION _____

When you write to a company or organization requesting information, you should keep in mind that you are asking them to help you. They are likely to do it for you because they perceive that it is in their best interest to tell their side of environmental issues to the public. You do not need to tell them your views or opinions—you simply want to find out their side of the issue or to learn some information. You want to make providing that information as easy and as agreeable to them as possible. Follow these guidelines and see the example on page 324. The superscript numbers in the example refer to the guidelines listed here.

1. Don't put off writing for information you need. It may take weeks!
2. Make your letter easy to read. Type it or write very clearly and neatly.
3. Be sure that the address is correct.
4. If you know the name of the contact person, be sure to spell it correctly.
5. If you don't know a name, address the envelope to "Public Information Office."
6. If you don't know a name, "Dear Sir or Madam" will do in the salutation.
7. Tell why you want the information.
8. Be brief and to the point. Reading a lot of unnecessary words from you takes their time. They want to know what you want, not what you think.
9. If you know of a publication by name, ask for it by name.
10. Whether you know of a specific publication or not, ask for any other pertinent information that they may have available.
11. Tell them when you need the information. If you don't have a specific date by which you need it, make one up or ask for it as soon as is convenient. This will help prevent your request from being set aside and forgotten.
12. Be sure to thank them.
13. Be sure to give your correct return address, including ZIP Code. An address label or stamped, self-addressed envelope would help them and would help eliminate a possible error on their part. Sometimes it is useful to have the information sent to your school's address. Check with your teacher. If you are having it sent to you at school, have it sent to you "care of" your teacher's name.
14. Include your area code and phone number so that they can call you if they are unclear as to what you want.

A Sample Letter Requesting Information

1234 Earth Street[2]
Anytown, CA 77777
October 15, 1993[1]

Office of Public Relations[3,4]
Acme Industrial Corporation
Someplace, NY 99991

Dear Sir or Madam:[5,6]

    I am a student at John Muir High School in Anytown, California. My Biology class is studying air and water pollution.[7,8] I understand that your company makes air and water purification systems. I would appreciate any information that you can send me about your products and how they work, including your booklet <u>Water Pollution and You,</u>[9] if it is available. I would also appreciate any other information that you have available on air and water pollution.[10]

    So that I can complete my project on time, I would appreciate receiving whatever information you can send by November 20, if that is possible.[11] If that is not possible, I would most appreciate a note letting me know so that I can plan accordingly.

    My address is given above. I enclose an address label sticker for your convenience.[13] If you would like to contact me, my telephone number is (111) 222–0000.[14] The best times to reach me are between 7:00 and 7:30 a.m. or after 4:30 p.m., Pacific time.

Thank you in advance.[12]

Sincerely.

Joe Citizen

APPENDIX IV: HOW TO WRITE A LETTER TO A GOVERNMENTAL OFFICIAL

Your letter can influence officials in a number of ways. Even though a legislator will probably not actually read your letter, it will be read by his or her staff, who will prepare a reply. The staff will keep the legislator apprised as to the sentiments expressed (for example, "Last week we had 74 letters in favor of that legislation and 13 against it.") They will also note the tone—was it well reasoned and informative or combative and antagonistic? If the letter is obviously written as part of a campaign by a group, that will be noted.

Do not be discouraged by the fact that a staff member will probably be the one who reads your letter. They are quite likely younger and more in touch with your ideas than the legislator is. They certainly have more influence on the legislator than you do. When you write your letter, keep in mind that it will probably be read by a staff member who is reasonably intelligent and informed, but who cares about what the legislator's constituency thinks. The following points will help your letter have the desired impact. See also the sample letter on page 327. The superscript numbers in the sample letter refer to the points listed here.

Letters to governmental agencies can be especially effective. The agencies generally do not receive nearly as much mail as legislators do, so they tend to pay more attention to each one. Assuming that you write to the proper agency, the staff of that agency already know and care about the topic. They need to know what the public thinks and knows.

1. Make your letter brief and to the point. Address only one subject in the letter.
2. Be sure that your letter is neatly written, preferably typed.
3. Be sure that you have the name spelled correctly and that you use the correct title.
4. If you are writing about a certain piece of legislation, refer to it by name and number if possible.
5. If you are not writing about a piece of legislation, clearly identify what your topic of concern is.
6. Show your understanding of the topic. Give a FEW relevant facts. If the topic has local implications (jobs, environment, etc.), mention that.
7. Ask the legislator to do something specific, like vote for or against, to co-sponsor, to tell you his or her position on the issue. Give your specific reasons for wanting that action.
8. If you can, mention his or her vote on a recent issue. This will show that you are paying attention to what he or she is doing.
9. You may want to ask for a response. In any case, be sure to give your return address.
10. When you receive a reply, and you will, send another letter. Thank him or her for supporting you or ask him or her to reconsider.
11. DON'T mention your membership in environmental groups. Letters that are written by an individual have more impact than do letters written as part of a campaign.
12. Unless there is a reason to do so, DON'T mention that you are a high school student. Legislators are most interested in the opinions of voters, and many high

school students are too young to vote. Also, being a student may imply that this is a class assignment rather than something that you really care about.

13. DON'T threaten in any way or try to impress the legislator with your influence or connections.

14. DON'T forget that local and state legislation is often just as important as national legislation and that it is usually easier to have an influence on more local issues.

Proper addresses and salutations:

The President:	**Your senator:**	**Your representative:**
The White House 1600 Pennsylvania Avenue, NW Washington, DC 20500	The Honorable (*name*) Senate Office Building Washington, DC 20510	The Honorable (*name*) House Office Building Washington, DC 20515
Dear Mr. President:	Dear Senator (*name*):	Dear Representative (*name*):
phone: (202) 456–1414	(202) 224–3121	(202) 224–3121

Sample Letter to a Legislator

November 14, 1993
The Honorable Jane Doe
Senate Office Building
Washington, DC 20510[2,3]

Dear Senator Doe:[3]

    I am writing to you because of my concern about Senate Bill 22222, the so-called "Wildlife Protection Act."[1,4] In spite of its name, this bill allows for clear-cut logging and other environmentally destructive practices within the range of threatened species of wildlife if it has been shown that the species of wildlife can be raised in captivity.[5]

    While it is important to continue to develop the ability to raise threatened and endangered species of plants and animals in captivity, captive breeding will never be a substitute for wild populations breeding in their natural environments. Even biologists who participate in captive breeding programs oppose this bill. The gene pool of a group of captive organisms is not large enough to adequately protect the genetic diversity of a species. Just as important, an animal in a zoo or in a captive breeding station is no substitute for one in the wild. Passage of Senate Bill 22222 would effectively eliminate the benefits of wildlife protective legislation of the past 20 years, including the Endangered Species Act of 1973.[6]

    Please vote against S.B. 22222 and urge your colleagues to do so too. If this bill passes, it will result in the elimination of many species of wildlife in their natural environments.[7]

    Your recent votes on S.B. 11111 and 11112 show that you are concerned about wildlife and the environment. I hope that you will continue your support by voting against S.B. 22222.[8]

    Please keep me informed of your involvement with this legislation.[9]

Sincerely,

Joe Citizen
1234 Earth Street

Anytown, CA 77777[9]

Bibliography

BIBLIOGRAPHY

When possible, I have provided the addresses and telephone numbers for the following publishers to facilitate obtaining the materials. They are the ones given in the books used or in other sources available to me. Since addresses and telephone numbers are subject to change, no guarantee is given as to the accuracy of these addresses or telephone numbers.

Altman, Paula, *Energy Education Resources—Kindergarten Through 12th Grade.* 1991; Energy Information Administration, National Energy Information Center, U.S. Department of Energy; 1000 Independence Avenue, SW, Washington, DC 20585; (202) 586–8800.

Anonymous, *California Endangered Species Resource Guide.* 1991; California Department of Education; 721 Capitol Mall, Sacramento, CA 95614; (916) 445–1260.

Anonymous, *Conservation Directory.* 1992; National Wildlife Federation; 1400 Sixteenth Street, NW, Washington, DC 20036; (202) 797–6800.

Anonymous, *Educator's Waste Management & Activity Guide.* 1991; California Department of Conservation, Division of Recycling; 1025 P Street, Room 401, Sacramento, CA 95814; (916) 323–3508.

Anonymous, *EdVentures in Population Education.* 1984; Zero Population Growth; 1400 Sixteenth Street, NW; Washington, DC 20036; (202) 332–2200.

Anonymous, *Endangered and Threatened Wildlife and Plants* (50 CFR 17.11 & 17.12). 1991; U.S. Fish and Wildlife Service, Department of the Interior; Washington, DC 20240; (703) 358–1706.

Anonymous, *Fifteen Simple Things Californians Can Do to Recycle.* 1991; EarthWorks Press; 1400 Shattuck Avenue, #25, Berkeley, CA 94709; (415) 841–5866.

Anonymous, *The Green Box.* 1989; Humboldt County Office of Education; 901 Myrtle Avenue, Eureka, CA 95501; (707) 445–7082.

Anonymous, *Group and Key Contact List.* 1992; U.S. Forest Service; 14th & Independence, SW, P.O. Box 96090, Washington, DC 20090; (202) 205–0957.

Anonymous, *Hazardous Household Products.* 1990; California Department of Health Services, Toxic Substances Control Program; 400 P Street, P.O. Box 942732, Sacramento, CA 94234; (916) 322–0476.

Anonymous, *Home Energy-Saving Practices Checklist, Winter Bill Workbook,* and *Your Summer PG&E Bill Workbook.* 1990; Pacific Gas and Electric Company; 77 Beale Street, San Francisco, CA; (415) 973–9017.

Anonymous, *If the Earth Were a Cookie.* 1991; activity published as part of the National Science & Technology Week packet by the National Science Foundation; 1800 G Street NW, Washington, DC 20550; (202) 357–9859.

Anonymous, *Parent/Student Water Conservation Checklist.* 1991; California Department of Water Resources; P.O. Box 942836, Sacramento, CA 94236; (916) 445–9248.

Anonymous, *Science Activities in Energy: Solar Energy.* 1980; U.S. Department of Energy, Education Division; 1000 Independence Avenue, SW, Washington, DC 20585; (202) 252–2000.

Blaustein, Elliott, *Antipollution Lab.* 1972; Sentinel Books Publishers, Inc.; 17–21 East 22 Street, New York, NY 10010.

Braus, Judy (editor), *NatureScope—Endangered Species: Wild and Rare.* 1989; National Wildlife Federation, 1400 Sixteenth Street, NW, Washington, DC 20036; (202) 797–6800.

Brouse, Deborah, and Pamela Wasserman, *For Earth's Sake.* 1989; Zero Population Growth; 1400 Sixteenth Street, NW; Washington, DC 20036; (202) 332–2200.

Butterfield, Charlie, and Marjorie McCandless, *Know Nukes.* 1982; Antioch/New England Graduate School; 103 Roxbury, Keene, NH 03431; (603) 357–3122.

Causey, Ann S., *Environmental Action Guide.* 1991; Benjamin/Cummings Publishing Company, Inc.; 390 Bridge Parkway, Suite 102, Redwood City, CA 94065; (415) 594–4400.

Cheryl, Dr. Charles (project director), *Project Learning Tree—Supplementary Activity Guide for Grades 7 through 12.* 1977; American Forest Council; 1250 Connecticut Avenue, NW, Suite 320, Washington, DC 20036; (202) 463–2455.

Cheryl, Dr. Charles (project director), *Project Wild—Secondary Activity Guide.* 1986; Western Regional Environmental Education Council; P.O. Box 18060, Boulder, CO 80308; (303) 444–2390.

Chiras, Daniel, *Environmental Science.* 1990; Benjamin/Cummings Publishing Co., Inc.; 390 Bridge Parkway, Suite 102, Redwood City, CA 94065; (415) 594–4400.

Chiras, Daniel, *Laboratory Activities Masters for Environmental Science.* 1989; Benjamin/Cummings Publishing Co., Inc.; 390 Bridge Parkway, Suite 102, Redwood City, CA 94065; (415) 594–4400.

Christensen, John W., *Global Science: Laboratory Manual* and *Teacher's Guide.* 1991; Kendall/Hunt Publishing Company, 2460 Kerper Boulevard, P.O. Box 539, Dubuque, IA 52004; 1–800–338–5578.

Clymire, Olga (principal writer), *California Class Project.* 1988; Orange County Superintendent of Schools; 200 Kalmus Drive, Costa Mesa, CA 92626.

Comnes, Leslie, *Toxics: Taking Charge.* 1989; Alameda County Office of Education, 313 West Winston Avenue, Hayward, CA 94544; (510) 887–0152.

Daniel, Joseph E. (editor-in-chief), *1992 Earth Journal.* 1992; Buzzworm Books, Inc., 2305 Canyon Boulevard, Suite 206, Boulder, CO 80302; (303) 442–1969.

Del Giorno, Bette, and Millicent Tissair, *Environmental Science Activities Handbook for Teachers.* 1975; Parker Publishing Co., Prentice Hall, Route 59, Brookhill Drive, West Nyack, New York 10994; (914) 358–8800. (out of print)

Drutman, Ava, and Susan Zuckerman, *Protecting Our Planet.* 1991; Good Apple; 1204 Buchanan Street, Box 299, Carthage, IL 62321; (217) 357–3981.

Enger, Eldon, and Bradley Smith, *Environmental Science: A Study of Interrelationships.* 1992; Wm. C. Brown, Publishers; 2460 Kerper Boulevard, P.O. Box 539, Dubuque, IA 52004; (319) 588–1451.

Geisel, Theodor Seuss, *The Lorax.* 1971; Random House, Inc., 201 East 50th Street, New York, NY 10022; (800) 733–3000.

Gould, Alan, *Hot Water and Warm Homes from Sunlight.* 1990; Lawrence Hall of Science, University of California at Berkeley, Berkeley, CA 94720; (415) 642–7771.

Harley, John P., and Bernard J. Nebel, *Environmental Science—The Way the World Works (Laboratory Manual).* 1990; Prentice Hall Publishing Co.; Englewood Cliffs, NJ 07632; (201) 592–2000.

Hocking, Colin, et al., *Global Warming & the Greenhouse Effect*. 1990; Lawrence Hall of Science, University of California at Berkeley, Berkeley, CA 94720; (415) 642–7771.

Javna, John, *30 Simple Energy Things You Can Do to Save the Earth*. 1990; The Earthworks Group and Pacific Gas and Electric Company; 77 Beale Street, San Francisco, CA; (415) 973–9017.

Johnson, Bob, *The Official Captain Hydro Water Conservation Workbook*. 1982; East Bay Municipal Utility District; P.O. Box 24025, Oakland, CA 94623; (510) 451–3444.

Levine, Michael, *The Environmental Address Book*. 1991; Putnam Publishing Group; 200 Madison Avenue, New York, NY 10016; (212) 951–8400.

McNeely, Jeffrey, et al., *Conserving the World's Biological Diversity*. 1990; World Resources Institute, et al.; 1709 New York Avenue, NW, Washington, DC 20006; (202) 638–6300.

Miller, G. Tyler, *Living in the Environment*. 1988, 1990; Wadsworth Publishing Company; 10 Davis Drive, Belmont, CA 94002; (415) 595–2350.

Myers, Norman, (editor), *GAIA—An Atlas of Planet Management*. 1984; Bantam Doubleday Dell Publishing Group; 666 Fifth Avenue, New York, NY 10103; (212) 765–6500.

Nebel, Bernard J., *Environmental Science—The Way the World Works*. 1990; Prentice Hall Publishing Co.; Englewood Cliffs, NJ 07632; (201) 592–2000.

Nilsson, Greta, *The Endangered Species Handbook*. 1990; Animal Welfare Institute; P.O. Box 3650, Washington, DC 20007; (202) 337–2333.

Schwartz, Linda, *Earth Book for Kids*. 1990; The Learning Works, Inc.; P.O. Box 6187, Santa Barbara, CA 93160; (805) 964–4220.

Seidel, Patricia, *Ecology Action Pack*. 1990; Symmetry Promotions Publishing; 109 Blossom Hill Lane, Chalfont, PA 18914; (215) 822–6042.

Simon, Sidney B., et al., *Values Clarification*. 1972; Hart Publishing Company, Inc.; New York, NY 10003.

Sly, Carolie (project coordinator), *The California State Environmental Education Guide*. 1988; Alameda County Office of Education; 313 West Winston Avenue, Hayward, CA 94544; (510) 887–0152.

Sly, Carolie (project coordinator), *Water Wisdom*. 1990; Alameda County Office of Education; 313 West Winston Avenue, Hayward, CA 94544; (510) 887–0152.

Tomera, Audrey, *Understanding Basic Ecological Concepts*. 1989; J. Weston Walch, Publisher; 321 Valley Street, P.O. Box 658, Portland, ME 04104–0658; 1–800–341–6094.

Tourtillot, Leeann, *Conserve & Renew*. 1990; California Energy Extension Service; 1400 Tenth Street, Sacramento, CA 95814; (916) 323–4388.

U.S. Bureau of the Census, *Statistical Abstract of the United States, 1991*. 1991; U.S. Government Printing Office, Washington, DC 20402; (202) 783–3238.

Wasserman, Pamela, and Andrea Doyle, *Earth Matters*. 1991; Zero Population Growth; 1400 Sixteenth Street, NW; Washington, DC 20036; (202) 332–2200.

Weaver, Elbert (editor), *Scientific Experiments in Environmental Pollution*. 1968; Holt, Rinehart and Winston, Inc.; New York, NY (out of print)

Wigginton, Eliot, *The Foxfire Book*. 1972; Anchor/Doubleday; 666 Fifth Avenue, New York, NY 10103; (800) 223–6834.